How Can Your Sun Sign Help in Your Career?

Ask yourself some simple questions. Do you have:

- A talent for coming up with ideas to initiate projects? You may be a Creative Aries, successful in fields of design and engineering.
- A strong desire for independence and risk-taking? Perhaps you're a Daring Aries, born to be a police officer, a federal agent or military strategist.
- Good taste and a discerning palate? Do you want a career that's both creative *and* practical? The Gourmet Taurus is ideally suited to a job in the food industry.
- A skill for managing money effectively? You could be a Financial Taurus, a prime candidate for a career as an accountant, financial planner or banker.

You may be a Public Service Cancer, or an Analytical Scorpio. For every sign there are many career choices—at least one may be perfect for you. Discover how to maximize your career potential in . . .

Most Pocket Books are available at special quantity discounts for bulk purchases for sales promotions, premiums or fund raising. Special books or book excerpts can also be created to fit specific needs.

For details write the office of the Vice President of Special Markets, Pocket Books, 1230 Avenue of the Americas, New York, New York 10020.

STAR SUCCESS

AN ASTROLOGICAL GUIDE TO YOUR CAREER

Karen Christino and Renée Randolph

POCKET BOOKS
New York   London   Toronto   Sydney   Tokyo   Singapore

An *Original* Publication of POCKET BOOKS

POCKET BOOKS, a division of Simon & Schuster Inc.
1230 Avenue of the Americas, New York, NY 10020

Copyright © 1992 by Karen Christino and Renée Randolph

All rights reserved, including the right to reproduce
this book or portions thereof in any form whatsoever.
For information address Pocket Books, a division of
Simon & Schuster Inc., 1230 Avenue
of the Americas, New York, NY 10020

ISBN: 0-671-75001-1

First Pocket Books printing October 1992

10 9 8 7 6 5 4 3 2 1

POCKET and colophon are registered trademarks of
Simon & Schuster Inc.

Printed in the U.S.A.

Acknowledgments

We would like to thank our wonderful family, without whose love, encouragement, patience, and understanding this book would not have been possible.

We also want to give special thanks to Lisa Kazmier for her remarkable ideas, her great interest in this project, and her first-rate editing of the book.

CONTENTS

Introduction
What Is a Sun Sign? ix

Part One: THE ASTROLOGY OF CAREER
More Than Just a Job 3

Part Two: YOUR CAREER
Aries 23
Taurus 41
Gemini 59
Cancer 76
Leo 95
Virgo 113
Libra 131
Scorpio 147
Sagittarius 164
Capricorn 181
Aquarius 198
Pisces 215

CONTENTS

Part Three: WORKING WITH OTHERS

Aries	235
Taurus	243
Gemini	253
Cancer	262
Leo	271
Virgo	280
Libra	289
Scorpio	297
Sagittarius	307
Capricorn	316
Aquarius	325
Pisces	335

Appendix

For Further Study	347
Suggested Reading List	350

Introduction

What Is a Sun Sign?

You probably already know if your sign is Aries, Taurus, or Gemini. Maybe you've consulted newspaper horoscopes, read some astrology books, or perhaps you have had your personal natal chart drawn up and interpreted by a professional astrologer. You might know that Capricorns are called penny pinchers, that Taureans like to eat, or that Leos always want to be the center of attention. But did you ever ask why this is so or what you're really saying when you state "I'm a Pisces"?

First consider that long ago someone divided our sky into twelve zones. These form a band around the Earth on the same plane on which the Earth circles the Sun, with each zone given a name, or "sign." From our viewpoint on Earth, the Sun and planets are placed within these zones. Since it takes a year for the Earth to circle the Sun, it also takes a year for all twelve signs to be the backdrop of the sky. On about March 21 of every year, we say that the Sun is in the sign of Aries. This coincides with the beginning of spring and the time when days will begin to get longer. In April and May the Sun is

INTRODUCTION

in the sign of Taurus, and so on, as the Sun moves throughout the zodiac, always in the same order: Gemini next, then Cancer, Leo, Virgo, Libra, Scorpio, Sagittarius, Capricorn, Aquarius, and Pisces. In the same manner, the Moon and each of the planets are located within a given sign at a given time and date. In a complete horoscope, each planet also has a sign, but since the Sun is the most important celestial body in our solar system, it's considered the most important in horoscope interpretation.

So when you say "I'm a Pisces" you're really saying that the Earth was in a certain relationship to the Sun at your time of birth; from our point of view on Earth, the Sun seemed to be in the zone we call Pisces. But what does this mean? How does it affect your life?

Astrologers believe that these positions of the Sun, Moon, and planets affect your characteristics, attitudes, and approach to life. We don't know exactly why, but we have studied the signs' effects on human behavior for thousands of years and found they consistently appeared to have an influence. Just as the Moon affects the tides and the Sun affects the length of day, so too does the Sun's sign at your time of birth stamp upon your psyche a certain approach to life.

Let's take a look at a few signs and how their meanings relate to life here on Earth. Aries is the first sign of the zodiac, and it appears in the spring. This is traditionally a time of renewal and birth. In the Northern Hemisphere, the days begin to get longer and we spend more time awake and out of doors. Animals come out of hibernation, and the sap begins to flow through trees. Leaves bud, and flowers start to bloom. Life is beginning anew, as it does each year in spring. Similarly, Aries natives are people with abundant energy. They love expressing themselves and beginning new projects. This makes perfect sense, of course. They are living proof of the vernal equinox and will be all their lives.

By contrast, in late December and January, when

INTRODUCTION

Capricorns are born, it's the coldest time of the year for us. Many areas have snow, and vegetation is minimal. Squirrels must live on what they've stored away during the year. Into this world the Capricorn babies are born. They can be gloomy and keep to themselves, but they manage to make a little go a long way. Doesn't that sound typical of someone living in the dead of winter, when coal and oil must be saved to last until the spring thaw comes in, when the fall's harvest must be meted out until new vegetation once again begins to grow?

Why Is a Sun Sign So Important?

The Sun gives us life on Earth and, of all the celestial bodies, has the greatest influence on us. It signals us when to wake up and when to sleep, when it's warm enough to go outside or when it's cold enough to go ice skating. In the same way, the Sun is the most important factor in a natal horoscope. While the other planets affect our lives and natures in many ways, the Sun is linked to one's character, one's will, and one's energy. The Sun also represents *you* in a horoscope and the manner in which you approach life, be it impulsively, cautiously, or questioningly.

The Sun is really at the heart of your creative drive and your will to be. It is the part of you that you're most easily in touch with, your consciousness and your basic life energy. The Sun is tied to your development of selfhood, your destiny, and the role you will play in life. Consequently, understanding your Sun sign can be a wonderful tool to determine "what to do" in life.

What qualities do you possess as a person? What are your strengths, your weaknesses? How can you use your strengths in a positive manner and utilize your weaknesses to your best advantage? What do you like to do? What things do you do well, and what things would you like to do better? Simple Sun sign astrology can help

INTRODUCTION

answer these questions by pointing you in the proper direction.

In this book we will be analyzing your Sun sign potentials to help you in a practical way toward setting and achieving your goals. Your career is one of the most important creative choices you can make in life. It should be an area in which you find great self-expression and self-fulfillment.

As the Sun is linked with your destiny and character, it is a good indicator of what you will look for in a career, your capabilities for advancement, and the way in which you relate to your success. It can pinpoint the talents that you will draw upon to get the things you want from the world.

Most important, Sun sign astrology can start you on a road to self-discovery that will continue for the rest of your life. Astrology can help you get in touch with the "real you," even when the ego or emotions get in the way. Understanding your Sun sign may introduce you to abilities you never realized you had before thinking through them. It can help you see that you may not have a talent for figures and keep you from trying to be an accountant. It can help put your natural affinities to work for you and direct you toward a more productive, successful, and fulfilling career. In addition, astrology can help you negotiate your chosen path by better understanding the people you work with every day.

We're all looking for that special niche in life—that perfect job or career opportunity that will be stimulating, engrossing, and enjoyable, as well as rewarding financially and emotionally. We hope *Star Success: An Astrological Guide to Your Career* will help you in your search. Good luck!

STAR
SUCCESS

Part One
THE ASTROLOGY OF CAREER

More Than Just a Job

We've written this book to help you use astrology to choose and develop your career. In our more than forty years combined of consultation, we've found career questions to be some of the most frequently asked. Those posed often involve choosing a field, being hired for a position, obtaining some kind of advancement or just trying to get along with others at the workplace.

Your job is important; for most of us, it's a necessity. If you don't get along with the purchasing manager and you have to order something, you're stuck! Work is not like your personal life, in which you can pick and choose many of the people with whom you associate on a daily basis. There will always be "givens" in any employment situation; the better you are at adapting to or working with these "givens," the more successful you will be.

Many people with regular full-time positions spend one half or more of their waking hours on the job! It seems reasonable to believe that they should get more from this effort than just a weekly paycheck. Think about your own experience. Has it been a chore to get up in the morning and go to work? Have you ever felt that you're in a rut, with no possibility of advancement? Or do you just feel slightly unhappy with your career or job choices?

You don't have to live this way! There are many, many people out there who love their jobs. But it's often a matter of chance that these people landed their positions. You can find a satisfying job as well. If there's one thing that astrology tells us, it's that *things change*. Even if you have financial obligations and feel you cannot easily make a career move, remember that opportunities will present themselves if you look for them.

If you are a young person or an older person returning to the work force, it's even more crucial that you make your first job one that will be rewarding. If you make the right choice, you can be happily employed for many years to come.

Today more than ever before, people are seeking freelance, part-time, or home-based positions. The rules seem to be changing, offering workers greater flexibility to find situations that are just right for them. The U.S. Department of Labor estimates that by the year 2000 the labor force may reach more than 140 million. This is great news for the job seeker. Somewhere out there, maybe even in your own backyard, there are job opportunities waiting for you, there's a growing population in need of goods and services, there are more people changing and growing and moving on.

What Do You Want to Be When You Grow Up?

Suddenly you *are* grown up, and this question is no longer fun. There are many career books on the market today that can help you in your search. Some will tell you what jobs will be wanted ten years from now, so that you can get a head start. You can find out what education you'll need and how to obtain the proper background. All kinds of books are written about many different fields, listing scores of possible positions, their job outlook, and probable pay.

But if you don't have a crystallized idea of what you'd like to do, you'd still be stymied. If you picked up the comprehensive *U.S. Occupational Outlook Handbook,* you'd have to wade through almost five hundred pages of information to get a good overview of the myriad of possibilities! Your mind will probably be so boggled at this point, and your body so fatigued from hunching over the book and turning pages, that you'll accept the first job offer that comes along.

Rational and persistent job seekers may find one of several other avenues open to them. Guidance or career counselors can be enlisted to offer their advice and experience. Aptitude tests are another great way of finding out what you do well. The problem is that most of us possess more than one marketable skill or talent and may not necessarily enjoy those things we do well. For example, many of us are expert dishwashers, and yet few will pursue this field as a career.

What Color Is Your Parachute? is a bestselling career guidance book that's been around for years. It's a job counselor in book form. In it are aptitude tests and all kinds of advice on getting a job, interviewing, and finding the right position. These things can be helpful to the job seeker—and in addition, they keep you busy while you wait for the phone to ring!

Yet the problem with all of these sources is that you'll always return again to *you. You* must give the counselor the input, *you* must sift through an entire book of advice until you find the bit you feel you can use. You must answer all the questions on the aptitude tests to get your evaluation. While you may see a nice graph of your talents, skills, and job desires, you still haven't answered the real question. You may find something like: "You'd succeed in an open-ended, service-oriented position that provides opportunity for independent input." But what does this mean? How can you use your traits to find a position you love? If you don't know, you may then return to taking the first position that comes along or the most easily accessible in the market, and you'll remain slightly happy or even unhappy.

Major career decisions call for a great deal of soul-searching. And in reality, you too are projecting and imagining what you think and feel to come to a conclusion. It's difficult at best to imagine that *one thing* you'd like to do above all others, if you haven't stumbled into it by sheer chance. If you haven't really *had* a career yet, your inexperience will only compound the problem: You probably haven't yet done all that you've now decided you want to do. But no matter what kind of help you get, only you can make the final decision. Your parents, spouse, and friends may make suggestions and recommendations, but you gotta live with 'em, pal! There's ultimately no one you can turn to but the Big Guy upstairs or that still small voice within, both of whom can be difficult to reach.

So what *can* you do? Are we really all alone in the cosmos, bits of flotsam tossed about by the sea of life? We don't think so. We've studied astrology for many years and can tell you honestly and frankly that we believe it works. It's as simple as that. And we also feel that astrology can help you take those most difficult first steps toward beginning a new career or jump-starting an old one.

Astrology and Your Career

The difference between using astrology to help you in your career and using any other form of guidance is just this: We can *tell* you something about yourself. Unlike anything else in the universe, astrology can tell you things that you may not have thought of, realized, or considered. Each of the twelve signs possess certain talents, characteristics, traits, and aptitudes. You can use these to zero in on a new field, advance in your current endeavors, or see how others in the workplace view you. Knowing a co-worker's birthday can help you to understand him or her better, and this will help you learn to work together in a more productive manner.

In fact, you'd be hard pressed to get this kind of objective character analysis from any other source. Close friends, relatives, and others you've known for years may know the "real you" better than we do, but they can't offer the kind of nonjudgmental, impersonal, objective advice that we can. Astrology is unique in that it's more specific than psychology and more applicable than an aptitude test.

Astrology is not a "fad," either—it's been around for more than three thousand years. That means that at least five hundred years before the Buddha was born, about one thousand years before anyone even heard of Jesus Christ, and more than fifteen hundred years before Mohammed left the earth, people found guidance via the stars. Ancient Mesopotamians, Egyptians, and Greeks practiced astrology. This is old, old stuff. In fact, since man first looked to the heavens, astrology has been around, and it developed hand-in-hand with its sister science, astronomy, from which it's currently split. Such lauded scientists as Pythagoras, Hippocrates, Ptolemy, Copernicus, Galileo, Johannes Kepler, and Sir Isaac Newton all believed in and practiced astrology, and most of their conclusions were based on their own observations and experiences. Albertus Magnus, Roger Bacon, and St. Thomas Aquinas all furthered the cause and study of astrology. In modern times, Carl Jung is best known among the famous proponents of this art/science.

Originally, astrologers worked mainly for kings, princes, and the nation as a whole, not for individuals.

For many centuries, astrology existed as a secret art, and practitioners were exclusive to heads of state. In contemporary times, astrology is accessible to all, and leaders such as George Washington, Teddy and Franklin Roosevelt, Winston Churchill, Ronald Reagan, and even Hitler have been known to use astrology to further their own agendas and those of their countries. Interestingly enough, these heavy hitters were all using it to *aid their careers*. We've got wonderful documentation of how astrologer Joan Quigley guided President Reagan's career from her book. We can easily conclude that one of the first and continuing uses of astrology has been as a tool to advance one's career.

Yet even today, with much popular acceptance of astrology, many people still feel it has secret or occult elements, unknown to the layman. This couldn't be farther from the truth. Astrology is as natural as the force of gravity, the orbits of the planets, and the tides here on Earth. It exists in a kind of no-man's land between the natural and the metaphysical sciences, being part of one and part of the other.

Astrology is the interpretation of how the regular and predictable motions of the planets, Sun, Moon, and sometimes other heavenly bodies affect us here on Earth. It places each of us within a system of order, makes us a part of the larger cosmos, and implies there are natural forces that we can utilize to work for our benefit. These natural forces are all there is to the "fate" many people see as being part of astrological interpretation.

How does it work? Well, there have been lots of theories involving relativity, electromagnetic influences, "rays," unidentified forces, and even the influence of the planets on our cells and bodily fluids, but they all remain theories. We do know, of course, that astrology does work, and it has proven itself over and over again to clients, relatives, friends, and associates. We've even convinced a few skeptics along the way as well! Who really wrote the Bible? We don't know. Who put those statues on Easter Island? How did they build the pyramids? We don't know. And, like astrology, another survivor of the ancient world, we may never really find out all there is to know about these subjects.

Back to the Twentieth Century

So, you say, I'm now aligned with the cosmos, humming the music of the spheres on my way to work. How do I get this mumbo-jumbo to help me? Countless astrology books have provided insight alone, but they usually stop there. And insight without a system to apply it to your life can be frustrating, at best. In the following sections of this book, we'll introduce you to some practical ways of applying your Sun sign potentials to everyday life on the job.

Understanding your own Sun sign and getting in touch with the capacities it represents are the first steps toward helping you in your career. You'll understand yourself, your motivations, and your goals a little better. We can help you with job-seeking advice and career suggestions that are uniquely tailored to each sign of the zodiac. Possibly most important, we can show you an objective view of how you interact with others at work and suggest ways to nurture positive traits and attitudes and minimize negative ones.

One of the most important concepts that astrology can introduce you to is the fact that all people are different. Of course, this is a truism, but astrology shows us just *how* different we all really are. We can gain enough insight to accept the fact that some people like to talk, some have naturally high spirits, and some just don't like to sit still. Can knowing this help on the job? You bet.

We feel that astrology is the only way you can truly understand another human being without spending months and years getting to know them. And there are many people we all know for a long time but never get to know well or understand. Personalities and outward appearances can get in the way of knowing what a person is really like. Yet the Sun sign provides an outline of the character. It may at times be difficult to observe, but even that Capricorn with the perky personality will basically be hard working, personally reserved, and somewhat insecure. Astrology can effectively help us "get inside someone else's head," so to speak. Once we can do this, we'll have a better idea of how to deal with them at work, and understand them as individuals.

There is always that person at work whom one coworker loves and another despises and cannot get along with. This is so because we all have different needs, desires, and attitudes. You have an edge over others if you can understand *their* needs, desires, and attitudes and learn how to adapt to them or use them positively to get the job done.

We truly believe that all signs can get along with all other signs at the workplace. We've seen the "terrible" Leo-Scorpio combination produce supportive coworkers, the "difficult" Virgo-Gemini combination achieve efficient results in a fun way, and the Capricorn-Libra mix get the job done together with finesse. Differences that may be more pronounced in a personal relationship can be worked through more easily at work because getting along is beneficial to all parties.

While you may be quite comfortable at work, your guard is never absolutely lifted the way it is in your close one-on-one relationships. Therefore it is easier to adjust *your* behavior when dealing with others. Here you have a better chance of acting in a logical and responsible manner, rather than on instinct and habit. You have specific goals that you'd like to reach, and these are often more important than your relationship with most of your co-workers. But oddly enough, if you try for practical reasons to get along with those you work with, you'll end up having better relationships as well!

Play by the Rules

We feel that you will express your Sun sign potential in many ways and that you can use it to help develop your career. There are endless facets to anyone's character, but most of us will demonstrate at least some of our Sun sign characteristics and, in many cases, most of them. We can also tell you what some of your career needs are, if you're ambitious, or need financial security, variety, or praise.

You bring your personality and character to any activity or relationship in your life, but we feel that there are two main ways in which your sign will be expressed in your career: through the *type* of job you want and through your choice of vocation, profession, or field.

For example, a Taurean would like a regular, full-time position that provides financial security. This is a *type* of position. He may choose to be a banker, a singer, or a horticulturist. These are examples of typically Taurean professions. In the same way, Aquarians need independent and possibly freelance jobs, dealing with other people regularly. They may choose electronics or computers as their area of expertise. Once again, you can see the difference between a kind of situation and a choice of field.

You may express your Sun sign energies through your choice of type of position, your choice of vocation, or in both of these ways. Most of us will generally use one or the other. If you "go with the flow" of these energies, we believe you'll find yourself more satisfied and successful. If you go against your natural tendencies, you'll have a more difficult time. Understanding your own self can go a long way toward achieving a rewarding career.

The other nice thing about astrology is that it breaks

down all kinds of barriers. When you hook into your Sun sign potential, you're suddenly no longer just a man or woman, black or white, young or old. You're an Aries or a Libra or whatever. While this may not help in terms of possible discrimination by others, it *can* help improve your own ability to get beyond physical characteristics or get beyond others' perception of these as possible liabilities. If you really feel you've been discriminated against, try to use our suggestions for boss and co-worker to get through to those short-sighted individuals. Astrology is not skin-deep!

In the hip and trendy seventies, astrology was "in" and droves of people had love-ins to celebrate the dawning of the Age of Aquarius (in actuality, it's still around the corner). "What's your sign?" was considered a good cocktail-party opener, first-date ice-breaker, and generally "cool" phrase utilized by the bell-bottomed populace. The nineties have ushered in a much more practical, conservative, and career-minded generation of adults. While your pleasant response twenty-five years ago to a newly discovered Virgo might have been "Far out, man!" today a more appropriate reply would be "You'll succeed if you work hard."

But to proceed with our studies we need birth information. Inaccurate birth data is the bane of the professional and amateur astrologer alike. A wrong date can give a very different horoscope interpretation, and when erecting a complete birth chart, even five minutes can occasionally change the horoscope wheel in critical ways!

Accurate verifiable data is often hard to come by, and even the astrological Rock of Gibraltar for data, the birth certificate, can be inaccurate. A woman we know found her birth certificate wrong because it said "P.M.," yet her family knew that she was born in the morning.

A recent conversation with a records employee in New York City revealed that these facts are really not all that important to the layperson. When Department of Health officials receive a doctor's certificate of a live birth and are not clear whether A.M. or P.M. has been indicated, they'll just pick one. Astrologers are outraged over this seemingly cavalier approach to very important information, yet in a world where civil service workers often feel overworked and underpaid, who can expect them to call a doctor or hospital to verify a time? "Get real!" they'll tell you, in no uncertain terms. And of course there *are* more important things going on in the birth room. The doctor usually cleans and examines the baby before writing down the time of birth. In a society where infants are sometimes even snatched from hospitals, can we expect a real and exact time on a birth certificate every time? Personally, we would like to see the institution of an official Virgo native in all delivery rooms with a multidial chronograph when the baby takes its first breath.

But for all of you Sun sign astrologers who are reading this book, remember that even the birth *date* itself can be misprinted, unknown, or changed. Adopted individuals may have a particularly hard time finding out their true date of birth, and often even as adults they do not have legal access to their birth certificates. In today's age of hospital births, most of us do know what day we were born. Yet it's not hard to imagine administrative personnel in these large institutions switching, misplacing, or miscopying data. Exhausted or overexcited parents can't be blamed for forgetting the actual birth date either.

For the older generations of people who were routinely born at home, it was even easier to mistake a date. A gentleman we know celebrated a Libra birth date for decades and then happened onto his birth certificate, which indicated he was born a week later, making him a Scorpio. Talk about an astrological identity crisis!

Another problem for Sun sign study are the people born on the cusp. Astrologers know that you're either one sign or another depending on the exact time of birth. A person born on March 21 can just as easily be a Pisces as an Aries: If you know your astrology well, you may be able to deduce which sign is really theirs. But occasionally there's an unknown quantity, such as the exact time of birth being questionable.

Even so, you might wonder how you can really get this all-important birth data from bosses, supervisors, and co-workers. It can be difficult, especially if the reason you want the data is to find out how to avert an imminent feud.

One good way is to let your own interest in astrology be known. Carry an astrology book, wear jewelry or accessories with your astrological sign as decoration, or use a personalized key ring or chain. All of these can spark casual conversation, and it's not difficult at this point to ask the other person for a birth date. Those who don't believe in astrology may be the most difficult to get dates from, but if you've been put in a "prove it to me" situation, you may wrangle the information through a philosophical discussion.

Just being conscious of birth information can prove to be helpful. Stories or anecdotes are often told about special birthday celebrations or events. A follow-up question about someone's exact birth date will appear casual or even be viewed as a healthy curiosity.

Many offices have birthday celebrations, and if one department knows someone's birthday, it quickly becomes common knowledge. Because of this nice practice, finding out the birth dates of your co-workers can become relatively easy. There's usually an individual entrusted with a birthday list, and if you ask to help with any upcoming parties, you'll probably get all the information you'll need.

If you are a secretary or assistant, you may come across your boss's information on a driver's license or some other personal document. This data is usually very accurate. Remember to exercise prudence with information obtained in this manner. Professional astrologers keep all birth data strictly confidential.

Pisceans can be evasive or inaccurate, but the notorious Scorpio wins the prize for withholding correct birth data. A birth certificate has recently been found that makes alleged Leo Andy Warhol actually a Scorpio! With conflicting information such as this, a little astrological logic is all that is needed. If he really were a Leo, he probably would not have lied about his birthday. If he were a Scorpio, he could have.

We have even had Scorpio clients who have had full charts done with inaccurate information. Sometimes it's only about fifteen minutes off, but for some reason, they want to be sure you don't know *everything* about them! We've often wondered how they sort through their interpretations in these cases.

In any event, Andy Warhol *is* the exception, and people with manufactured birthdays pretty consistently keep the birth *day* intact. Just like the criminal whose alias retains the same initials as his real moniker, there's something primal and real about your birthday. Just remember that it's also something private and personal at times.

When in doubt, when dealing with cuspers, or if you just lack full information and don't want to wait till your boss is drunk at the Christmas party to pry, simply observe. Read about how to recognize the boss and co-worker types for each sign in question. Watch how this person interacts with others and you'll learn a lot about how to treat them yourself. When the pieces come together, read our advice for that sign. You'll probably find that if you've studied the real *character* of a person for a period of time, you'll have some clues concerning their Sun sign.

While accurate birth data is essential, it can be found if you're patient, innovative, and know your astrology.

How to Use This Book

Turn to Part Two for advice on your own career. First-time job seekers, career changers, and those currently working or returning to the work force can equally use this information. Most of us need to work for a living, and for those of you who do, Part II will have an immediate and obvious use. But all of you lucky people born into wealth or success can also use our advice. Perhaps you're a businessperson bored with your current position—you're committed to your lifestyle but are looking to branch out with something more rewarding. Maybe you're a mother at home with young children who would like to begin working part-time. Are you looking to invest in your own business and wonder what field is appropriate? We can help you too.

We have defined "career" as any field of pursuit that will give you satisfaction, a sense of self-worth, and some financial return. You don't necessarily have to go to college to have a career, but that may be necessary for certain professions. You don't have to spend frustrating years "working your way up" to an ultimate payoff at age forty-five unless you choose to, and you don't have to spend eight hours of every day doing the same thing to have a career, either. Your career is not necessarily how you earn your living, although it's nice when these two factors can come together. So before you read any further, throw out all those old, tired ideas. You don't have to be a doctor, lawyer, or even an Indian chief to have a rewarding career that is everything you want it to be!

As no sign begins and ends on exactly the same day each year, you'll find that our Sun sign chapters have overlapping dates. If you were born on the cusp you might need to find out your true Sun sign by having an inexpensive computer chart drawn up. Or you may have enough experience to read both signs that correspond to your birthday and understand which sign you really are.

Think about your own behavior and needs as you read. None of us will relate to *every* trait of a given Sun sign, and it may be helpful to highlight those sections that you feel are the most appropriate. You will probably relate more strongly to either a type of job or a profession ruled by your sign.

Think about our sections on possible problem areas carefully. It is quite difficult to take the objective view and recognize when *you* are at fault. Negative characteristics can often appear to be coming from the outside, from other people with whom you work. Yet if you find you're constantly having the same problem crop up with various others, your own behavior probably has something to do with it.

Try to keep an open mind. Usually your most problematic behavior is the most deeply rooted. You might possibly be denying to yourself that a problem exists. If this is the case, you're also denying yourself the opportunity of coming up with a solution and improving your work.

For each sign of the zodiac, we've included examples from real life. Most of them are designed to show you the many different ways in which the Sun sign energies can be used effectively toward career development. They are usually "success stories" to get you thinking in the right way. But they are all *true*, whether they are examples of celebrity lives or those of the guy and gal next door. Rich and famous people are not the only ones who succeed in the world, and we can all succeed in little ways every day on the job.

Each Sun sign in Part Two has a vocational unit. One of the major ways in which you can express the sign's energy in your career is in your choice of profession or vocation. Included are mini-quizzes to help guide you toward an area of concentration. When you've completed them all, you should find quite a few selections that will appeal to you.

The dutiful Capricorn and practical Virgo will probably follow the instructions to the letter. Imaginative Cancerians or spontaneous Aquarians will probably not want to go through the trouble! If you feel limited by the format of the quiz, skip it. But don't overlook the many vocational choices appropriate for your sign. You may skim through them all or ponder them in depth. In other words, use our material in whatever way you feel is the best for you.

Be creative. While we can make many suggestions, we can't decide exactly what you should pursue. Take our suggestions and guidelines as the first step in your career search. Improvise! Of course, there are any number of things that a particular individual will be involved with throughout his or her lifetime; you may well find more than one category that appeals to you.

Because of the unique natures of the twelve signs, everyone will have different work experiences. Some signs, like Gemini, Virgo, Libra, Sagittarius, Aquarius, and Pisces, typically look for variety. These people will usually have more diverse work situations and may change jobs or fields more frequently than others. Due to this dazzling diversity, we simply couldn't list *all* of the many positions possible. On the other hand, signs like Taurus, Scorpio, and Capricorn usually prefer to stick with one specific vocation or situation for much longer periods of time.

Part III deals with the others that you'll encounter at the workplace, specifically your co-workers and your boss. By understanding *their* Sun sign attributes, you'll be better able to adapt to their strengths and weaknesses.

This section also includes gift-giving suggestions for the signs because, as we all know, the office gift can be a real sticky wicket. What gifts are personal and yet impersonal enough to be given to others at the office? We often don't know a co-worker's likes and dislikes all that well, and a group gift presents further problems. We hope you'll find the solution to many of them by using our guide.

We cannot guarantee you'll gain wealth, acclaim, success, or a promotion from following our advice. Astrology is partly a metaphysical science that deals more with intangibles like happiness, well-being, and using your natural characteristics to their best advantage. We do hope this book will help you find some self-knowledge and a better understanding of your unique place in the scheme of things. And if you gain even some small insight into your path in life, you will be better able to find success in your career and working relationships and satisfaction with your choice of profession.

But what happens if you find you're still tearing your hair out? You're not a Libra's Libra or a Virgo's Virgo? Other factors in your natal horoscope could be giving you a greater affinity for another sign. If you're one of those few people who simply does not relate to your Sun sign, turn to the last section of this book for further ways to use astrology to help in your career endeavors. Anyone who wants more information will find it useful.

Part Two

YOUR CAREER

ARIES
March 20 to April 21

"Be more assertive, more able to deal with conflict."
—Gloria Steinem, *Esquire*

Bighorn

Aries is the ram, a male sheep. Although most sheep today are domesticated, originally they were wild animals, which roamed the fields and hillsides. Living in herds, the individuals were able to withstand fierce winter storms and climb to the heights of tall mountainsides. Aries natives have these daring, spirited, and independent characteristics common to the wild ram.

Rams, of course, are also known for their tough horns, which they use in battle. They'll butt a competitor directly with their head and horns at the slightest provocation. This metaphor is one of the most evocative of Ariens. Possessing tremendous energy, they'll fight first and ask questions later (like "Ram"-bo). Aries people are always candid and frank, and will face challenges head-on. They are ambitious, driven, and at times even headstrong.

Like the ram who races to the mountaintop first, Ariens enjoy leading, beginning new projects, and providing the impetus to move ahead. There is a wonderful simplicity to the Aries person, who believes exclusively in the strength of the self. They are quick to react and have great decisive capacities. Ariens will never "sit on the fence" and will jump over it as soon as they possibly can! These people are completely unself-conscious, taking action in an almost instinctive manner.

The phrase "don't fence me in" was probably coined by an Aries native. Because Ariens need to do and act based on their own judgment at all times, they ordinarily hate any restrictions or impediments to their career progress. Independence is the name of the game for these lively people: The ram would rather lead the herd than follow.

Aries people can come on too strong at times, especially when they get their horns twisted, but they never hold grudges and will forgive and forget as a matter of course. They are gregarious, friendly people who need others around them most of the time in order to be happy—part of their ancestral tendency toward being a member of the herd, perhaps? Arien energy well directed toward a career can lead, challenge, and benefit all of the sheep involved!

Get to Work! What to Look for in a Career

Aries is a fire sign and is ruled by the planet Mars. Both of these accentuate your high energy, courage, and need for exciting and stimulating positions. You will thrive on challenge and be stimulated by competition. All Ariens need to be physically active, and most Aries people prefer positions that allow them to move about at will. Some of you may opt for physical work with tools or machines that can utilize your tremendous energy positively.

You are an outgoing individual and you need to direct your abundant energy toward your career goals. You'll be happy in positions that allow you physical freedom, a flexible schedule, and the ability to make your own decisions. Heavy restrictions and office routine can cause you to rebel. You must be able to move ahead in terms of activity, job responsibility, and leadership. If you are in a dead-end job, with no hope for a promotion, you should quickly seek one in which your enterprise is rewarded.

You need to be among people on the job—to talk, share your feelings, and generally have a good time. You should try to secure a position in which you're actually dealing with people as part of your job, or else one that places you as part of a group or team. The best position will allow you to work as an independent unit of a group effort. Here you will find the camaraderie, appreciation, and acceptance from others with which you are most comfortable. You are naturally competitive and will thus appreciate the opportunity to test your skills against those of your friends on the job.

You'll succeed in sales, marketing, or promotion positions. You also can enthuse others through your powerful self-expression, especially useful in meetings or presentations.

You may be easily tempted to take the first offer that comes along just to get going! Before you accept any position, however, take a moment to ask yourself some questions: On a day-to-day basis, will you enjoy the people, schedule, and activities involved? Does the position seem involving and offer at least some opportunity to lead or initiate action? Is the job promotable? If you are satisfied with your own answers, accept the position. If you have doubts, it's best not to leap in just yet. A job search can be tedious business, and you won't like to be idle, but if you wait and seek out other possibilities, you will probably find something more suitable.

Many Ariens succeed in the military because of the

opportunity for physical challenge and the ability to move up to positions of power. Most Ariens succeed as "self-made" people, and the military can also offer an internship of sorts: You learn the job by doing. The planet Mars, representing the god of war, is also associated with Aries, making many born generals, on the battlefield and off.

Certainly, Four-Star General Colin Powell has used many of his Aries characteristics in his career. The son of poor Jamaican immigrants, Powell took the initiative to leave the South Bronx and attend college. Joining an ROTC program, he quickly rose through the military ranks to become the highest-ranking officer in America —clearly a leader! Powell served in two tours of duty in Vietnam and led the 1989 invasion of Panama and the 1991 war in the Persian Gulf. While cautious about recommending the use of force too quickly, Powell is the typically self-confident Aries: When the decision has been made, he's committed, even to risky military action. Appointed chairman of the Joint Chiefs of Staff in 1989, Powell has selected a career that utilizes his Arien abilities in the best possible manner.

What's Your Line? Your Vocational Choices

Aries fields include those relating to activities that combine the use of the mind and body. Many are action-oriented and some are physically demanding. Talents in the constructional or mechanical areas are common to many of you and can be used in an endless number of practical jobs. You can hold executive and administrative positions and, when in the proper field, will easily advance to leadership positions. Choose a field in which you feel you can direct your energies in a positive and practical manner.

An Aries man became a police officer, working in a motorcycle patrol and as a mechanic for police vehicles.

STAR SUCCESS

Later, he continued law enforcement work as a court officer.

David Letterman has used his charming Arien personality and quick and acerbic wit to make him a top talk-show host. He exhibits typical Arien directness and likability, but, true to his sign, he's not always tactful. His youthful enthusiasm is an Aries trait that is evident at any age.

Aries Liz Claiborne worked for twenty-five years as a designer before using her enterprising abilities to launch her own firm. She had a clear idea of her buyers: active, Aries-type working women. The company has done tremendous business as a result and in recent years has worked to modernize textile production in the United States—the manufacturing side of business also ruled by Aries!

Put a checkmark next to each question that you'd answer with a "yes." If there are several checks for a few career groups, review these first and think about the career suggestions we've listed. If you believe that one of these areas is right for you, investigate your selections further or those closely related to them. Also take a look at the rest of our suggestions for other possibilities.

___ Would you like independent control of your own duties while working as part of a team?

___ Are you attracted to working with heavy machinery?

___ Do you feel you'd like physical activity as part of your job?

___ Does seeing the actual results of your work bring you satisfaction?

___ Would you like to make a big difference to many?

You are a Constructive Aries. Your energy and need for activity can take you out in the open in the construction field, building roads, factories, shops, homes, offices, or bridges. If you like working with equipment, you should try becoming an assayer, industrial or metallurgical engineer, instrumentation technician, mechanical drafter; forklift, crane, motor, or power saw operator; truck or tractor driver, brakeman, or locomotive engineer. Skilled workers in stone, iron, steel, cement, concrete, brickwork, and metals can all be Ariens. Ariens enjoy work with metals and machines, so work as a tool and die maker, lathe worker, welder, printing-press operator, typesetter, mechanic, machinist, or foundry worker could also be appropriate. Other careers in this group relate to the installation, repair, and maintenance of business machines, refrigeration, air-conditioning and heating equipment, aircraft, cars, trucks, buses, and vans; or textile (especially wool) processing, sales, and distribution.

___ Do you have a talent for coming up with ideas to initiate projects?

___ Would you be able to increase efficiency?

___ Do you like to face new challenges on a regular basis?

___ Would you enjoy turning your ideas into real projects?

___ Do you have problem-solving abilities?

You are a Creative Aries. Because of your fresh, exciting, and efficient approach, you can succeed in the fields of design and engineering. Aries designers can be especially adept in the fields of industrial design, product efficiency, lighting, graphics, and exhibits. Aries engineers have many diverse areas of specialization to choose from, including electrical, mechanical, aeronautics, recording, construction, civil, metallurgical, petroleum, and efficiency. The positions of millwright or telecommunications specialist could be rewarding for you. You could also succeed as a manager or group leader in these or related fields.

___ Would you enjoy the element of the unexpected at work?

___ Do you need independence?

___ Are you able to react to emergencies swiftly and with a cool head?

___ Do you like to take risks?

___ Are you comfortable with using firearms or other potentially dangerous equipment?

You are a Daring Aries. There are many dangerous jobs and positions in government and service that can utilize your ability to leap to decisive action at a moment's notice. You may choose to become a police, corrections, or parole officer; federal agent; alcohol, tobacco, and firearms inspector; firefighter; SWAT-team member; detonation expert; military strategist or aide-de-camp, combat specialist, or martial arts instructor.

Positions in civil service and politics are possible, as they will utilize your enjoyment of dealing with others. You may also want to try becoming a war correspondent or crime reporter.

You could also be attracted to jobs such as pilot or test pilot; race car or test car driver, parachute jumper, stunt driver, or stunt double for films; shooting instructor or hunter; driving, flying, diving, or skydiving instructor.

There are also many jobs in the munitions field that you may enjoy. These include work in the manufacture of, sale of, or training in the use of guns, rifles, revolvers, and other firearms; and fireworks, armaments, and appliances relating to military work.

___ Are you skillful, with good hand-eye coordination?

___ Do you like to work with metal tools or mechanical instruments?

___ Can you be expedient and quick?

___ Would you like dealing with others to make their lives better?

___ Do you need to control your own duties?

You are a Human Service Aries. There are many positions that can utilize your talents while providing you with lots of activity. The positions of barber, hairstylist, meatcutter, butcher, animal groomer, sheep shearer, driver, chauffeur, fence installer, and landscaper are all positions that deal with the public in some way but allow you to actively be in charge. There are also many possible jobs in the medical field for you, including surgeon or surgical technician; neurosurgeon; eye, ear, nose, and throat specialist; sonographer, electrocardiograph operator, X-ray technician or CAT scanner, emergency medical technician, or crisis hot-line operator.

___ Do you enjoy sports?

___ Do you have lots of physical energy?

___ Would you like to work with others?

___ Are you physically skillful and coordinated?

___ Would you like to be part of a group effort?

You are a Sporting Aries. Many positions in the fields of physical fitness and sports can utilize your tremendous energy and are available to you. These include especially work in team and contact sports such as baseball, football, basketball, soccer, and hockey as a player, coach, manager, trainer, press spokesman, agent, recruiter, or equipment manager. You could succeed in and enjoy work as a fitness or exercise instructor, weight trainer, or fight trainer. Reporting on sporting events for television or radio might also be exciting for you.

___ Do you like dealing with people?

___ Would you like to use your personality to help you succeed?

___ Can you take quick action when necessary?

___ Do you enjoy pointing the way for others?

___ Would you like to work independently?

You are a Public Aries. Your work should deal with the public in some way. You can utilize your outgoing personality and aggressiveness to succeed in many different jobs. You could enjoy work in sales, as a direct sales representative, advertising representative, or product manager. Some specific Aries fields that you can combine with this type of work include positions in auto-parts equipment, cars, machinery, or firearms sales.

Your ability to lead and excite others can be put to good use as a company promoter, publicist, headhunter, floor broker, trouble-shooter, labor leader, lobbyist, explorer, or guide. You could function well as a television reporter, activist, dispatcher, expediter, traffic manager or production coordinator.

___ Do you enjoy beginning new projects?

___ Do you feel you want complete control of your work?

___ Can you develop the discipline necessary to follow through on an important venture?

___ Do you have an easy time telling others what to do?

___ Can you sell yourself?

You are an Entrepreneurial Aries and should own your own business. Your enthusiasm, assertiveness, and natural high spirits can help you succeed. Consider any of the areas outlined above or become a freelancer or consultant in your field of choice. If you choose this route, you must learn to follow through and complete long-range projects, something many Ariens can find difficult to do.

Happy Hunting! How to Get That Job

When considering a career, all Ariens are encouraged to *think*. You are spontaneous, active people who do not usually plan for the long term. Yet your vocation is one area in life in which you can obviously benefit from doing this. Take some time to think about what you really need and want and even consider what you'll want to be doing a year from now. "I don't know" will probably be your immediate response, but if you imagine what type of position you're really qualified for *today* you can project into the future.

What positions can you land now that will keep you busy but will be exciting in themselves? How many of these jobs offer the opportunity to advance to a position of more independence or in which you can lead others, say within a year or so?

Don't be put off by the fact that you may not be able to find your "dream job" right now. All of us need to work our way up to some extent. Aries natives often seek immediate gratification in career goals—and sometimes get it. But more often than not, you have to compromise a little. If you are a good, reliable, and enthusiastic worker, your supervisors will soon know that you're motivated, ambitious, and can get the job done.

Having trouble just *thinking* about all this? Then talk to some friends or acquaintances who are entering a similar field or pursuing a job right now. Others who've been successful in landing positions can lend advice from experience. You will want to go forth on your own, but discussions can help you to realize in your own head what is right for you. At the same time, you can get some invaluable advice from those who've already been there.

A lot has been said about tapping the "hidden" job market, and you are just the one to do it! How? Ask. So-called "hidden" jobs are those that are not advertised or solicited. But you are gregarious enough to introduce yourself to others in your field and inquire about positions. Most people will respond to your friendly and candid manner.

Or go directly to hirers or directors of personnel in those firms or types of businesses in which you have an active interest. Ask questions, make suggestions, collect information. Always leave your resume or business card. You never know when someone may quit and create an opening for you. You can find lists of firms in your field or city from many resources at your local library. Talking to people in general can be helpful. You may find out about opportunities from friends or acquaintances. Follow up on all leads, drop by, or call.

Internships can also be advantageous because they'll actually allow you to *do* a job in order to find out about it. Many schools or trade organizations offer internship placement as part of their regular programs. If they don't, take the initiative and create your own! A young Aries woman we know was going to school while working full time. She was required to do an internship and the school had specific organizations where these programs existed, all quite a distance from her home. With a little investigation, she found a few similar organizations in her area and was able to arrange for a position near her home. The school ultimately approved of her plan.

Remember, though, that internships are often low-paying or may only offer a stipend for a season's work. If you can be an intern as part of a training program, it will transfer as course credit. If you are on your own, however, be willing to pull in your belt for a while if you go this route. One final note: While internships can offer job experience and contacts, they are not guaranteed to lead *directly* to a salaried position!

Once you have an interview scheduled for a new job, you need to shift your mode from aggressive to pleasant. While you Ariens are confident, self-assured, and open, some individuals may find you to be a little too brash, bold, or frank at times. Try not to come on too strong, talk too fast, or say too much.

If asked about a previous unsatisfactory job experience, keep the facts to a minimum. If you offer too much information, you may get excited about your problems and begin re-enacting an argument. If this happens, the interviewer could see *you* as excitable and difficult to work with. You should always remain calm, cool, and collected while interviewing.

Your energy can be expressed more positively by being enthusiastic about the position and asking pointed questions. Some hirers can be vague about a situation, responsibilities, expectations, and pay. Get all the facts through direct inquiry.

Demonstrate your skills, if possible, too. Ask to see and try out the equipment you may use. If the position involves sales or dealing with the public, show the charm and honesty that you will be using to get your job done.

Aries people know they are capable of handling most tasks, whether or not they've done them before. You may thus be tempted to exaggerate on your resume. Please avoid this practice. Exaggerations can be checked through references and may lose you that job you so wanted.

Your excitement may cause you to fidget, pace, or move about too much while you wait for your interview, but try to relax. You Ariens can be quite impatient and restless, so bring something to occupy yourself and to center your mind. A book, mini electronic game, or a Walkman can all offer absorbing and nonintrusive activities suitable for a waiting room. You could also chat quietly with others or review any company-related materials in the reception area.

Just don't get too impatient and leave in a huff! You may be walking out on a very good job. A good receptionist will warn you if the interviewer is running late. You may ask if not told, but don't make a pest of yourself by inquiring "How much longer?" every ten minutes. Even good business people can run from thirty to forty-five minutes late. Don't be insulted, aggravated, or angry at these realities of the business world. If you have somewhere else to go, inform the proper person. You can probably be bumped up or rescheduled. And if you've kept yourself occupied and relaxed, the waiting period will go much faster, and you'll be more confident and collected for your all-important interview.

Getting Ahead: How to Do Your Best on the Job

Aries is the sign of the pioneer, and besides having the capacity to enjoy beginning new projects, you can inspire and lead others as well. You are self-motivated and can come up with new ideas and activities for yourself and others. Your optimism can also inspire others to do their jobs well, and your quick mind and imagination can cope with changing circumstances. You can also enthuse others through your powerful self-expression, especially useful in meetings or for presentations.

You Aries people are doers and like to see the tangible results of your work. When you've got a task that inspires you, your energy will be inexhaustible. You'll always cut to the heart of any matter or project, serving the most basic needs with direct implementation.

Because of your speed and dexterity, you can accomplish many tasks at once, physical as well as mental. You can be a successful jack-of-all-trades, trouble-shooter, or manager regardless of your job title, which will earn you the immediate appreciation of your superiors.

An Aries chef we know enjoys his position because he heads a team where each member is responsible for their own job. Yet he makes all the menu decisions, keeps the group running efficiently, and institutes ideas for new systems and dishes. The position utilizes his tremendous energy and decisiveness, especially during peak meal hours, when the staff is kept very busy and orders must be served quickly.

As you're used to keeping up a fast pace, you'll be cool and in control when in crisis situations. In fact, you almost thrive on them! A crisis or deadline can inspire you to work even more quickly; be careful at these times not to sacrifice accuracy and attention to detail. While in positions where quick decisiveness, firmness, and authority are all-important, you'll function very effectively.

Ariens on a career track are not afraid to admit their great drive and desire for success. Because you are one of the most ambitious and motivated signs of the zodiac, you will be intensely passionate and driven once on the right course and will be determined to succeed and advance. Opportunities will be quickly seized in order to demonstrate to others your capability and strength. You strive for success and position; money and security will likely follow but are not as important in the Arien scheme of things.

You'll do well in competitive situations that allow you to directly conquer obstacles. In the rare instances when you fail, you'll easily pick up the pieces and aggressively begin again to meet new challenges. These are ways in which your powerful energies can be positively directed.

Your temper may get the better of you at times, but you usually just need to let off steam in order to be yourself again. It can always help to share your feelings with others on the job. Avoid building up problems, however, by discussing them again and again. Seek out solutions to problems with certain personalities that crop up on a regular basis by talking with others or instituting new procedures. As you can at times simply have a conflict of personality with a client or co-worker, it may ultimately be of help to discuss problems of this type with your supervisor.

Others may not understand if you do have an outburst. Try to control your voice, as well as what you say. After you've cooled down, a relaxed discussion can smooth things out, but make sure you're cooled down first! Another shouting match could easily occur if you get yourself worked up again.

You can jump to conclusions as well, so don't be afraid to admit when *you've* made a mistake and raised your voice when you shouldn't have. Be especially cautious about this when around supervisors: You may feel they're not really in charge, but they nominally are. Many an Aries has lost a job through too quick a use of direct and heated repartee with a superior.

When properly directed, your energy can't be beat. However, some Ariens jump too quickly into projects. Make a conscious effort to pause and reflect before you take action. Consider all possible outcomes. This will be difficult for you but will result in greater success. In your zeal to get things accomplished, you may overlook important details and deliver work in a slipshod fashion. Check and double-check! This need not be boring or wasteful of time if you concentrate on different specifics each time.

While you respond well to current emergencies, you may not naturally plan ahead to avoid them in the future. This can result in great inefficiency, as you'll be repeating mistakes that could well be avoided. When the crisis has passed, come up with ideas or ways of making sure it doesn't recur. It will be most helpful if you can get someone else to implement these changes for you.

As you Ariens are always in the "now," you may abandon projects that take too long to accomplish or impulsively redirect your energies in another direction. This can be a shortcoming on the job. If you are assigned a large project, break it up into many different parts. Set small hourly or daily goals toward your larger end. In this way you'll have a feeling of accomplishment each day, as well as variety and stimulation on a regular basis, and will finally achieve your overall objective.

You'll probably be bored by routine, so avoid this when possible. If not, at least vary your tasks in some way. Do the less enjoyable ones first so you can look forward to those that you enjoy.

You can be distracted by demands from others that crop up suddenly, as you like to handle problems at once. Yet you can in this way lose sight of other priorities. A daily list of "things to do" can be helpful. Whether or not you get everything done today is not significant, but you'll have a reminder when a crisis gets you off the track. Also, you don't have to act on everything that's presented to you at once. You work best when addressing one project at a time. If you organize, prioritize, and wait for the proper opportunity, you'll use your time more effectively. Completely unexpected demands may need the input of others: Ask for it when you need it.

In getting along with others on the job, it's best to remember that most people aren't as frank and candid as you. You are direct about what you want and need, but many others—especially Scorpio, Cancer, and Pisces people—will only imply or use indirect methods to get their ends accomplished. Your direct forcefulness will get beyond tendencies such as these in others, but you can benefit from trying to understand their points of view. Encourage discussion with those who aren't so clear-cut and attempt to see what they really want. It may seem silly to you, but you can work more effectively with others if you realize how different many of them are from you.

In meetings, keep an open mind in discussions and don't let yourself get too perturbed. Try to listen more to what others say: You may find someone else's input to be of value. Avoid being bossy and controlling, especially with those weaker than yourself personality-wise. Not everyone exists on your energy level, but all have different perceptions, skills, and ideas to offer if encouraged.

You can be impulsive in financial matters, and this is often an important consideration in the business world. When possible, get input from others or devise checks and balances to help you avoid overspending.

Yet you know how to take a risk and can succeed by taking action. You Ariens are naturally confident, often tireless individuals and will seize opportunities as they are presented. You'll enthusiastically dive into a new position, and if offered a promotion, chances are you'll prove that the confidence placed in you was correct.

If you're unhappy with your work, don't just explode and quit. Things can change if you try in a rational way to encourage others to help you. Think first! Don't make a rash decision that could affect your career adversely. If you feel absolutely thwarted in expressing your potential, however, it's best to move on.

You may want to tell everyone just what you think of them before leaving, but don't ever allow yourself to! One of them may be in a position to help you in the future, so save your most honest and candid statements for your closest friends and family.

Do

- Get an active position.
- Try for leadership positions or those in which you can work independently.

- Use your outgoing personality.
- Be decisive and efficient.
- Set daily goals.

Don't

- Lose your temper or be too blunt.
- Be impatient and impetuous.
- Dive into a project before thinking it through.
- Allow yourself to be distracted from finishing projects.
- Be too aggressive or competitive.

TAURUS
April 20 to May 22

> "Classic. That means enduring quality."
> —I. M. Pei, *Newsweek*

No Bull

Taurus is a bull. Think about him left quietly alone in his field or stall, and you have an accurate picture of the Taurean nature: calm, serene, and placid. Taurus enjoys the simple things in life, takes things easily in stride, and doesn't get excited quickly.

To ancient man, owning cattle meant wealth. These animals provided meat and milk for food, their hides were made into leather, bones were used as fertilizer, and the horns were made into tools. They have always been used as beasts of burden as well, because they are strong and stable. If you were a primitive man and had a few head of cattle, you had it all.

Taurus people are by nature down-to-earth individuals. Not surprisingly, they are attracted to the finer things the world has to offer. Taurus people are extremely security-conscious and enjoy domesticity. They seem to have a knack for attracting money and material wealth: Is it any wonder that the term for an optimistic market is "bullish"?

Oxen, mentioned by the ancient Hebrews in the Bible, were painted by cave dwellers in early Europe and are seen on Egyptian monuments as well. The bull has staying power, and Taureans are persistent, consistent, and stubborn. Patient and committed, they stick to their goals and follow through, no matter how long it takes. Like oxen, Taurus people have a great capacity for hard work—they are practical and purposeful. And they also love the earth and have an affinity for the natural world.

Some bulls today are just kept for breeding purposes. Now you understand why Taureans are such sensualists! They love physical pleasure, good food and drink, and the creature comforts that the world has to offer. Many become connoisseurs, as the Taurean ability to love and appreciate beauty is strong.

The eye in the constellation Taurus is a reddish star, said to symbolize anger, but Taureans have calm dispositions. They rarely lose their tempers and will put up with an extraordinary amount of abuse. But when enough is enough, they'll exhibit an extreme temper. Yet a *lot* of aggravation and goading is necessary before they explode.

Get to Work! What to Look for in a Career

Your primary drive is toward security, and thus money becomes an important issue. You can usually be counted on to find situations in which you will be solidly reimbursed for your hard work. You need to earn enough money so you can buy the things you want and those that make you feel most secure: a comfortable home, warm and attractive clothing, and good food. You'll feel best when you can point to a sound financial reward as representative of your ability, dedication, and hard work.

You should also seek out the security of employee benefits, such as a savings plan, medical insurance, retirement plan, paid vacation, and an annual bonus. These are becoming harder to find, but they can add an additional and significant reimbursement to your take-home pay. You should look into them, ascertain which are most important to you, and actively seek them from prospective employers.

You will always prefer a strong structure and regular work schedule. Whatever your hours, you need to know in advance that you have regular days and times when you're expected to be at work. You'd also like to be able to go to the same location every day as well. And if you can find a position where your supervisors and co-workers will remain fairly constant, you've found the ideal! Taureans like and need familiarity and stability, as you find changes on a regular basis to be emotionally draining.

All Taureans should work in a calm and pleasant atmosphere. While you can put up with a lot, noise, shouting, emotionality, and undependability of co-workers can make you frazzled. An environment of this type will eventually take its toll on your health and should be avoided. Seek instead a more businesslike, friendly, and relaxed atmosphere.

You Taureans also do best in comfortable and practical surroundings. If you sit in a chair, it must be a good one; if you work regularly with tools or machines, they must be of the proper quality to accomplish the task at hand. It also follows that work for a firm that's unwilling to provide you with the bare necessities is not for you. Avoid unstable, financially troubled companies that have trouble paying their telephone and other monthly bills! Problems of this type are always indicative of a much greater instability in finances or management.

The lush and plush will always appeal to you. You will find it most relaxing and soothing to work in a gorgeous atmosphere, with soft music and well-mannered associates. This is certainly not a necessity, but it would be an extra bonus for any Taurean.

You should also seek a job that you can love. You *will* find it if you try! A Taurus airline flight attendant we know enjoyed her position but wanted something she truly loved. She studied candy making and cake decorating on the side, eventually beginning a small catering service. Because of her persistence and patience, she now plans to open her own restaurant.

You should be comfortable in the knowledge that your skill or trade is needed and that you could easily find a new job, if necessary. In career planning, you should seek a field of specialization that will be able to provide for you and your family ten or twenty years from now. You might want to check out the *Occupational Outlook Handbook* in your local library. You may find a promising new field or a specialization in your current choice that will provide you with earning ability year after year.

Make sure you get a solid foundation in whatever field you decide on. Learn what prerequisites are necessary for success and get them under your belt. This can be done through education, internships, or on-the-job training. Most trade and business schools and adult-education programs offer part-time schedules, often specifically designed to help the worker learn skills that are directly applicable to the job market.

What's Your Line? Your Vocational Choices

Taurus is an earth sign, and you can do well in the financial and business arena in any number of positions. Work utilizing your physical strength to accomplish practical tasks can be a good opportunity.

Most people born under this sign have a great affinity for the finer things in life. Thus you have an appreciation of beauty on a number of physical levels, most notably touch and taste. You may have an interest in the food industry, luxury trade, or creative work because of these gifts.

Barbra Streisand has used her beautiful voice to create a career in the performing arts. Growing up poor in Brooklyn, this stubborn Taurean stuck to her goals to succeed against the odds. While Taurus specifically rules singing, it is also associated with other creative arts. Streisand followed hit records with acting in such films as *Funny Girl, Hello Dolly, The Way We Were,* and *A Star is Born.* Her career grew slowly but surely, and she's held on to the wealth and property she's accumulated along the way.

Taureans are natural business persons, and eventually Streisand took charge of her productions as well. She not only produced and directed *Yentl* but starred in it, co-wrote the screenplay, and recorded the music. Most recently, she directed and starred in *The Prince of Tides.* Streisand's four-disc retrospective album "Just for the Record" spans over thirty-five years in the recording industry and is a great testament to the Taurus staying power.

Another musical Taurus with a long, successful career is "Piano Man" Billy Joel. He sings, plays piano, and composes his own songs—all three Taurean careers.

Judith Jamison has used her natural Taurean grace and strength to become one of the foremost dancers of our era. True to her constant Taurean nature, this versatile performer's success is mainly due to her fifteen-year relationship with the Alvin Ailey Dance Theater. Founding her own company in 1988, she was asked to take over Alvin Ailey's after his death. Committed to her own dancers and board members, Jamison merged them with the Ailey company and continued managing and choreographing for this highly successful group.

Put a checkmark next to each question that you'd answer with a "yes." If there are several checks for a few career groups, review these first and think about the career suggestions we've listed. If you believe that one of these areas is right for you, investigate your selections further or those closely related to them. Also, take a look at the rest of our suggestions for other possibilities.

___ Do you have artistic taste?

___ Would you like a career in the creative arts?

___ Could you handle a career that may not always provide a solid living?

___ Are you good at expressing yourself?

___ Would you like to see the tangible results of your work?

You are a Creative Taurus. You have distinctive talent and the ability to soothe and relax others through your creative projects. You may want to become a singer, cartoon or ad voice-over artist, musician, disc jockey, composer, actor, dancer, choreographer, artist, sculptor, or writer to express to others your understanding of beauty and reality. You may also have a gift for decorating or design, leading to work as an upholsterer, drapist, interior decorator, or floral arranger.

You can also use your artistic talents to get into the production or administrative end of the creative industry. You could make a more solid living as a set or prop designer, recording engineer, record producer, musical arranger, voice coach; administrator in a radio studio, film or video production house, broadcasting station, or theater; producer of films, plays, or videos and associated positions; artist's agent or theater or house manager.

___ Are you attracted to things of beauty and value?

___ Do you have good taste?

___ Would you like the opportunity to earn a high income?

___ Do you feel you can develop a discerning ability?

___ Would you like to work in an upscale industry?

You are a Luxury Trade Taurus. You can use your appreciation of fine objects to help others enjoy them as well. You would enjoy work as a fine-art appraiser, art-gallery manager, curator, makeup artist, image consultant, display artist, clothing designer, fashion forecaster, perfume manufacturer, or salesperson of art objects, fashions, or cosmetics. You could develop your talents to become an art or fashion writer, reviewer, and critic as well.

You could also become involved in the sale, manufacture, design, appraisal, wholesale, or retail trade of gems, jewelry, furs, sculpture, antiques, lingerie, silks, satins, linen, leather, or other fine ornaments.

___ Do you want the opportunity to earn a high income?

___ Do you understand how to manage money effectively?

___ Would you feel confident enough to handle the finances or investments of others?

___ Do you have a realistic and practical outlook?

___ Are you interested in a field where your services will always be necessary?

You are a Financial Taurus. There are all kinds of positions in the financial field that would be right for you. You could function well as an accountant, actuary, auditor, treasurer, purser, credit interviewer, monetary exchange agent, coin dealer, collector, land developer, insurance agent, appraiser, or cashier. Some more creative positions in this area include work as a financial planner, controller, financial trust officer, stockbroker, trader, financial agent and/or advisor, loan officer, negotiator, and security manager. There are numerous positions in the banking industry that you would enjoy, and most banks also have excellent benefits packages.

___ Do you have a discerning palate?

___ Are you attracted to the food industry?

___ Would you enjoy providing delicious food for others?

___ Would you like a career that's creative but practical at the same time?

___ Are you willing to work with government regulations and restrictions?

You are a Gourmet Taurus. The food industry is a large one with many types of positions, from the creative to the practical and managerial. You should consider becoming a bakery or pastry chef; candy maker; chocolate, sweets, or confectionery manufacturer. Use your good taste as a gourmet cook or chef, cruise-line chef, or wine merchant. Your creativity may lead you to become a food stylist, cake decorator, or garnish specialist. Your business ability and reliability can be put to good use as a food service supervisor, caterer, restaurant or kitchen manager, food technologist, steward, goods manager, or food inspector.

___ Do you like to work with your hands?

___ Would you like to get back to basics in your work?

___ Do you appreciate seeing and feeling the tangible results of your work?

STAR SUCCESS

___ Could you enjoy work that is physically demanding?

___ Would you like to help society meet certain basic needs?

You are an Earthy Taurus. You'd enjoy physical, practical jobs in which you really get something accomplished. You may want to try your hand at becoming a woodworker, cabinetmaker, upholsterer, furniture maker, stagehand, stage carpenter, lumberjack, bricklayer, road repairer, materials tester, construction worker or inspector, grainery operator, heavy equipment or construction machinery operator, industrial truck and tractor operator, farm equipment mechanic, fruit or crop dealer, leather worker, shoemaker, butcher, domestic, or civil engineer. Use your experience or training in one of these areas to become a labor boss or administrator. If you are sports-minded you might try becoming an acrobat, gymnast, boxer, wrestler, discus thrower, skater, swimmer, or long-distance runner. Some other physically demanding jobs include work as a trainer, exercise or aerobics instructor, or dance teacher.

Work dealing with the natural world would also be to your liking. You may want to become an environmentalist, forest ranger, natural historian, horticulturist, botanist, geologist, earth scientist, soil conservationist, or erosion scientist; geophysicist or seismologist; agricultural scientist, economist, technician, or inspector. You may find work as a rancher, farmer, livestock or poultry breeder, or beekeeper to your liking. In the health field, you might enjoy work as a throat specialist or a massage therapist.

___ Would you like the opportunity to earn a high income?

___ Do you want the security of a vocation that will always be in demand?

___ Can you recognize and appreciate things of value?

___ Would you enjoy dealing with commercial or personal property?

___ Can you work well with the needs of others?

You are an Estate Taurus. You'd enjoy work in the real-estate or property-ownership field. You could profit by becoming a real-estate agent, investor, appraiser, manager, or salesperson. You may want to become a property or estate planner, real-estate attorney, or landlord-tenant lawyer. Your creative talents could be put to use as an interior or exterior designer or decorator, structural engineer or architect of solid structures (such as stores, bridges, roads), landscaper, or landscape architect.

___ Do you want to be completely independent?

___ Are you confident of earning an income on your own?

___ Could you handle money and investments well?

___ Can you take initiative and action?

___ Could you work hard without supervision?

You are an Entrepreneurial Taurus. Many people of your sign succeed as business owners. Make sure you have an idea that is financially viable and that will be enjoyable for you. Look over the lists above or use your own talents and creative ability to guide you to a venture that's right for you.

Happy Hunting! How to Get That Job

Your Sun sign gives you the tendency to resist change: You may have difficulty beginning your job search due to inertia. If you are currently employed, it may seem easier for you to stay where you are. You are able to put up with the most difficult situations. But remember that a steady diet of unhappiness at work will eventually eat away at your sense of well-being. If you have definitely decided it's time to leave, begin your new job search in at least some small way.

If you're currently unemployed, your present lifestyle of sleeping late, spending time on special interests, and hanging out may appeal to you more than making the effort to find a position. You can easily slip into an indolent lifestyle and will really be better off once you're in a more purposeful routine. While it will probably be a trying experience to call and write strangers, as well as to go to irregularly scheduled appointments, you must do it in this interim time. Make the decision to pick yourself up, dust yourself off, and get a job!

Once you've really decided to act, you will have no problems. You are a hard worker and will follow through on your promises to yourself. Like the tortoise in the old fable, you will win the race through slow and steady progress. You have a natural ability to go after exactly what you want and will not swerve or falter. You make progress in some small way for each effort you put forth.

Capitalize on your patience and persistence by committing a set amount of time to your job search each day or each week. You can use this time in any number of ways: researching the job market, responding to ads, visiting agencies, or scheduling appointments. Don't limit yourself to just one method of looking for a position; investigate all possibilities.

While you will probably be committed to a specific

goal, it may be necessary to compromise. Don't limit yourself by stubbornly insisting on having it all right now. You will probably get everything you want eventually through your strength of will and determination. Yet if you've decided on a creative career, you'll probably have to accept less pay. If you want a really stable and secure position, you may not be able to get other job perks. Evaluate the current market, your experience, and value to an employer. Decide what's most important to you and be prepared to cut corners in other areas. Otherwise, be ready to spend a great deal of time searching.

You have a natural grace and refinement and can easily make a good impression in an interview. You should dress conservatively and appropriately for the position you're interested in. Don't overdress—avoid chunky jewelry and strong cologne unless going after a strictly creative job where you'll want to show off your unique taste.

Taureans don't mince words, and you will get right to the point when asked questions. But be prepared to elucidate and elaborate. An interviewer wants to hear you talk and wants to understand your thoughts, feelings, and background. One can't get to know you if you answer simply "yes" or "no." Many interviewers will begin by saying "Tell me a little about yourself," and you should be ready to respond in an interesting manner. If necessary, prepare some material beforehand. Include your ultimate career goals, past experience, and personal assets.

Allow yourself the time to make a thoughtful decision. Don't let a prospective employer pressure you into making a commitment immediately. Someone who really wants you will be willing to wait a few days for your response to an offer. Secure a second interview if you need to have more questions answered. If a firm springs an offer on you and demands an immediate response, just say "yes." You can always change your mind after you take the time to think it over. Or use your grace of manner to let the employer know what your reservations are—you may get a better deal.

Be certain to negotiate exactly what you want in terms of salary, benefits, and vacation time in advance of accepting the position. Many firms make promises that they don't deliver. Be aware of the telltale signs of a successful business as well: cheerful and relaxed employees, a neat and attractive workplace, and sufficient staffing.

If possible, try to see your actual workplace. Atmosphere and environment can mean a lot, as can your co-workers. If you feel comfortable in the place that's been designated for you, you'll feel better about the job as a whole. Once again, if you have reservations, bring them up right away.

Getting Ahead: How to Do Your Best on the Job

Your pleasant personality and natural good manners make you an asset to any workplace. People will be easily attracted to your quiet courtesy, amiability, and affable good nature. Your ability to bring beauty and harmony to the working atmosphere will help everyone feel more comfortable.

Your greatest asset is your determination and dedication to your goals. You will singlemindedly pursue them with patience, persistence, and tenacity. You have the ability to work your way up along traditional lines and will not be swayed by difficulties or obstacles in your path. These will simply serve to make you more committed in achieving the results you want.

As a realist, you know what will or won't be possible. You know that your slow and steady approach will work. When others have quit in disgust or frustration, you will continue your increases in stability, security, and financial remuneration.

You are unhurried about each next step in your career path and will carefully consider any action before proceeding. You will easily build a solid foundation and will have the security of knowing that you deserve and can handle your current position.

A Taurus writer we know realized that he needed further training in order to advance in his field. He was rejected from several graduate schools but, undaunted, applied again the next year and was accepted. His realistic outlook helped him in school—he worked hard to improve his craft and made many personal connections. While the field is a difficult one to break into, he realized that his persistence would pay off. He mailed out many manuscripts to no avail, but eventually he received some acceptances and ultimately earned grants and other awards. He is now well on his way to a successful career.

You have a solid, thorough mind, and while you may take some time to digest new facts or learn new skills, once you do so you will never forget them. As an earth sign, Taurus likes to reduce situations and problems to their most simple and basic elements in order to evaluate them and make sound decisions. You will weigh all variables before making a decision, and once that is done you will stick to your convictions, acting only when you've convinced yourself that it's the best course of action.

You naturally have a sensible, sound, and businesslike outlook. You understand instinctively how to work with money to produce significant returns, while maintaining a secure foundation. You know and can estimate the value of things in the real world and won't take unnecessary risks. You will be conservative, especially when utilizing company funds, and are careful and prudent in the spending and accounting of time and money.

You are hardworking and will bring much strength, stick-to-itiveness and endurance to your job. You are an employer's dream because you will be willing to do whatever it takes to get the job done. You'll deal well with difficult personalities, complex situations, and emergencies with the same basic and unruffled view that you bring to everything else. When you are responsible for completing a project, you will go about it in a deliberate manner and work early or late if need be to accomplish your task on time and within budget. You take pride in accomplishment, rely on yourself alone, and don't often ask for help or favors unless necessary.

While you prefer a pleasant atmosphere, you can deal with almost anything that comes your way in the course of a work day. You can even work through illness and discomfort if need be and take stress in stride.

You work best when you're on your own and able to exercise your strong judgment. You also prefer to be able to work at your own pace and will work most effectively when you can proceed step by step in a relaxed manner. You will finish whatever you begin and can be relied upon in times of crisis.

You are usually straightforward and truthful. You can be trusted to keep your word and will keep business confidences easily. Because of your solidity and integrity, you can become a Rock of Gibraltar to co-workers.

You can succeed in almost any type of position. As an employee, you respect your superiors, but you can be a gentle but firm supervisor as well. You have no ego problem with work and will never resent those in authority; rather, you will work with and for them to attain your goals.

Many Taureans do well when working for one particular firm over a long period of time, and employers will reward you for your loyalty. Conversely, you can also do well if you stick to one particular vocation over the long haul. Your rewards will be cumulative, and in these ways you can gain in security. Your ambitions will be achieved over time, and you could build up a sideline career while holding down a secure position. We know one Taurus construction supervisor who kept his job through many years while playing in a band on weekends. Over the years, he purchased two condominiums, a house, and even a restaurant. He plans to pursue music full time and enjoy his properties and family.

If you don't maintain an active interest in your work, you may become apathetic or lazy. If you find yourself becoming bored or indifferent, chances are that there's not enough to keep you busy. Most employers will happily give you more work if you ask for it. Or set about making some functional or aesthetic improvements to your workplace until you become busier.

If you wish to remain with your current employer, seek out your supervisor to see if there's the possibility of a transfer to something more interesting or perhaps a promotion in the wings. You must assert yourself if you seek a change within the existing structure. If you're a good worker, it will probably only be a matter of time before you see a change.

You will stand up for what you believe in, which is typically a great asset, but on occasion may be problematic. Try to be reasonable if you disagree with supervisors, and remember that they will do what they choose in the long run, no matter how strongly you state your case.

Many Taureans become obstinate, and you should avoid this at the workplace. You need to work with others, and compromise is often necessary. While your firmness and patience are important attributes to utilize in achieving your career goals, they are not necessarily the best when working on projects with co-workers. The democratic principle of social equality usually prevails here. Try to learn the give and take of good relationships. While you may get what you want by demanding your way, you'll damage your working relationships. You should also try to be aware of constructive criticism. Other people have different ways of looking at things and may help you to improve your performance and efficiency. Even if you don't like to change the way you usually do things, logically you know there's always room for improvement.

In these high-tech times, you also need to get used to change. You'd prefer that things always stay the same, but today's business world is one of technological innovation and personnel movement. As many firms fare poorly under harsh economic conditions, there can be moves, layoffs, and other events that will indirectly affect you. Be as adaptable as possible to these outside circumstances if you are otherwise happy with your job. Use your sensible and creative mind to keep you alert to contingencies. When in doubt, ask your supervisor for more explicit instructions on how to proceed.

You always follow instructions to the letter, but you should guard against performing tasks by rote. Shake yourself up a bit now and then and do things a little differently. You can more easily make mistakes when you're not paying attention to habitual tasks, so don't allow yourself to be dulled by routine.

All of you Taurus people need plenty of rest in order to function at your best. Make sure you don't skip meals, either. A good breakfast of protein-rich foods or whole-grain cereals will keep you going through the toughest morning. While you Taureans have strong physical constitutions, you can easily wear yourselves out by neglecting proper sleep, nourishment, and relaxation. Put these on your priority list, especially in times of stress. Even Taureans cannot ignore stress forever, so do your best to unwind when you can.

Your tendency to put up with difficult situations may keep you in a position that you're unhappy with. If your pay and benefits are good, you might stay on for years of disgust rather than make a change. You can find a better opportunity if you look for one. Realize that your disposition and skills are worth a lot in themselves.

Take your time, but set about to make a change! If you're feeling depressed on your way to work, take stock of your situation. Are you moving ahead in this firm? Are you happy with what you're doing and with your co-workers? Are you being paid a fair wage for the work you do? If the answer to any of these questions is no, you should at least try to change things. If that becomes impossible, do yourself a favor and look for something better or begin your own venture on the side. You seek stability and security above all, but if you must put up with abuse in order to have them, you're doing the wrong thing.

You can find that ideal job if you put your mind to it! You naturally know how to leave with grace and tact. Get your former co-workers' addresses and phone numbers to keep in touch—not everything has to change in order to improve your work situation!

Do

- Find a job you'll love.
- Take initiative.
- Use your patience and persistence to realize your goals.
- Be willing to accept new and better ways of doing things.
- Create a pleasant work atmosphere.

Don't

- Stay in a job you dislike simply for security.
- Let your work and routine become merely a habit.
- Demand that others do things your way.
- Be stubborn at the workplace.
- Overwork or overstress yourself.

GEMINI
May 21 to June 22

"Can we talk?"
—Joan Rivers

Twice as Nice

The sign Gemini is symbolized by the mythological twins, Castor and Pollux, which are also the two bright stars in the constellation of Gemini. Geminis are witty, with quicksilver minds. An air sign, Gemini enjoys talking, learning new things, and exchanging ideas with others. Think about a pair of twins who have grown up sharing everything together. Each chatters away, always has a companion, and is totally comfortable in the other's company. This is how an individual Gemini person acts with others: open, straightforward, and communicative. Friends, relatives, and associates take the place of the missing mythological twin, as Geminis find it necessary to seek out company in order to feel whole themselves.

Castor and Pollux weren't identical, by the way. Sons of Zeus, they were fraternal twins only; Castor was mortal and Pollux immortal. A certain duality as well as changeability is implied by the duo. Most real twins stress their differences rather than their similarities and often develop quite separate interests. This characteristic, too, is common to people born under the sign of Gemini. They have a wide range of interests, activities, and associates, know a little about a lot of topics, and are also adaptable to their circumstances. The Gemini mind and moods are so fast moving that other more staid zodiac signs might regard them as two-faced.

The mythological Castor was known to be a wrestler, while Pollux was a boxer. All Geminis are dexterous with their hands. They are clever handymen and enjoy physical activity. Most Gemini people have excellent coordination as well—possibly the result of the twins' ability to keep in step with each other since ancient times!

When Castor was slain, Zeus saw how lost Pollux was and allowed them to live together forever in the sky. Similarly, Geminis will also continue to seek out relationships and companionship on earth. If they can use their ability to get along and communicate with others on the job, they'll be on their way to happy and satisfying careers.

Get to Work! What to Look for in a Career

Most important, you need to find a position that offers change and variety. You will be stimulated by a situation that allows you to handle many different tasks: You will never be content to do the same thing all day. You will be most happy if you are able to use your own judgment as well.

You need to have a degree of freedom on the job. If you're in a situation where you must get permission from a superior to move about, that job is not for you! By the same token, if you exclusively must be responsible for staying at the workplace to wait for appointments or calls, that position is probably not for you, either. You work best in an unrestricted environment where you can get up and attend to the current task at a moment's notice.

If you are tied down by routine or restrictive responsibilities, you will quickly become bored. Your attention will wander away from your work, and you'll soon be socializing or making personal calls. Avoid all of this by making sure you find a position that stimulates you mentally and that provides at least some freedom and diversity.

You should also look for a position that gives you the ability to interact with others. Whether it be working in a large office, dealing with outside people as part of your job (such as in sales or customer service), or working as part of a team, you must have others around you who will provide needed stimulation and unexpected challenges.

But most Geminis have highly developed nervous systems and many can be high-strung individuals, and you may become overwrought or exhausted by too much of a good thing! While you need an exciting atmosphere full of people and ideas, too much stimulation could make you feel "wired." No one can keep moving *all* day long, and you should always vary your work day with rest periods and breaks. Take some time to let yourself relax and settle your mind. Frequent breaks of short lengths are probably best, but in the course of a hectic work day, you will probably ignore this advice and forget about reserving time for yourself. Make an extra effort *not* to. Find a position that allows you to take a break when you need it.

Find, if you can, a job in which you'll also have a quiet atmosphere in which to work. You can become distracted from the task at hand by noise from office machines or idle chatter. Your concentration may be shattered by the smallest of intrusions. The ideal position will offer you a private office or cubicle, conference room, or library for quiet time when you need it.

In career planning, you should try to think of the big picture. Does your current interest or employment provide you with a decent wage and promise of security? If not, you'll soon be driven off your course by necessity. You should find a field that will be around for a while.

The best careers are developed over many years. You Geminis like so much change and variety you may impede your career growth by job-hopping. If you can find a career that offers enough variety within itself, you will be better able to stay with a particular field for many years. Try also to isolate a specialization that provides diversity and mental challenge.

What's Your Line? Your Vocational Choices

The involvement and use of your intellect and mental functions provide the basis for most Gemini positions. Many can also make use of your physical dexterity. All can benefit from or often demand variety.

You have so many interests and skills that you could do just about anything or become involved in many diverse vocations in a lifetime. The following lists feature many true Gemini positions but can be expanded on by your own ideas.

In the case of Gemini Bill Moyers, he began his career as a reporter while still a young teenager. The Gemini ability to use words, ideas, and communication is natural to Moyers, who worked as a Baptist preacher and television news assistant director while in college.

Moyers's career reflects the many-faceted Gemini nature. He's best known for his work on educational television, most notably "Bill Moyer's Journal," and as a correspondent, news analyst, and commentator for CBS News. His observations, panel discussions, and interviews are always thought-provoking, and his many Emmy and Peabody awards attest to his reputation as one of the most well-respected broadcast journalists today.

Joyce Carol Oates epitomizes the Gemini as a writer. Her versatile mind is responsible for her prolific work and the need for a diversity of style and format. She's written novels, short stories, poems, plays, criticism, and essays, as well as editing the work of others, and she continues to teach creative writing at Princeton University as well.

When Gemini energies are properly directed into a career, great amounts of work can be accomplished. Joyce Carol Oates exemplifies this tendency: She's authored over twenty novels and dozens of short stories and frequently contributes to periodicals.

Roger Ebert is also a Gemini who's primarily a writer, but his work draws more on the Gemini analytical ability. He began his career as a reporter but eventually switched to film criticism. By the time he was twenty-five he was reviewing for the *Chicago Sun-Times* and continues to do so today (newspapers are specifically ruled by the sign Gemini). Like most successful Geminis, Ebert, too, has found diversity in his career in viewing new films on a regular basis. Best known for his television programs "Sneak Previews" and "At the Movies," his friendly arguments with fellow critic Gene Siskel (Geminis love debate) are what have always made the shows popular and remind one immediately of the archetypal Gemini twins.

Comedian turned talk-show host Joan Rivers uses her great Gemini communicative ability to help us see the lighter side of life. Her quick wit, split-second comebacks, and gossipy manner are all typical of her Sun sign, and her sharp tongue and astute observations owe much to her critical Gemini abilities. Before launching her comedy career, she worked in publicity and retail, both also Gemini avocations.

* * *

Put a checkmark next to each question that you'd answer with a "yes." If there are several checks for a few career groups, review these first and think about the career suggestions we've listed. If you believe that one of these areas is right for you, investigate your selections further or those closely related to them. Also, take a look at the rest of our suggestions for other possibilities.

___ Would you like to actively use your mind at work?

___ Do you express yourself well?

___ Are you interested in language and its usage?

___ Are you looking for a job that presents great variety?

___ Do you have a need to express your views and opinions or help others to do so?

You are a Communications Gemini. This is an extremely wide and versatile field, which is why you're probably attracted to it! There are many careers that can make use of your excellent reading, writing, and language skills. You could become a writer or editor of plays, documentaries, short stories, commercials, magazine articles, comedy, television shows, or books (you can choose novels, nonfiction, humor, or biographies). You could also function well as a newspaper journalist, press secretary, speech writer, freelance or ghost writer, advertising copy writer, or television or radio newscaster or announcer. Your analytical and critical abilities can be put to good use as a literary agent, librarian, or critic of books, television, or theater.

You could become a lecturer or orator and write your own work. You might be qualified to be a linguist, interpreter, telecommunications specialist, auctioneer, communications consultant, information specialist, or media spokesperson.

STAR SUCCESS

___ Are you interested in travel?

___ Would you like to go from place to place as part of your job or help others to do so?

___ Do you like to deal with the public?

___ Do you think you could repeat the same task with different places and people?

___ Do you have a mechanical inclination?

You are a Traveling Gemini. There are many jobs that relate to the travel industry and vehicles themselves that may be of interest to you. Many of these positions deal with the public, such as railway jobs—including train or subway motorman, engineer, conductor, administrator, supervisor, or maintenance operator. Drivers are often Geminis, including chauffeur, bus or taxi driver, or other support positions in a limousine or car service. Running a messenger service or becoming a service representative, travel agent, tour guide, or airline ticket agent might also be appropriate for you. If you have a faculty for mechanics, you could become a car, bus, or aircraft parts sales representative, mechanic, or repair shop manager.

___ Do you have good skills for detail work?

___ Would you like to deal with the public?

___ Can you understand and communicate well with others?

___ Do you find sales and trading stimulating?

___ Do you have the ability to accommodate the needs of others?

You are a Commercial Gemini. You would enjoy work in wholesale or retail trade in any number of businesses. Some specific Gemini fields include work in a bookshop, the stationery or paper trade (including pens, ink, pencils, and artistic supplies), or as an employment counselor or placement agent. Others include audio/video sales or service person; computer hardware and software designer, manufacturer, or salesperson; museum worker or guide; car insurance sales agent. Any position in commercial, retail, merchandising, sales, and marketing could be good for you, including buyer, window-display artist, bookkeeper, or manager.

___ Do you have creative talent?

___ Would you like to express yourself as part of your job?

___ Can you handle the uncertainty that's often part of temporary or freelance work?

___ Would you like to work with your physical as well as mental skills?

___ Do you have physical coordination or manual dexterity?

You are a Creative Gemini. There are all kinds of positions in various creative disciplines that could be stimulating and rewarding for you. If you have a good eye or drawing skills, you should seek work as a commercial artist, illustrator, cartoonist, animator, calligrapher, or graphics designer. Your ability to do fine work can also be put to good use in jewelry or handicrafts design or manufacture. The Gemini communicative and mental ability could help you succeed as an actor, dancer, musician, songwriter, composer, director, sound designer, or acoustics expert. Some off-beat creative jobs for Geminis include inventor, copyright or patent clerk, graphologist, illusionist (especially card tricks and sleight of hand), juggler, mime, and manicurist.

STAR SUCCESS

__ Would you like to be of service to others?

__ Could you deal with people as part of your day-to-day duties?

__ Would you like to use your mental abilities to solve problems?

__ Do you want a position that offers variety and diversity?

__ Are you good with facts and figures?

You are a Human Services Gemini. Once again, there is a tremendous variety of positions that you'll be suitable for in business, industry, and the service sector. You could become an attorney, politician, diplomat, mechanical engineer, teacher, tutor, private management consultant, broker, trader, fundraiser, efficiency expert, expediter, trouble-shooter, market survey specialist, computer programmer, or computer-data consultant.

A few other positions that you may enjoy include social worker, human relations aide, federal agent, postal service worker, traffic specialist or inspector, notary public, vocational counselor, or youth-group or recreational leader in your community. Some health-related positions that you might find stimulating include psychologist, respiratory therapist, speech pathologist, or audiologist.

__ Do you want to work with your hands as well as your mind?

__ Can you concentrate on details to get a job done?

__ Would you like a position in which you can finish many small projects in the course of a day?

__ Do you have physical coordination or manual dexterity?

___ Do you think you could handle routine work at times?

You are a Precision Gemini. Your ability to do fine detail work can lead you to become a dentist or dental work craftsman, delivery route driver, or jewel sorter, polisher, or cutter. Others include communications-equipment technician, carpenter, handyman, watchmaker or repairer, bookbinder, book manufacturer, or printer. Some positions draw more on your mental side, such as executive secretary, administrator or assistant, bilingual secretary, typist, files or mail-room manager, word processor, or receptionist. Other ideas are restaurant host or maitre d', telephone operator or answering-service attendant, clerk, page, and box-office manager.

Happy Hunting! How to Get That Job

Since you are by nature a communicative type, you should start your job search by talking! Whoever you run into in the course of your busy day should be told of your plans. You probably have quite a large circle of acquaintances, and you'll find many leads just by asking around.

To speed up your job search, enlist the help of your telephone. With postal fees skyrocketing, it's often cheaper to place a phone call than to send a query letter and resume, and you'll usually get immediate information. Call prospective employers, friends, relatives, acquaintances, co-workers—anyone you can think of who may be able to give you some job-hunting ideas or information on possible openings.

Your search should also include local and city newspapers. Skim the Help Wanted section to get an idea of what's being offered in your area. Don't forget to look up related jobs in addition to the particular position you're after. In this way you may isolate a prospective employer who could have an opening for you in the future. Make a quick call and you just might be invited to fill out an application.

The key is to collect as much information as you can. If you're persistent and follow up on all leads, you'll develop a wide pool of opportunity. It helps to seek out as many possibilities as you can: Out of a dozen employers, only one may have the right job for you.

Since you'll probably be using your phone a lot, it can help to get a few special services. Call waiting is inexpensive and gives you the convenience of having a second line when you need it. Employers who have many people to call may pass you over if they get a busy signal. You can thereby make the best use of your time by continuing an active search while not tying up the line when important calls are coming through.

It can also help to invest in an answering machine to catch your calls when you're out on interviews. The cost of these has gone down greatly during the last several years, and you can buy telephones with answering machines attached for a better price than purchasing each one separately. This is a good investment, which will help your social life after you've landed the job!

Use your fluency with the written word to produce a top-notch resume that really tells it all at first glance. Your writing style can also be helpful when it's necessary to introduce yourself by mail: Bring up any significant facts that aren't appropriate for the resume. And don't forget thank-you notes! They always make a good impression but can also serve to remind the interviewer of your interest.

Your conversational ability puts you in a superior position when it comes to job interviews. Employers will be attracted to your charm, easy manner, and intelligence. Don't allow yourself to talk too much, however. Many Geminis get excited by the direction of a conversation and don't know how or when to stop. Be cautious and answer only the questions that are asked of you. Make yourself aware of how the interviewer is reacting.

Small talk is always necessary when meeting strangers, but your conversation must have substance as well as style. Avoid diversions and make sure you specifically address the questions at hand.

As you are adaptable by nature and can easily deal with many different personalities, adapt your mode of dress to the position when going on an interview. You tend toward the conservative, but be aware of how one is supposed to look in the job you want. Err on the side of conventionality.

Most important: Relax and enjoy yourself! Let the interviewer see how easily and effectively you can deal with others. See many people and make a lot of appointments. You'll have fun meeting new people as you learn more about many different organizations and possibly get more leads. In a short time you're sure to find something just right!

Getting Ahead: How to Do Your Best on the Job

Your flexibility is perhaps your greatest asset on the job. You can adapt to changing circumstances or the demands of a supervisor. You don't worry when plans must change, as you find new situations stimulating and challenging.

Your quick mind is always there to help you chart a new course or change methods in order to get the job done most effectively. You are not held down by preconceived notions or old ways of doing things. For you the best method is always the one that works to solve the current problem at hand, as you like to experiment with new ways of accomplishing tasks simply because they're mentally stimulating.

You always enjoy an intelligent challenge and are good at problem-solving. You will keep yourself occupied with discussion, examination, and experimentation until you come up with the best solution. Your often brilliantly logical mind will easily offer any number of clever alternatives, and you can function well in a think tank or brain-storming session. Realistic and objective, you can dispassionately review a problem on an abstract level in order to come up with the best course of action.

You also easily accept suggestions from others and have no prejudices about what will work before you think things through. You are decidedly not an egotist (with twins there's always someone else to think about) and will not let yourself become involved in power struggles or competition with associates. You would prefer to remain on an equal, friendly footing with all and to consistently enjoy pleasant business relationships. Your advancement will be the result of your intelligence, ability to interact with others, and doing a job well, rather than heavy ambition or struggle.

As an air sign, your mind is a great asset that can be used on any number of levels. You seize all that is presented to you, and you're interested in really understanding and exploring the tasks you're presented with. You are always a realist, and your views cannot easily be clouded by emotion or desire. You are a rational person with imagination and ingenuity who can analyze components, causes, and effects, and combine these quickly for the best result. You always try to organize thoughts into a logical order. Nothing will be missed by your sharp eye, and you can critique and reappraise business situations in a flash.

You have a real fluency for the written and spoken word, and this can be of great use in correspondence, proposal or draft writing, business discussions, meetings, or telephone work. Because you are quick and often have a highly developed sense of humor, you get along well with others. You are charming, likable, and easy to be with and thus are popular with co-workers. You can make others immediately comfortable and familiar with you, and can use these skills to deal effectively with everyone. You handle people with diplomacy and can influence them through your ability to see and understand both sides of a question at once. With your finesse you can soothe angry customers, reconcile co-worker differences, or act as a go-between to disparate parties.

The Gemini character is multitudinous and multifaceted. You'll be able to work well with business machines or mechanical equipment and can become known as the Mr. or Ms. Fix-It of the office. Or you'll be a Mr. or Ms. Do-It-All, like a Gemini technical director we know who enjoyed working in the theater, where he would do a variety of tasks. He organized work schedules, drafted set construction plans, supervised carpenters and painters, and hung and focused lighting instruments as part of his job. In a business where the unexpected always seems to happen, this Gemini reveled in practical problem-solving as he met sudden crises and acted on swift decisions.

You need to be busy and active, and when you are you'll contribute much to your employer's goals—being ready, willing, and able to meet opportunities as soon as they come your way.

Your need for excitement and change may well get in the way of keeping to one career track. Try not to switch jobs often; you may do this just for the sake of change and thus can short-circuit your career. Remember, most employers want to hire people who will stay with the firm for at least a year or two. You can also try to circumvent the boredom factor by opting for multiple part-time positions, temporary, or freelance work.

If your job is not stimulating, you may have difficulty concentrating on the task at hand and can waste time in idle chitchat. Alternating tasks can have a beneficial effect, as can talking to others about business matters rather than gossiping. Instead of letting your attention wander to unimportant things, cultivate more useful conversations, or tackle miscellaneous chores. Once you learn to control and concentrate your mental energies, you can accomplish a tremendous amount of work.

Learn to take pride in what you do. You may turn in sloppy or incomplete work just to get it over with quickly. If you are bored with or tired of a repetitive task, return to it later with a fresh outlook or different point of view.

You have a tendency to learn a little about a lot of things rather than a lot about a few things. Learn at least one skill, subject, or specialty in real depth. You will find that if you stick to a single topic, there are always new and fascinating things to learn about it. Many corporations will even help you attend school if your learning will benefit the job. Specializing can also make you the *one* person whom others will seek out for advice and information.

In business conversations, learn especially to organize your thoughts and questions before making a call or attending a meeting. You can be distracted and scatter your mental energies, and you might entirely miss the point you needed to make! Outlines can help provide you with a point of reference. Concentration is a good habit that all Geminis should learn to practice.

In general, stick to the facts. Your discussions can be so fluent that you may have a tendency to expand on the facts or imply more than is true. While this can be an asset to good story-telling, it's not good for business purposes. Decisions can be made by superiors, customers, or clients based on your recommendations, and if these aren't founded on simple facts it may backfire on you. Double-check all sources, and don't take rumors or gossip for the truth. Research and verification can be stimulating or fun, as you'll be met with many different people and ideas.

Hopefully you've found a position that enables you to move about from place to place. Don't overdo it, though! Don't ever let socializing get in the way of your work. Schedule regular, short breaks instead.

If you do find yourself confined to a desk or office, don't despair. Today's world of technology can provide you with many ways of being elsewhere while remaining in one place. Use your phone, fax machine, computer modem, or bulletin board to communicate with others while you stay put. Or encourage others to come to you if necessary.

Because you seek out the new and really are alive in the present (rather than the past or future), you can become forgetful or unpunctual. Don't let other things distract you on your way to important business appointments. Get a good, large watch and appointment book. Train yourself to refer to these with regularity, and jot down notes or reminders. Organize and preplan your time. Set an alarm to remind you when to begin a new task or move on to a new project. With these tricks you can still concentrate on what you're doing *now*, while keeping yourself apprised of what is required *later*.

Try to keep your word as well and follow through on projects. After the numerous events of your busy day, you may not recall whether you really said you'd deliver those reports tomorrow or not. Write down important promises to co-workers and remember to consult that list! Or ask your co-workers to remind you with a call, note, or visit. If a project is that important to them, they'll follow up.

In many jobs, you will have to account for expenses. While money is not of the greatest importance to you, you should learn to use it effectively at work. Dealing with money on an abstract level is easy; it's the practical experience that may throw you. Once again, a journal can help. Keep track of all expenses by jotting them down; get a company credit card and *always* get receipts. If you can train yourself to consistently do these simple things when spending company funds, you're sure to be reimbursed properly. And whether or not you care about being reimbursed, the company will appreciate accurate records about what expenses you incur on the job.

Don't overwork: If you're really stimulated by your job, you may do so. Many Geminis suffer from stress and nervous tension. Learn to recognize the warning signs of overwork. Take a break, a day off, or a long weekend away from the cares of your job when necessary.

Business opportunities can come your way in an effortless manner, and you'll usually be quite willing to accept something new and different. Make sure your changes are lateral ones or promise advances in pay or the interest level of your work. Don't skip around to many different types of jobs unless you've made a conscious decision to change your career direction.

Get the names, addresses, and phone numbers of co-workers and important associates before you leave—they may be helpful later on, and you'll probably want to keep in touch. You instinctively know how to leave graciously and may even convince people to cheer you when you go!

Do

- Adapt to circumstances.
- Try to keep at a task by making it fresh and interesting.
- Cultivate concentration and relaxation when appropriate.
- Slow down and organize your mental and physical pace.
- Utilize mental skills, calendars, and reminders.

Don't

- Let yourself become distracted on the job.
- Socialize too much.
- Scatter your efforts.
- Allow yourself to breeze through important tasks.
- Overwork.

CANCER

June 21 to July 23

"Look for the new, imaginative, and humanistic."
—Nam June Paik, *American Film*

Crustacean

Cancer is the crab—the only crustacean of the zodiac. There's so much imitation crabmeat sold in supermarkets these days that it's hard to remember what the real thing is like. But we must, for Cancer is the genuine article. In restaurants crabmeat is usually served flaked, already removed from the shell. But sometimes you'll get the whole body on your plate or perhaps just the claw. Then you realize that this little crustacean is a tough nut to crack—and so are Cancerians.

Like the crab, Cancer people are very soft and delicate inside but often have a tough outer shell. They are sensitive, gentle people who are easily hurt, so they become protective of themselves and their feelings. If you don't know them too well, you may just see the exterior facade. In business they can appear gruff, stand-offish, or even stuck-up; these behaviors are the "shell." Cancerians take a long time to get to know others well and to feel comfortable and secure with them. It's not until then that they'll let down their defenses.

If you think about the hermit crab, you'll have a good image of a Cancer person. He has no shell, but he must find one at all costs or be devoured by some sea predator! When he finds a shell, he sticks with it and spends most of his time in it alone. Cancer people seek security above all else and often find their homes to be refuges from the outside world. They are generally reserved and put emphasis on their family and maintaining their security.

When Cancerians find the things they want in life, they dig their claws in and hold on. This holds true for items of sentimental value and jobs, as well as relationships. The crab has eyes at the ends of its movable antennae and thus very good vision. Cancerians look to the past as well as the future, but they will proceed slowly to protect and expand their base of security.

Cancer is a water sign, ruled by the changeable Moon and therefore the tides and the sea as well. Their moods and feelings are changeable; Cancers are sensitive and reactive. They are often imaginative, creative, and ambitious people, but in a quiet way. And yes, they can be "crabby" when they're hurt, when things aren't going their way, or just because of a bad mood.

Young crabs can grow new legs to replace those that have been damaged or lost, and the Cancerian, likewise, has the ability to keep on keepin' on. They are tenacious and persistent people on the job, yet adaptable to circumstances. Yes, they will complain and retreat into their shells at times. But they will slowly and effectively work their way toward their goals.

Get to Work! What to Look for in a Career

You should take some time to think about the practical side of your job requirements. You Cancerians should ideally have a regular schedule, job stability, and financial security from any position. What kind of pay do you need? It may be helpful to list your expenses (including those for enjoyments and recreation) to get an idea of what you need to earn. If you can't manage to pay your basic household expenses plus put a little away for a rainy day, you'll feel anxious and pressured.

While money is an important concern for you, you'll do even better if you find your position emotionally rewarding. Many Cancerians succeed in the business world because they are adept at helping things grow and develop. If you can see your firm, department, or group move forward as a result of your efforts you'll get great satisfaction. Cancer is a nurturing sign by nature, and you might also seek a job where you can nurture and help other people to grow.

You must also feel that you can move ahead in some way, whether it be in terms of position, money, responsibility, security, or benefits. Yet remember that if you seek a really satisfying job, you may have to compromise on pay.

Cancerians' families are important, and you'll want to be at home as much as possible. You probably won't want to work too far from home, as travel can add unnecessary time to your work day. Would you consider moving to another city for an ideal opportunity, or are your roots firmly planted now?

The demands of home and family may incline some Cancerians to opt for part-time work, but this is not always an option. Realize that many full-time positions can take up more than forty hours a week because of commuting, overtime, and special projects at work. Yet you can find career-track positions in business and industry that are strictly nine-to-five if you need to.

All of you Cancerians should consider the alternative of a home-based business. You'll feel great satisfaction in building your own opportunities while staying right at home. A talented Cancerian chef we know loved his job and was soon the manager of an establishment. On the side he handled catering jobs in which his whole family helped out. Eventually, he opened his own firm, managing cafeterias and catering. Another Cancer enjoyed staying home while her children were growing up, but as she felt the need for some career development, she began writing. She soon sold a series of magazine articles and eventually wrote a book. With the help of the post office and a home computer, she had created a business that allowed her to work at home.

Positions with a regular schedule are best for you. You like to settle into a routine, and atmosphere is especially important. Look for a position in pleasant surroundings with friendly associates. Decorate your personal space with things you enjoy: Pictures of family and home, plants, and even soft music can make you feel at ease in your working environment.

What's Your Line? Your Vocational Choices

You Cancerians are like parents—with a need to help children, adults, and businesses grow, develop, and mature. Many Cancerian occupations have something to do with the basics: food, clothing, and shelter. From the simplest variation on this theme (grocer or baker) to international commodities trader, Cancer rules them all.

The other side of Cancerian occupations deals with the inner life and psychological well-being. Cancer's need to offer public service in the form of social work is reflected here, as are creative positions in the arts and design field. You can create your own "families" at work and are often comfortable working at home or with your closest relatives.

Bill Cosby is a Cancer who's been in the public eye for

over twenty-five years. He began his career as a comic in order to finance his college education. Cosby's gentle, "real life," family humor epitomizes the Cancerian's traits, as do the careers of some of the characters he's made famous: an agent working for the U.S. government, a physical education teacher, and an obstetrician. Bill Cosby has the Cancer talent of knowing just what the public wants and needs, which is the secret of his phenomenal appeal in television, records, commercials, and concerts. Financially, he's built an empire that includes real-estate investments.

Cancerian Norma Kamali has succeeded in designing clothing that women will buy and feel comfortable in. She is also said to be reserved and shy, and she avoids public appearances. However, she's garnered great publicity for her fashions, including the enormously popular sweatshirt line and retro designs, all reflecting Cancer's interest in clothing, comfort, convenience, and nostalgia. She even serves as a saleswoman in her shop—another Cancerian job!

Cancerian Faye Wattleton was the president of Planned Parenthood, the oldest and largest family-planning service in the United States. A former nursing instructor and mother, she's used her caring and supportive nurturing instincts to help millions of women across America take control of their reproductive lives through family planning. Wattleton is very much a public figure today, hosting a TV talk show dealing with women's issues.

Put a checkmark next to each question that you'd answer with a "yes." If there are several checks for a few career groups, review these first and think about the career suggestions we've listed. If you believe that one of these areas is right for you, investigate your selections further or those closely related to them. Also, take a look at the rest of our suggestions for other possibilities.

___ Do you really enjoy food?

___ Are you convinced that the public's need for convenience is profitable?

___ Do you like the feeling of helping others with their basic needs?

___ Are you skillful, capable, and reliable?

___ Do you feel you could fill the wants and needs of the public?

You are a Nourishing Cancer. Those fields relating to the provision of foods and food services for others could be rewarding for you. These include the baking, canning, packing, and food-processing businesses. You could succeed on many employment levels in firms dealing in coffee, tea, refreshments, or food. Work in restaurants and fast-food businesses, or as a caterer, baker, grocer, or chocolate or candy maker can all provide enjoyable and profitable jobs for Cancerians. You may also profit from a career as a food stylist (that is, making sure the hamburger looks fantastic in an ad) or food, restaurant, or wine critic.

___ Is the welfare of your community or region important to you?

___ Would you like to be of service to others in a practical way?

___ Do you instinctively feel you know what needs to be done?

___ Do you get emotional satisfaction from giving something of yourself to others?

___ Are you efficient, responsible, and personable?

You are a Public Service Cancer. You can earn money and help others by satisfying some of their basic needs in life. You should try a job as employee, manager, or owner of a hotel, motel, restaurant, bed and breakfast inn, or boardinghouse. Involvement in the management of apartment houses, homeless shelters, day-care centers, group homes, or orphanages could also be good for you. Working as domestic help—as a cook, housekeeper, companion, personal shopper, dry cleaner, or live-in help for the elderly or disabled—for individuals or large institutions could benefit you. Designers, dress makers, and seamstresses can be Cancerians. Other positions in this category include security specialist, house manager, and foster-home placement officer.

You can get great emotional fulfillment from giving your help to the public, your community, or another regional or perhaps global group. Possible positions for you include family-guidance counselor, relief-agency worker, consumer-affairs advocate, social worker, teacher (especially early education), and occupational, behavioral, or physical therapist. You could serve as a local historian, genaeologist, museum worker or curator, assembly or council person (or other local offices), family or real-estate attorney, city or county worker, home inspector, child-protection or support investigator, political liaison, or lobbyist. Military personnel can also be Cancerians and may specifically serve as supply handlers, naval personnel, or navigators.

The other side of the public service sector career is seen in positions dealing directly with the public: salesperson, cashier, tour guide, cruise-ship manager, and pollster. Cancer's natural affinity for the public and likable manner will help you succeed in these areas.

___ Are you interested in the business world?

___ Are you good with money, figures, and trading?

___ Do you want a career with great earning potential?

___ Would you like to help others feel more
     secure?

___ Do you feel you have a good idea of what the
     public wants and needs?

You are a Commercial Cancer. Cancerians exhibit a wonderful aptitude for understanding and utilizing the value of a dollar and can capitalize on changing markets. Positions in the real-estate field could be right for you, including work as a developer, broker, agent, apartment manager, super, appraiser, or even builder. In finance, work as an auditor, economist, accountant, actuary, insurance-claim representative, property assessor, cost analyst, money manager, financial planner, purchasing or acquisition agent may be of interest to you. Other related positions in this group include commodities dealer or trader, labor specialist or manager, market research analyst, antiques dealer, insurance agent, and art or collectibles dealer.

Cancers can be attracted to the security of the business world, and many fields in the commercial area would be ideal for you. Sales administrative positions with firms that manufacture or distribute home appliances are good choices. Work as a sales representative, distributor, wholesaler, or merchandiser for large chains could be lucrative for you in the fields of food service, home improvement, and hardware. Retailers and shop owners also fall into this category.

___ Are you interested in the workings of the
     planet Earth?

___ Do the life sciences interest you?

___ Do the real basics of life appeal to you?

___ Can you encourage others to know more?

___ Would you like your job to deal with the natural world in some way?

You are a Down-to-Earth Cancer. Cancerians often like to stick with the basics and investigate the subjects relating to the growth of our planet and the organisms and societies that depend upon it. Some positions of possible interest to you could be conservationist, miner (especially silver), pearl harvester, geologist, silversmith, or precious-gem merchant. Others positions include agricultural, biological, or metallurgical scientist, researcher, technician, or engineer. Also urban or regional planners, civil engineers, anthropologists, historical preservationists, archaeologists and genealogists can all be Cancerians. Landscape architect, gardener, horticulturist, and commercial boat or ship owner are all specific jobs with appeal for Down-to-Earth Cancerians.

___ Are you interested in birth and children?

___ Would you like to work in a scientific field?

___ Could you see yourself helping others through the conception and birthing process?

___ Do you feel drawn to helping those who cannot care for themselves?

___ Do you need an emotionally rewarding position?

You are a Nurturing Cancer. Your keen interest in the birth process and parenting can lead you to many jobs in which you can help others at crucial times in their lives. Such positions as obstetrician, pediatrician, midwife, nurse (especially of children), family planner, population-control expert, or Lamaze instructor would be excellent for you. Those with a more scientific bent could try a job as sonogram technician, diagnostician, fertilization or biological testing specialist, biomedical engineer or technician, neonatalist, or embryologist. Related fields include microbiology, genetics, anatomy, gerontology (a rapidly growing field) and physiology (as it relates to growth and reproduction).

___ Are you able to use your imagination in a creative way?

___ Do you want to bring your talents before the public?

___ Would you like to have a career relating to your own self-expression?

___ Do you think you could help others achieve a more relaxed and rewarding existence?

___ Do you feel you can communicate emotionally with others?

You are a Creative Cancer. You might want to consider one of these positions as a sideline, as most are not that secure. Yet all can be developed into a regular income with time. Your imagination and emotional power can help you succeed as an actor, photographer, filmmaker, or artist. You may enjoy writing as a career, especially books for children or about family life; fiction could include romance and melodrama. If you are musical, you could consider becoming a performer or songwriter and may do well with pop or easy-listening music. Designers and decorators of homes, offices, gardens, and museums could all be Cancerians as well.

___ Would you like to build an income on your own?

___ Do you have obligations that keep you at home?

___ Do you have a unique product, service, or skill to offer others?

___ Would you like to be in complete control of your own career?

___ Do you like to make your own hours?

You are an Entrepreneurial Cancer. You should own your own business or other venture that can possibly be run from the home. Look over the other quizzes for an area of special interest. Most new firms go out of business before the first year is out, so proceed with great caution. You have the tenacity to develop success over time and may want to start while still holding another job.

Happy Hunting! How to Get That Job

Whatever your career goals or ultimate dream may be, when considering a career, you Cancers should think about something you'd be *comfortable* doing—something you'd feel you could handle *now*, without too much stress or anxiety. You are very much in tune with your inner feelings, and a position that doesn't feel quite "right" to you, for whatever reason, will probably remain that way for some time to come.

Take it slow and easy. You probably have lofty ambitions, but remember that we all have to start somewhere. If you need to enter your field at the bottom rung of the ladder, realize that you will slowly and surely work your way up.

Any job search can be trying as well as time-consuming. Odds are you will probably find yourself rejected more often than not, and it's important to not take this personally. Keep your chin up. This can be the most significant advice, because you'll feel better, look better, and interview better if you're in a positive frame of mind.

A real job search can last for many months, and you may be tempted to settle for less than what you really want. Consider all the future implications if you choose this course of action. Once within a firm, there may be the possibility of switching departments and usually the opportunity for advancement.

If you are committed to finding that ideal job, keep yourself occupied during your job-searching weeks. Stay in touch with good friends and family. Hobbies and home-improvement projects can be inexpensive activities to help fill your time. It's best not to be too fixated on one particular or specific type of job. Think about alternatives and assure yourself that your goals are practical ones.

All close personal contacts should be enlisted to help in your job search. Family members, community groups, or local organizations well known to you can provide advice, experience, and possibly even opportunities. Professional or trade publications in your field may also provide you with leads, ideas, or even help-wanted ads.

Cancer people can dwell on the past and may be inhibited about starting something new. You generally feel uncomfortable about making changes in your life, even when excited by the prospects. You may also feel ill at ease in calling potential employers or even interviewing. You can circumvent this by answering ads that require a written response. You'll more easily express yourself while writing quietly from home in familiar surroundings. It will also be easier for you to be more assertive about your strengths and experience.

Ultimately, you will have to face that interview. Because you can be shy and retiring, you may feel apprehensive about doing this. Don't go into the interview feeling that it is a do-or-die situation. It's only your attitude that will change, and nothing more. Perhaps you can have a nice phone conversation with the interviewer beforehand, going over the basics of the job as well as your qualifications and needs. If the company is a big one, you may find out more about it from your local library or friends who have had experience with the firm. If you follow these steps, you won't feel you're going into the interview totally cold. You'll also find that you'll be more prepared, relaxed, and knowledgeable.

If you are planning a major job search, it may be good for you to go on as many interviews as possible. You *will* get used to it! You'll find that you're asked a similar set of questions each time, and with practice you can polish your responses.

Often the people that are conducting the interview do not do this every day; they're just the people who need to hire someone. You'll eventually be able to take advantage of their lack of experience by responding to open-ended questions in a positive manner. Know exactly what you'll say about your past experience, career goals, and salary expectations for each particular position you're considering. Cancerians can usually profit from being a little more pushy than they think they should be. You can be insecure, so toot your own horn a little here! No one else is around to speak up for you, and what you say about yourself will be taken as fact.

Dress comfortably, in something that makes you feel good about yourself. Although you may feel inwardly reserved, Cancerians generally make a good impression. With your unassuming manner, you put others at ease. You are also naturally responsive to the personality, manner, and moods of others, and you respond well to cues. If the interviewer is chipper, you'll brighten up. If one is serious, you'll instinctively echo that tone as well. Because of this "hidden" aptitude, interviewers will feel you are more like them and will take to you immediately.

If you are put off by the interviewer's manner or personality, don't let that end the opportunity for you. You may not be dealing with this person on a regular basis. Wait till you meet your prospective boss and co-workers before you make any judgments.

Your instincts and impressions are a big part of your decision-making process, so put them to practical use.

Many firms interview several candidates on the same day, and this may give you the impression that they're busier or less organized than they usually are. If it's possible, try to come back on more than one occasion. Or use your time waiting to see the boss to observe the surrounding atmosphere. Make sure you see the space where you'll work. Could you see yourself as a part of this environment? Would you feel comfortable and at ease working here? Did you like the people? These are some of the important questions to ask yourself before making a decision.

Getting Ahead: How to Do Your Best on the Job

Cancerians want and need security from their jobs, and you can help increase this by being a steady worker. As time goes by, you'll find the benefits accrue. Salary and vacation time, of course, go up the longer you stay with a firm. Larger companies may even offer profit-sharing or retirement plans after you've been with them for a while.

Induce others to be helpful and cooperative by setting a good example yourself. Try at all times to keep any moodiness at home; you'll find your work can become a wonderful diversion from personal problems if you let yourself become completely involved with your tasks and associates. You'll also find that a regular smile at the workplace will encourage others to do the same.

You need to develop warm relationships, and a regular, long-term position can help you do this as well. Take the time to have lunch or coffee with those associates you like.

Cancerians generally have a great sense of responsibility on the job. Your work is important to you from a practical viewpoint, and you'll do everything possible to insure that your work satisfies both you and your supervisors. You are generally reliable, dependable, and hardworking on a day-to-day basis, and able to give extra effort when necessary.

You are very ambitious when motivated but will never be aggressive. You are determined and tenacious in following your goals, and you know how to seize an opportunity, no matter how small. You can cope with changing circumstances, and can also adapt your ultimate goals to suit practical considerations.

Cancer people are emotionally drawn to the past, their own as well as history in general. You like to save and collect things, and these qualities can be put to good use on the job, too. You can easily gather and absorb information, and you Cancerians generally have excellent memories. Many different positions require the collection and organization of information, and these may be suitable for you, too.

As Cancer is cautious and security-conscious, you'll protect your employer's interests. You will never take unnecessary chances and will be a cautious spender of company funds. You instinctively know how to hold on to and use money, and you can succeed in any type of position that involves finances, budgeting, or managing costs.

You have a rich emotional life and can benefit from using your imagination on the job. You have the ability to come up with ingenious solutions to problems and can see simple solutions that others might overlook. You also have a knack for knowing just what the public wants and can succeed in customer service, public relations, or any business geared toward broad sales.

All Cancerians can benefit from using their practical natures more. You generally rely on instinct and feelings to help you make decisions, but business is business, after all. You have an able intellect: Use it more for objective analysis and evaluation.

Cancers do resist change and like to cling to old ways of doing things. You can be adaptable to new ways, but it takes you a long time to get used to them. Keep an open mind on the job. If the boss wants to computerize the office, you'll probably dread it, but realize that you have to move ahead with change and that greater efficiency can often be the result.

Because of your characteristics of going along with others and liking a nonstressed position, you may take the easiest way out of a problem. You could also follow the line of least resistance in your career goals and may end up with a job that doesn't interest you at all. Try to stick up for what you believe in: The easiest solution is not usually the best and is certainly not the only way. Encourage yourself to be more assertive about what you want—though you may have to shake things up a bit to do so! Don't act just because someone else wants you to.

You are very sensitive and can be insecure, often having a hard time asking for that promotion or raise. Think about your attendance record, loyalty, and accomplishments and compare them with others at your workplace. You'll probably come out ahead. If you've done a good job for someone for over a year and haven't gotten a raise, you do need to ask for one. Be prepared to ask for more than you think you'll get. You tend to underestimate yourself! If you feel you can't face the boss personally, ask a close supervisor to intercede for you or write a memo.

Always try to take criticism objectively and not personally. You are in a business situation, and others will encourage you to get the job done correctly and more efficiently. Remember, too, that others are not as sensitive as yourself and usually don't mean any harm when they speak brusquely or bluntly. Take this to heart, especially with Aries, Sagittarians, or Scorpios on the job.

You may have a tendency to be somewhat self-involved in your business life and can "look out for Number One" to the exclusion of all else. It can benefit all of you Cancerians to see the larger picture and to view yourself as part of the overall company, not just subjectively. You can also become like the hermit crab and close yourself off from others. Keeping up a positive attitude and maintaining relationships on the job can improve on this trait. You will also benefit from simple physical movement about the workplace, as you may have a tendency to become too placid and rooted in one place.

Cancer is very protective of the emotional self, and if you're having a particularly difficult time at work you'll probably opt to take a few days off. You can benefit from rest, and a break from routine may brighten your spirits and freshen you psychologically. Be careful, however, not to get too carried away with this tactic. Calling in "sick" on a regular basis does little to help the career, and you will lose credibility. Others may feel you lack responsibility if you don't consistently face your work problems.

Conflicts are generally not resolved on their own, no matter how you may try to avoid them, and associates can become resentful if you run away whenever the chips are down. If you feel your position is too draining and takes too much of your energy with no reward, it's time to make a change! Whether it be to take action now or begin a new job search is up to you. But avoidance will only compound your problems over the long term.

If you must take time off for personal reasons, try to discuss it with those in charge beforehand. Most people are quite understanding if you take a mature attitude and attempt to work out your priorities in a straightforward manner.

The most important advice we can give you is to leave your home and family at home. Personal obligations will be your top priority, no matter how ambitious you become. But you must guard against allowing your personal life to interfere with business. We all have periods of crisis, when we must take time off or keep in close contact with loved ones on the phone. Too much of this, though, can ruin any career. Keep personal calls to a minimum, but if you must, try to schedule them for your lunch hour or regular breaks. Many supervisors will resent long phone calls, especially if they coincide with less productivity on your part. If you maintain your regular schedule, you'll probably be emotionally stronger to help those who need you the most.

All hard-working Cancers can expect a promotion or better job offer at some point. A job description can sound frightening and threatening, but once you've laid down a routine and have loosened up a bit, you'll find your tasks become second nature. Yes, you probably will feel insecure, and you may even feel badly that your good friend in the next cubicle didn't get a promotion also, but you are adaptable and won't turn down this chance to prove to your supervisor that the confidence in you was not misplaced. After you've accepted the promotion and learned the responsibilities and routine involved, you'll wonder why you ever thought it would be beyond your capabilities.

If you are unhappy now and want to move on, remember to keep all your bases covered. Don't leave one job before you have a firm offer of another. Schedule interviews during lunch or after hours. If you have vacation days coming, use these, but schedule them beforehand. You never know how long your search will take, and you don't want to make things more difficult where you are now if you end up staying. Above all, don't just sit back and hope something comes along. Be assertive, and take action to find that ideal position.

Do

- Cultivate self-confidence and assertiveness.
- Strive to be more realistic and logical.
- Use your imagination and versatility.
- Learn to accept constructive criticism.
- Utilize your good memory.

Don't

- Resist change.
- Rely exclusively on emotions and feelings.
- Be oversensitive to others on the job.
- Feel inferior.
- Bring your personal life into the office.

LEO

July 22 to August 24

> "It's a great feeling to be powerful.
> I've been striving for it all my life."
> —Madonna, *Vanity Fair*

Big Cats

Leo is the big cat of the zodiac, just like the lion is the big cat of the jungle. The Leo native also takes to the business world as Elsa in *Born Free* did in returning to her natural habitat. Sure, she loved playing around with her soft human companions and was reluctant to leave the fun-and-games crowd. She even had a few problems adjusting to the rough-and-tumble land. Yet she soon responded to the challenges of survival and made her way proudly on her own.

Leos have big, big hearts and innate childlike qualities. They love to play and have great creative capacities. Have you ever observed kittens in a pet-store window? They hold your attention because they are fun-loving and can come up with 101 uses for a scratching post. So can Leos. Their creative inspiration and dramatic flair make them a dynamic asset for many businesses, as well as problem-solvers of the best stripe. A little self-absorbed? Yes. But when Leos lose themselves in a project, there's a lot of energy directed in a positive manner.

Like the lion, cheetah, and panther, Leos are self-assured, confident, and dignified. There's a vital, strong will in the Leo nature, as well as a great deal of pride, which constantly seeks to prove itself. Leos rise to the occasion, are courageous, and like to be in the spotlight. They need to take the lead and are comfortable in positions where they can command.

Sound a lot like the king of the jungle, don't they? But these big cats have such generous, warm, and honest natures that they are usually kind to their "subjects." Leos really are loyal, optimistic, and magnanimous. Yet like all self-satisfied kingly types, they can become "fat cats" if they're not careful: a little too lazy, a little too boastful. Leos love to be praised and fussed over. Like Morris in those television commercials, they may become pompous, easily spoiled, presumptuous, or obstinate.

But most Leos can easily use the positive aspects of their character to help them succeed on the job. See the complete concentration in the lioness as she stalks her prey? Quietly collected, yet intent on the goal at hand, she'll wait for her chance, leap out, and prevail. Keep this image in mind as you think about Leos and their careers.

Get to Work! What to Look for in a Career

Leo is a strong and powerful fire sign, and if you are career-oriented, you will not be happy simply being stable and secure. You need an opportunity to compete with others, and you should seek an active, challenging position. As long as a job is stimulating for you, you will stick with it. However, if you don't have this kind of opportunity on a regular basis, you will soon become frustrated and unhappy.

STAR SUCCESS

You'll also want to find a position in which you can learn and develop your career. You must be able to feel that you are moving ahead, that you are continuing to grow as time goes by. You have a healthy ego and need to see that your work has been appreciated and rewarded. Most Leos enjoy recognition from co-workers and superiors. You can live without this, however, if you receive the ultimate rewards: a position of greater importance and an increase in salary. You'd love your own office, private phone line, expense account, company car, or enough money to buy a designer wardrobe.

You are an independent person and need to be able to take control over your work. Only then can you take pride in your job. If you need to perform routine tasks solely to the specifications of a supervisor, you're in the wrong place. You also need to have a nice place to work, one that you can show off to your friends and family.

Many Leos enjoy high-profile positions. Because of your charm and charisma, you will be an effective speaker and can make any subject appear interesting. You may opt for a position in which you can appear before the public. Your poise and ability to attract attention can be used in such diverse positions as reporter or receptionist, or in any involving public speaking. Other executive positions, political appointments, and jobs dealing with celebrities or VIPs can also satisfy your need to be seen.

Leo is a creative sign, and you'll want to find a career in which you can exercise your imagination and ability to inspire others. You often have exciting ideas and should have the opportunity to implement all of your talents. You need to seek a position that will be personally satisfying, fulfilling, and enjoyable.

When planning a career, Leos should ask themselves one simple question: "What do I love to do?" You will do your best and advance more quickly when you're inspired. As philosopher Joseph Campbell put it, "Follow your bliss." What would you like to do, even if you had to *pay* to do it? If you like to dance and attend parties, for example, you might think about working in a health club, a dance club, a record company, or even a catering service.

What motivates you? Could it be putting your best foot forward? If this is the case, a career in sales might be perfect. There you would constantly meet challenges while selling your own personality. Likewise, being a teacher, acting as a host or hostess for a classy restaurant, or becoming a museum tour guide would also satisfy this need.

What's Your Line? Your Vocational Choices

Your idealism, energy, and determined nature will help you succeed in a variety of fields. From playground director to cardiac specialist, a Leo's heart needs to be in the job! Working creatively, with children, in speculative fields, or in sports are all positive outlets for Leos.

Leos want and need to be in the limelight, and show business and all its related professions can easily attract you. Superstar singer Madonna is a Leo, and she has utilized many of her Leo attributes toward a successful career. She's always the center of attention in any project she's involved in and has become the head of a multimillion-dollar business. She uses her leonine creativity to write her own songs and uses her image in her videos to attract attention. This gets her more recognition, which generates more interest in her concerts and other performances.

Director-producer Blake Edwards is also a well-known Leo, and although he's not directly in the public eye, he's in complete control of his films. He takes risks with unusual projects, often writing the screenplays he directs. Most Leos who are in command of a creative venture will continue along this rewarding path. With a Hollywood career spanning over four decades, Edwards certainly has the Leo staying power. From serious films such as *Breakfast at Tiffany's* and *Days of Wine and Roses* to the farcical *Pink Panther* series and high comedies like *10* and *Victor/Victoria,* the writer, director, and some-time producer continues to entertain movie audiences worldwide.

Many Leos also succeed by developing a loyal group of clients and co-workers. Edwards has a regular team of technicians and players, including his wife, Julie Andrews, whom he often casts in the starring roles.

Of course most Leos will not actually get involved in show business, but there are thousands of other jobs that reflect many of Leo's talents. An executive in a catering firm loves her job because Leos love making things special. Her work often involves creating an atmosphere for weddings, sporting events, and other celebrations, where she leads and directs the preparations. She also coordinates special events, booking hotels, transportation, and entertainment for large groups of people while still being in charge.

Put a checkmark next to each question that you'd answer with a "yes." If there are several checks for a few career groups, review these first and think about the career suggestions we've listed. If you believe that one of these areas is right for you, investigate your selections further or those closely related to them. Also, take a look at the rest of our suggestions for other possibilities.

___ Do you love children?

___ Would you like to share your special knowledge with others?

___ Do you have leadership capabilities?

___ Could you get satisfaction from helping others?

___ Can your own enthusiasm stimulate others to reach their greatest potential?

You are an Educational Leo. You could succeed in positions where you teach, guide, or instruct others. These jobs include teacher, lecturer, or administrator for schools, camps, theater arts, music, or other creative organizations. You may enjoy counseling positions, such as camp director, child psychologist, or guidance or employment counselor. Youth-corps recruiters, sports coaches, and trainers can also be Leos.

Health-related positions are included in this category, such as back, spine or heart specialist, cardiologist, optometrist, opthalmologist, or any other technical work with optical equipment, such as an astronomer.

___ Does the entertainment field excite you?

___ Are you moved to express dramatic feelings in some way?

___ Do you like to be in the spotlight?

___ Do you have a flair for showmanship?

___ Would you like to have a "fun" job?

You are a Showman Leo. Positions relating to television, film, or theater production could be ideal, and becoming an actor, director, or producer would all be excellent choices. There are many other types of jobs for you to choose from, including ballroom dance instructor, puppeteer, animal trainer, circus performer, or video-arcade proprietor. Bandleaders, singers, and musicians can also be Leos. Careers in modeling, makeup, or fashion may be good for you. Drama coaches, theatrical managers, casting agents, and stage managers are also included in this category. Work at carnivals and amusement centers such as Disneyland are possibilities. You could lead or organize festivals, weddings, children's parties, and other celebrations.

___ Do you enjoy taking risks?

___ Are you a gambler at heart?

___ Does the potential of a high income excite you?

___ Do you like to work with money?

___ Would you enjoy working with others in a glamorous field?

You are a Speculative Leo. Positions in the trade or financial markets can utilize your talents. Stock-market brokers, futures traders, and investment specialists can all be Leos. You may enjoy working in the financial or banking field in other areas, such as personal services, gold or other precious metal investments, or as a consultant. Professional gambling is another field for you, and Leos can succeed working as organizers of gambling events for fundraisers. Blackjack dealers, croupiers, casino or off-track betting managers, and other positions affiliated with this industry should be considered. Some Leos can earn a living as professional gamblers themselves (although this career is better as a sideline, even if you feel you're lucky!).

___ Do you love competition?

___ Do sporting events excite you?

___ Do you have a lot of physical energy and enthusiasm?

___ Would you like to be the center of attention?

___ Do you have a theatrical flair?

You're a Sporting Leo. There are all kinds of positions available that relate to sporting events, and many Leos make excellent professional athletes themselves. The solo sports such as boxing, judo, tennis, track and field, golf, and gymnastics are all good choices, but theatrical sports such as professional wrestling or cheerleading can also attract you. Leos often make excellent athletic coaches and trainers. You should also consider the positions of sports reporter, promoter, reviewer, or announcer on the local, regional, or national level. Administrative, organizational, and managerial positions related to these fields would also be appropriate for you. One of the ultimate Leo jobs in this area is to own or manage a team or a stadium.

___ Would you enjoy a high-profile position?

___ Do you have creative talent?

___ Can you think on your feet?

___ Do you become inspired by sharing your ideas with others?

___ Are you comfortable working in the business world?

You are a Business Services Leo. There are many positions in the business world that could utilize your talents in a regular or freelance position. The fields of promotion, publicity, advertising, or public relations could be good choices for you if you like to reach the public. Creative positions in business also include graphics designer, art director, photographer, or copywriter. Designing shop windows or constructing displays in retail stores are also possibilities.

The sales field is ever-expanding, and you may find your personality and confidence useful here. You would do well in convention booths, product demonstrations, or in other direct solicitation situations. Advertising account executives or sales managers are leadership positions in which Leos could also succeed.

___ Are you still a kid at heart?

___ Do you enjoy using your creative talent and imagination?

___ Does glamour, beauty, or fashion excite you?

___ Do you want to help others enjoy themselves?

___ Is there something you really feel drawn to say or do?

You are a Creative Leo. There are many fun, exciting, and creative fields in which you could excel. Salespeople specializing in glamour or children's products could be Leos. You may like a position such as runway or showroom model, tour guide, hospitality manager, ballroom dance instructor, or even receptionist or restaurant host or hostess. Any consulting position could be good for you, but particularly jobs as special events coordinator, image consultant, interior decorator, or wedding planner. You could serve well as an entertainer or social organizer for cruise ships, resorts, or spas.

Many artists, writers, and other creative types will fall into this category. Jewelers and jewelry makers are specifically ruled by Leo and can run their own businesses. You could succeed in the fashion industry as a designer, an administrator, or a boutique owner. The writing of children's or romance books is another Leo occupation. Leos may want to work in and eventually own a ski or beach resort, park, dude ranch, restaurant, nightclub, or disco. Toy manufacturers and inventors are also leonine types.

___ Do you want to build something on your own?

___ Do you feel you can take the responsibility for managing an operation?

___ Are you organized and efficient?

___ Are you looking for something really challenging?

___ Do you have a talent or skill that you can turn to good profit?

You are an Entrepreneurial Leo and should own your own business. Many Leos find this the most rewarding career of all. Look over the other quizzes to locate possible fields for yourself. A photographic studio or TV/video store might be appropriate for you, and other Leo products include paper and greeting cards. A card or gift shop could be of great interest to you.

Happy Hunting! How to Get That Job

Once you've identified a field it's time to actually begin a job search. You Leos are very good about keeping your sights on future goals and will work hard to achieve them. This works very well for your career, as you'll usually pursue one course of action over a long period of time.

Important authority figures in your life, such as parents or a special teacher or friend, should be looked to for career guidance or advice. Seek out professionals in your vocation of choice who have succeeded, or read about a celebrity who's done exactly what you dream about. Use their examples to help you plot your own course. Once you've done your homework and some soul-searching you will probably find it easy to spring into action.

You really have the ability to project a strong image in terms of your personality as well as your physical self. If you are currently jobless, you need to project an aura of self-assurance and success by paying extra attention to your appearance and dress. Identify the style you'll need to achieve for the position you're currently seeking and adopt it now. Everyone will naturally see that you belong there. If you're after a corporate appointment, wear a business suit as often as you can. If you're looking for a creative position, dress in a trendy style appropriate for that job.

Whatever you wear, *look good*. Look professional. You never can tell when you'll run into a prospective employer or someone who knows a potential employer. First impressions last. If you shake hands with someone for the first time wearing jeans and sneakers, you're going to have to work doubly hard to sell yourself as a connoisseur of fine wine! Yet if you want to be the high-school football coach, you may be okay.

Tell everyone you know that you're looking for a job. You'll be surprised to find how wide your circle of acquaintance really is. Situation-wanted ads could also work for you, as you know what you want, as well as your assets and skills. These ads may be somewhat expensive, but they are one way in which you can get the right employers to come to *you*.

Try to meet people in person whenever possible. Although you may have a charming phone manner or writing style, Leos do best in person. Don't be forward, but try to take control of the situation by asking, "When can I stop by to meet you?" or "When are you interviewing?"

For any interview, dress tastefully—Leos have a tendency to overdo it. Both sexes should always stress understated dignity in their appearance and avoid excess jewelry or cologne.

Be a winner. You naturally give off an air of confidence, capability, and self-assurance. Show that your business experience or previous background has been successful. Who would hire the person who laments "I really *need* this job" over someone who calmly states "I feel I could be an asset to your firm, and I think I'd have an opportunity to grow here"?

Leo sincerity and spirit always go a long way in first interviews and any subsequent follow-ups. You are good at talking about yourself. What do you feel sets you apart from the crowd? What qualities or experiences do you have that exemplify your most sellable traits? Zero in on a few of these so you're prepared when an interviewer makes an open-ended statement like "Tell me about yourself." But stay focused and let the interviewer ask questions to guide you. This is not the time for a twenty-minute monologue!

Don't complain about previous bosses or be overly frank if asked why you left your last position. You don't have to go on at length about either of these. Once you've provided simple answers, the interviewer will move on.

Think about the interview as being like a game of "show and tell" (this is a sure way to get your Leo juices flowing!). While most job applicants just "tell," a Leo executive assistant looking for a new position in publishing recently brought along with her resume a copy of her listing in *Who's Who of American Women*. She also had a copy of a book she worked on at an earlier job, pointing out the acknowledgment for all her hard work. This Leo used her creativity to come up with a different way of demonstrating her abilities and landed the job. You can, too.

Not all employers check references, but most know that they should. Your photocopied letters of recommendation or lists of names and numbers to call will inspire confidence. Offering references up front shows you have a good relationship with the people you've cited, and you've also made the interviewer's job easier!

Don't be put off or insulted if you are asked to take a test of your skills. The employer does not yet know you personally! Think about the test as a chance to dramatize all that you've reported about yourself: It's a good way to prove you can do what you've said you can.

Finally, be persistent. If you've been told that there's an opportunity sometime in the future, don't hesitate to follow up or keep in touch. If you decide to stop by, do just that; don't hang around for a long conversation. Your interest and enthusiasm will be better remembered if you keep it short and sweet!

Getting Ahead: How to Do Your Best on the Job

You Leos take a great deal of pride in everything you do, including your career. If you have a clear-cut goal in mind and work hard to achieve it, you should easily advance in your chosen field. Alex Haley is a good example of a Leo who succeeded through determination. His pride in his heritage led him to ghostwrite *The Autobiography of Malcolm X;* then his love of his family led to a twelve-year period of research into his past. The final result was the blockbuster book *Roots,* which has sold millions of copies. Made into a TV miniseries in 1977, *Roots* captured one of the largest television audiences ever. Had Haley been less confident or resolute about pursuing this project, it never would've been completed.

Your kind, generous nature gives you the ability to deal effectively with others at the workplace. You genuinely like other people and make and keep friends easily; others are quickly attracted to your warmth and spontaneity. You openly give of yourself, which can make you a popular co-worker and employee.

You like to help people as well, and this tendency can be applied to any profession that is in the service sector. You are able to make others think of *themselves* as special when you can perform a task with or for them. You easily develop long-lasting business relationships because you prefer to positively work out your problems with others for the benefit of all. Your even-tempered disposition, too, can make others just like to have you around.

You are frank and will express exactly what you feel. Superiors do not intimidate you, and you will speak up if you feel someone is being treated unfairly. Others will appreciate your candor and respond in kind. You readily admit your own mistakes and quickly take action to correct them.

You have much vitality and energy, and you welcome the opportunity to give your all. Leo has a natural strength and endurance, so you have the ability to work hard and long if you are committed to what you are doing. Once directed, your powers of concentration are great. You can inspire others with your enthusiasm.

You will also make good impressions through your speech and writing. You know just the proper way to express yourself and the ability to dramatize or lend excitement to your chosen topic can also be utilized in meetings, seminars, and reports.

Leos have great self-confidence. You are strong and forceful and can center your energies with remarkable power. You can be decisive and are calm and cool in emergency situations. A Leo in a competitive business situation may be aggressive but will never be unfair. You are stimulated by the game and like to win. The affinity for command and leadership is strong, and your self-promotion often contributes to your success.

You Leos can excel as team leaders or managers. Your enthusiasm and energy are infectious, and you lead with a firm hand. You have a good concept of the power structure and feel comfortable in a position of authority. You are also cognizant of exactly where you fit into the scheme of things and will be respectful to those above you. You will do what you have to do to get the job done, but at your own pace and in your own way. You can become obstinate if pushed: Any efforts to control you will be met with stubborn resistance. You easily delegate work to employees or those working with or for you. You love titles and, when granted one, will live up to the responsibilities that go with it.

There is a great desire to prove yourself at all costs, and if truly career-driven, you can gain money, power, respect, and public acclaim. You will seize opportunities quickly if they are presented. Usually a combination of hard work, commitment, and luck forms the typical Leo success story.

But your kind, open nature can backfire at times in the workplace. Someone who appears nice will always *be* nice in your opinion, and you may misjudge others. You can be manipulated, and you may be subject to flattery because of your genuine naiveté. Try not to trust anyone too soon, or share your ideas, judgments, or ambitions with others too quickly. Remember that true relationships must be built over a long period, and this certainly holds true for those with your co-workers.

You Leos always like to share your experiences, talk about yourselves, and have a good time. That's fine after hours, but don't put this above your work! On the job your first priority is getting your tasks accomplished—chatting and joking can wait until later. Of course, everyone needs and deserves breaks, but be careful not to overextend these.

Be conscious, too, that others may find you too bold, competitive, or even arrogant. People of a quieter nature can be intimidated by your up-front strength and determination, and those with less expansive natures may feel you're a show-off or that you're conceited (yes, Leos can be both!). Try to become aware of how others respond to you, especially superiors and important co-workers. You may need to lower your performance a few decibels! Show an active interest in other people at the workplace, and try not to be the center of attention *all* the time.

Leos sometimes promise more than they can deliver. Don't exaggerate what you can accomplish when on the job. Consider carefully what you can and cannot do before making any commitments, and make sure you follow through on all your promises.

Your own pride can also become a debit at times. You

don't like to admit you can't handle a project alone, can't meet a deadline, or have a personal problem interfering with your work. You may push yourself too hard to accomplish a task that could've easily been shared. Try to delegate work if possible. Tell your supervisor when you've been given too much to do. Remember that it takes longer to do a job right; rushing or cutting corners will lower the quality of your work. Admit to *yourself* when you're overworked or stressed out. All it may take is one day away from the office to set yourself right again.

Your sense of self-confidence can lead you to take necessary risks at work and make these successful. But some Leos can become foolhardy and begin to believe *everything* will go right for them. This is gambling, pure and simple. And it's fun, which is why you could want to indulge in it! Work, however, is not the place for gambling, unless you're a stockbroker or running a numbers game. Confine yourself to prudent or calculated risks at work and save your glee for the casinos and your personal funds.

Your Sun sign can make you stubborn and sometimes opinionated. You have the ability to make up your mind quickly and act on your decisions. Yet others whom you have to deal with will have their own viewpoints as well, and it may be necessary or diplomatic to discuss the issues and come to a compromise in order to work together. Don't force your judgments on others; if you present your arguments in a persuasive manner (one of your talents), you may be able to sway others to your side.

Keep in mind that co-workers are just as proud to do their jobs well as you are, even the least experienced member of the team. Treat all with kindness and respect. You will find that other people respond better to encouragement and geniality than to being ordered about like a servant.

You can also be impatient, and in especially stressful situations you can lose your temper. Try to curb these tendencies. While it might be appropriate occasionally to raise your voice to make a point you feel strongly about, do this consciously and in a dignified manner. Even when the boss is wrong, avoid a showdown! Opt instead for a low-key meeting, sensible letter, or memo.

The final and often fatal Leo shortcoming is laziness. If you find your work boring or uninteresting, you may have a tendency to goof off. The only remedy is to find a position that excites and stimulates you. If you're stuck where you are for the moment, try to make your job more fun. Infusing your work with imagination will help you like it more. Turn the mundane task into an event, at least in your own mind, and take pride in *whatever* you do. If you're doing your simple tasks well, you'll be in line for a promotion sooner. Or let your supervisor know you'd like a change or transfer when the opportunity arises. Your candor and honesty will help you realize that you're just not cut out for *every* task.

For most Leos, steady work over a long period will pay off in the end, but the big break may come quite suddenly or unexpectedly. You can often be lucky, and you may find yourself whisked away from your regular work to an exciting new opportunity with more responsibility, creativity, or leadership potential. You will most likely accept the new position with gusto. But if you're having difficulty adjusting, remember to take things slowly and get your bearings first. No one expects you to know how to do everything right away. Delegate work when you can and need to, and don't be too proud to ask others for help or advice.

You do enjoy being the big fish in a small pond, but only if the pond is stimulating enough. But if you're in a position you feel is stagnant, unpromising, or unpromotable, take action to go somewhere else. It always helps to keep up good relations with your former employer; you'll never know when you may want to return. If you're having trouble with associates now, keep it to yourself and try to work things out for the moment. Get some good letters of reference from people you trust.

That lucky break will come to you, but not unless you promote yourself and wait for the right opportunity.

Do

- Use your engaging personality.
- Utilize your confidence, self-assurance, and leadership ability.
- Rouse enthusiasm in others.
- Work independently.
- Use eloquence in speech and writing.

Don't

- Boast or be presumptuous.
- Demand constant praise and attention.
- Be too competitive.
- Demand special privileges.
- Trust everyone.

VIRGO

August 23 to September 24

> "Never compromise on quality."
> —Debbi Fields,
> *Working Woman*

The Harvester

The sign Virgo is represented by a girl with a sheaf of wheat. The wheat is ripe for the harvest, ready to be threshed and ground into flour for the nourishment of us all.

It's not surprising, then, that Virgo, an earth sign, is concerned with health, nutrition, and the maintenance of the physical body. Virgos are persnickety about what they eat, and they often have sensitive nervous and digestive systems. The food of choice: whole-grain wheat, of course. Whole grains provide protein, vitamins, and even fiber, all essential to the growth and functioning of the human body.

The Virgo symbol also suggests someone who has a job to do. She's holding one ear of wheat, but there are many more to gather. Since the beginning of the industrial revolution, machines have replaced scythes as harvesting tools, but it still takes plenty of time, skill, and patience to get the crop in, not to mention the processing afterward. Virgos are known for their hard work, dedication to duty, and no-nonsense approach to life. They need to find something to do that makes them feel like they're doing important work. A serious girl, this Virgo maiden!

Straight from our bread basket, you may think Virgo is too out of touch to know about anything other than cereal. Not so. Remember that wheat is one of the most highly valued crops and has been for centuries. Virgos know this. They recognize all things of worth, know how to handle money effectively, and will put their effort into earning their share. Always discerning, Virgos know quality when they see it. Because the Virgo maiden has spent eons meticulously separating the wheat from the chaff, she can never be fooled by second best!

Get to Work! What to Look for in a Career

Your needs in work and career are quite simple, straightforward, and important. If you don't have the basics you will never be happy, no matter how interesting or promotable your position is.

You should seek a job that provides you with a regular schedule, and your work should not be allowed to become disruptive of your life. While you are quite adaptable and will not be thrown by the ordinary demands of occasional overtime, a job that routinely sends you to different places during odd hours can become debilitating for you. It's certainly not necessary that you always remain in one place as long as you have a sense of routine. If you must go out on sales calls, always do it on a set day. You'll find that once a habitual work routine is established, you'll look forward to and appreciate special jaunts.

Your position must provide you with commensurate

pay. You are always willing to work hard for what you receive, but you shouldn't put up with a situation that isn't advantageous to you. You certainly don't need a lot of money, but you should be able to expect a regular wage. Commission situations can give you anxiety unless there's enough of a base salary. Whatever you accept you'll have to live with for some time, and your current salary will have a lot to do with what you can expect to earn several years from now. Don't forget how much health-care insurance plans will afford you if they're offered by an employer, and how much they'll cost if you must pay the premiums yourself. Add these expenses into your calculations for determining what you can expect to earn.

Your work atmosphere can also be quite important, and you should try to find a field as well as a specific position that provide a quiet and dedicated work atmosphere. You will do best in a workplace where everyone has a job to do and takes their work seriously. Noisy, disruptive, or cavalier co-workers will keep you from doing your best.

You'll work best in a pleasant businesslike environment where all the basics are provided for you. If you must hunt for a pencil daily or don't have free access to a phone, duplicating machine, or other necessary equipment, you could become anxious and your attitude and work will suffer. A well-equipped, organized workplace will add to your productive capacity.

You need a career that will keep you busy and in which you'll be of service to others. You must feel that your work is significant, even if you are only providing a small part of a final product or service. For this reason many Virgos go into the health-care field, often performing small tasks that are quite meaningful as well as important to our society as a whole.

You should learn a basic skill or trade that will always be bankable. No matter what your ultimate objective, you need to feel secure along the way. Work as a word processor, for example, can net you good pay while you become a successful novelist. You may not always find a job as a nutritionist, but your skills as a medical technician or aerobics instructor are ones that will always be profitable for you, in cities as well as smaller towns. Learn some basic skill or trade of this type early on in your career. You can then build on that strong foundation and will know that no matter what happens you can always find a job!

What's Your Line? Your Vocational Choices

You Virgos have good minds and also enjoy doing practical tasks. You are efficient, careful workers, who can accomplish the most demanding assignments. Many Virgo people gravitate toward careers in which they can serve others, even in an indirect way.

Violinist Itzhak Perlman is a Virgo who has worked hard to overcome his handicaps. At the age of four, he was struck by polio and as a result needed crutches to walk, but he continued with his violin lessons. With Virgoan dedication, the Israeli native appeared on *The Ed Sullivan Show* at thirteen, toured the U.S., then attended the Julliard School in New York. Perlman is known to be a perfectionist and has exquisite coordination and technique—all Virgo traits. He certainly knows a good value when he sees one: His Stradivarius violin is considered to be one of the finest ever made, and it is quite necessary to his profession.

Since Virgo is an earth sign, the violinist is characteristically down to earth about his music: He plays country tunes and jazz as well as the classical repertoire. Virgo often likes to help others in some way, and Perlman has found an outlet through furthering the rights of the handicapped.

Mother Teresa is a Virgo who epitomizes this sign's

need of dedication to a cause. Virgos are often noted for their intelligence, and she began her career by teaching high school in India. After nearly twenty years of teaching, Mother Teresa felt a call to help the poor by living among them. Drawn to the health-care field, she spent several months in intense medical training (an activity also ruled by Virgo).

Mother Teresa then began a school for the poorest children and later opened a home for the dying poor. As Virgos are always clean and orderly, so was her shelter. Typically Virgoan, Mother Teresa is said to be extremely down to earth, with a calm manner and good sense of humor. While her group can never expect to wipe out world poverty, they help individuals all over, including a new home for AIDS babies in Pennsylvania.

Debbi Fields is a Virgo who has succeeded in the business world by her commitment to a high-quality product. Growing up in a modest home, Debbi held several jobs but felt she could only be really satisfied by running her own business. Before she turned twenty-one, her husband had loaned her the money to open a small shop, and Mrs. Fields Cookies was born.

Debbi Fields has always enjoyed her work and has thus found it easy to reach her goals. Using only the best ingredients and stressing customer satisfaction and service, she now has hundreds of stores across the U.S. and overseas. Her high standards also include not selling any cookies over two hours old. These are given to charities —yet another Virgo concern!

Put a checkmark next to each question that you'd answer with a "yes." If there are several checks for a few career groups, review these first and think about the career suggestions we've listed. If you believe that one of these areas is right for you, investigate your selections further or those closely related to them. Also, take a look at the rest of our suggestions for other possibilities.

___ Are you exact in your use of language?

___ Do you enjoy communicating with others?

___ Do you possess a sharp mind?

___ Would you like to use your skills to help others learn?

___ Do you find satisfaction in developing your mental dexterity?

You are a Communications Virgo. You can succeed in any number of positions that utilize your mental capabilities. Some of these stress written work like book, magazine, or newspaper publisher, editor, copyeditor, proofreader, researcher, or author, especially of nonfiction, technical, or medical subjects. Others include literary critic, speech writer, ghost writer, reporter, courtroom stenographer, or graphologist. Positions dealing with the spoken word include actor, announcer, teacher (especially of English, history, or business), or telephone operator. Some related jobs include inventor, historian, postal service worker, and book or stationery store owner, manager, or associate.

___ Do you have scientific skills or talents?

___ Are you good with detail work?

___ Would you like to work in a clean and orderly environment?

___ Can you handle work that may be exacting and repetitive?

___ Would you like to do a job that has a significant impact on others?

You are a Medical Services Virgo. You could succeed in the medical field or those related fields that involve improving our physical well-being. You might enjoy work as a scientific researcher, technologist, or experimenter in such fields as agriculture, biology, microbiology, or chemistry. Positions in sterilization or the pharmaceutical or sanitation fields could also be to your liking. Try work as a druggist, smog-control technician, or environmental, industrial, or sanitation engineer. You may choose work as a mathematician, meteorologist, or materials-testing technician.

There are many jobs specific to medical work that you might enjoy. These include internist, veterinarian, anatomist, diagnostician, audiologist, allergist, pathologist, respiratory therapist, physical culturist, immunologist, nurse, clinical or medical lab technician, medical photographer, dental hygienist, prosthesis manufacturer, hospital or nursing-home administrator, public-health aide, consumer-safety inspector, medical records manager, or biomedical equipment specialist.

___ Do you want to serve society?

___ Do you understand how to make yourself useful?

___ Are you willing to put time and energy into working toward realistic goals?

___ Do you possess investigative or scientific abilities?

___ Would you like to help others help themselves?

You are a Human Services Virgo. Your talents could best be utilized by helping others improve the quality of their mental, emotional, or physical lives. You would find satisfaction being a rehabilitation counselor, medical ethics counselor, sociologist, economist, social worker, day-care worker, child-support investigator, drug and alcohol addiction educator, placement counselor, occupational planner, physical therapist, emergency medical services (EMS) worker, psychological counselor, psychiatrist, mental health aide, speech pathologist, or training and development specialist.

Other positions in this category include public health inspector, disease-control worker, hospital safety officer, smog-control officer, weather forecaster, business-home economist, and regulatory inspector.

___ Are you concerned with health and fitness?

___ Do you believe in a natural approach to life?

___ Would you like a position that provides a necessary service for others?

___ Can you judge quality and value?

___ Would you like to help others be their best physically?

You are a Natural Health Virgo. Many people are now more conscious of health and fitness, creating a growing field. You could succeed as a spa, gym, health food, or diet center employee, health inspector, allergist, food critic, homeopath, dietician, nutritionist, home economist, herbalist, or massage therapist.

The field of agriculture and produce is also appealing for you. You could work as a farmer or distributor dealing with cereals, vegetables, fruit, or cotton. Work as a restaurateur or chef, lawn and pruning service manager or worker, horticulturist, gardener, woodworker, or carpenter might also be to your liking.

Jobs in the many service firms that relate to physical hygiene could also be right for you. Try becoming a beauty parlor or barbershop manager, hairstylist, manicurist, hair waxer, or tanning-salon technician. Other service positions relating to home and clothing include home or office cleaner, tailor, dressmaker, or sewing goods salesperson.

Some purely service-related jobs include flight attendant, waiter or waitress, hotel manager or clerk, linen supervisor or housekeeper, custodial worker, or vending-machine serviceman. Virgos often love animals, and the occupations of animal groomer, trainer, veterinarian or assistant, zookeeper, or animal rights activist would all be good choices.

___ Are you good with detail work?

___ Do you get satisfaction from putting things in order?

___ Are you a good judge of value?

___ Do you enjoy the rewards of accomplishing practical tasks?

___ Would you like a position that provides a necessary service to others?

You are an Exacting Virgo. You can put your talent for detail and organization to good use in any number of business or industry jobs. You would be an excellent administrator or assistant in any field, especially those outlined below.

Many Virgos enjoy work in the financial field, and if you are one of them, you should consider work as a business lawyer, stockbroker, investment advisor, accountant, financial auditor, cost and valuation manager, income-tax preparer, purchasing agent, bank teller, or cashier.

Statistical positions for which you are highly qualified include bookkeeper, government recorder (for census and other vital statistics, property, or traffic), numerical controller, librarian, computer programmer, word processor, data-entry keyer, transcriber, data retriever, stenographer, and typist. Other related work includes systems analyst, market research analyst, mapmaker, secretary, mail carrier or sorter, and book binder.

Positions in precision work include work as a clock or

watch repairer, film editor, graphic designer, sound mixer, music transposer or transcriber, precision assembler, photo-lab technician, needleworker, pattern designer or cutter, upholsterer, carpet installer, wallpaper hanger, painter, or handcrafter.

___ Do you have a valuable skill, service, or product?

___ Would you like to reap great rewards for your work?

___ Are you independent?

___ Can you consistently meet deadlines?

___ Do you have the ability to make sound business decisions?

You are an Entrepreneurial Virgo. You should own your own business. Your ability to work for what you want, need to seek perfection, and sound business sense can all lead you to success. If you are not sure of a field, review the above lists.

Happy Hunting! How to Get That Job

In seeking employment, don't be modest in assessing your value. You are the ideal employee. In your responsibility to work, realistic attitude, and willingness to do what needs to be done, you win points again and again. Even in a tough market, it's difficult for most employers to find the right person who knows how to work and is committed to the goals of the company. You are someone who can become indispensable, yet your employer won't know that until you've worked for several months.

Therefore you need to try extra hard to get your foot in the door. It's unfortunate but true that most people can't judge you on your work habits but must go by your initial appearance and conversation. Do your best to show exactly what you can offer. Write a resume that indicates what you do best. Consider including such things as "100 percent attendance," "most accurate column addition in the firm," or "trained in CPR" just to let them know exactly what you have to offer. List *all* of your skills at the bottom, especially typing speeds, equipment you can use, or even having a driver's license. All can become important to specific job situations.

Try to include letters of recommendation from previous employers. These will most accurately describe your assets as an employee. For first-time job seekers, letters from teachers or personal references can help, too.

It's always good for Virgos to be properly trained, and you should upgrade your skills as it becomes necessary. When seeking a new position, make sure you are at least as well qualified as the others. Take a refresher course, find out about new technology, or become certified to operate the latest machinery. The more skills you possess, the better able you'll be to compete in the job market. These can also be added to your resume and might prompt an employer to invite you for an interview.

Your attention to detail is one of your greatest assets, so put it to good use in job hunting. Follow all leads, leave no stone unturned, and don't dismiss any possible opportunity.

Work can beget work: Your current position can help you find a new one. Co-workers may be able to recommend a firm they've worked for previously. You've probably developed colleagues in other firms who know what a good job you do. These people will ordinarily be in related fields and may know of openings; ask them when you next meet or talk on the phone. For students or those new to the job market, internships and recommendations from associates there can serve the same purpose.

The interview is a key factor in landing a job, and you must learn to make it work for you. You will most likely be neatly and appropriately dressed and intelligently spoken; both of these will go a long way toward impressing your orderliness on the interviewer.

Before your job interview, you should investigate the market for your specific position to ascertain what your salary range should be. Many firms, especially smaller ones, will ask *you* what you expect to be paid before making an offer. They already have some idea of what they're willing to pay, but they want to see what you have in mind. You must be able to quickly respond.

If you're already working in a field, you've probably got a good idea of salary trends. Keep your request in proportion to what you've earned before, as employers may verify previous pay. If you're switching fields or just entering the job market, there are many resources available. Classified ads will often carry pay figures, so check these over a period of time. Ask others you know in the field or call a trade association or other group. General wage guides can also be found in most public libraries.

Consider your own wants and needs. You'll probably expect less in order to work near your home as opposed to commuting an hour to a big city. In tough economic times, salary rates drop due to high employee availability, so keep this in mind as well. Think about exactly how much you need to earn to support yourself. You should come out with a range of a minimum you need and a maximum that you'd accept in the best circumstances. Start by asking for something near the high figure—no employer will offer you more money than you request! Most will try to compromise with you and offer a bit less. If you're working with an employment agency, it still helps to know the ballpark. Your agent may not hold out for a top salary you feel you can get unless you insist and have the resources to prove it.

You easily analyze business situations, people, and procedures, but keep your advice and opinions to yourself in the interview. Unless you're up for a job in which you'll be directly participating in improving operations, comments of this type will be out of place in an interview. Save them till you've landed the job and know people better. Keep answers succinct and concentrate on asking questions that will help clarify the situation for you. After all, you may not want to join an organization that isn't run smoothly and efficiently.

Getting Ahead: How to Do Your Best on the Job

One of your greatest assets is your quick and able mind. Your analytical abilities can easily be put to use to solve day-to-day problems at work. You are a realist, and as such your observations, deductions, and decisions are sound and accurate.

You concentrate on the facts, and your business life will reflect your basic understanding of the "whys" and "hows" of what it is you do. You will rely on experience rather than the opinions of others. You have the ability to examine the minutest detail and can discriminate based on the slightest difference. You like to make your own decisions and can make constructive suggestions for improvements.

A Virgo paralegal we know works for a real-estate attorney and accountant. She enjoys her job and has kept it for many years because she has excellent skills to handle detail-oriented tasks. Some of her duties include keeping balance sheets and bookkeeping for clients, billing, and checking tax returns, and home closing documents for accuracy.

Efficiency is of importance to all Virgos, and you will seek the easiest and most productive way to go about your work. You are neat, clean, and fussy about your work habits. You can be painstakingly careful in seeking to attain perfect results. You'll take the time that is required to do your job properly and cannot allow yourself to relax until you've finished a project.

A Virgo film editor advanced because his work was

precise and accurate. He was his own best critic and would work diligently until a job was done to his satisfaction. Attention to detail and clean work are necessary, and he scored points with employers because of his quality output. Eventually he became a producer and director because he understood so well what the final product needed to be.

There is usually a great aptitude for facts and figures in the Virgo nature, and you can use this productively on the job. You have a head for statistics and seek to express yourself always in the clearest, most precise way possible. You write effectively because you quickly get to the point.

You have organizational ability and can easily prioritize your work. You can bring order out of chaos and constantly look to maintain a systematic way of doing things. You know immediately where to find that specific piece of information you need in a hurry. And you save time, too, and enjoy any improvements or innovations that can aid you in performing your work more efficiently.

You enjoy working with money and can bring your skills of accuracy and precision easily to financial affairs. You'd make an excellent bookkeeper, auditor, accountant, or analyst. You almost get a thrill from balancing a checkbook or rectifying a bank statement. If you don't choose to specialize in this manner, your instinctive understanding of the effective use of money can be used in any position you choose. You are conservative in spending, but you know a good bargain when you see one and will seek the maximum value for your dollar.

Perhaps your most important asset is your ability to work hard. You'll go about completing the most difficult tasks in the same way that you do everything else—by taking them apart into manageable pieces. You show great zeal in attacking a large project and seeing it through. Your reward is knowing that you worked to the best of your ability. You won't get excited or put off by demands such as overtime, big projects, or mundane chores; you'll view them instead as challenges, roll up your sleeves, and quietly begin.

You have a great feeling of responsibility about your work and are self-motivated to achieve. You are punctual, and you do your best to make the most of your time. You discipline yourself because you have a natural need to work hard. You do it not to gain attention or recognition from others but simply because it gives you a sense of personal satisfaction. Your ideals are the highest of all.

Self-sufficient, you gravitate toward working alone because you can do your job diligently, at your own pace and to your own satisfaction. Yet you are versatile and can easily adapt to many different situations. You can work within an existing system and will work with and around it to get your tasks accomplished. You can do any number of tasks well and have the ability to juggle several projects at once.

You work easily with others because you will be thoughtful and considerate, carrying out your responsibilities to the best of your ability. Your calm, patient manner can inspire others to feel reassured in getting the job done.

Your practical outlook will help you advance as time goes on. You are able to plan ahead and will work for what you want. You realize what is possible and will take the requisite steps to gain added responsibility and pay. Your reliability, consistency, and constructive attitude will insure that you get ahead.

While you are excellent when dealing with facts and figures, all Virgos can benefit from using their imaginations on the job. You stress specific issues in speech and writing, but your ideas and good sense of humor can always help to spice up your communications, making them more pleasant and accessible to others. In your desire to be purposeful you may forget the niceties and should consciously remember them. Strive to be more friendly on the job—enjoy your lunch-hour breaks. Don't let yourself work to the exclusion of all else. In order to fully enjoy your work, you've got to learn how to have a little fun as well.

You can also lose yourself in the trivial points and you may not "see the forest for the trees." Try to always see the forest! Use your organizational ability to see the larger picture and keep that in mind at all times. Learn which details *are* important and which may be less so. It can be helpful in your communications with superiors and co-workers to learn how to summarize or generalize. Your boss doesn't always need a blow-by-blow account of what you've been doing for the past eight hours. Think of what he or she needs to know and only fill in specifics when asked.

Your excellent sense of discrimination can aid in developing the quality of your work, but many Virgos can become hypercritical. Being too harsh on yourself can lead to low self-esteem, overwork, and anxiety. Do your best, but remember that we can't expect perfection on this earth. Strive for improvement the next time rather than redoing the same presentation endlessly.

You can have a tendency to underestimate yourself. If you have doubts about your worth as an employee, compare yourself to your co-workers. You'll probably find that you come out ahead. Speak up when you feel you're not receiving your due. You may feel too reserved to ask for a raise, but situations do occur where you can be overlooked. Be businesslike and don't let yourself be exploited.

For example, don't always be the one to volunteer for overtime. While you like to please and will feel obligated to stay late if asked, make sure it's your *choice* to do so. Don't consistently stay late out of a sense of responsibility. Yes, there are others who can do the work and you do have a life outside of work. If you give in to superiors too often, it will always be expected of you. Also, make sure that you're paid your overtime and keep close track of your extra hours.

You can bite off more than you can chew and are prone

to overwork, even when working your regular schedule. You might exhaust yourself physically and emotionally if you're not careful. Remember that a well-rested and refreshed person is more efficient and productive. Plan and work ahead of deadlines when possible and don't allow yourself to worry about work piling up. Do what you can and advise your supervisor if you're under too much pressure. Your boss may be able to reassign or delegate extra work to others. Concentrate on your assigned priorities.

Try not to criticize others. You may feel that you could do a better job, and probably could, but your relationships will suffer if you begin to routinely offer unsolicited advice to your co-workers. Always be constructive when you offer any opinions. Steer clear, especially, of offering criticism to supervisors when it's not requested. If you have people working for you, try to remember their good points as well as their shortcomings. Don't nag about small details. Many people are quite sensitive to critiques of their work—if you must do it to improve performance, phrase it pleasantly and be constructive and supportive.

Your reserved nature will cause you to shy from the spotlight, and this is good for many positions. As you advance up the career ladder, however, you will find more social or political obligations creeping into your work life. While it's difficult for you to play games, they may become necessary to your career advancement. A certain amount of networking is essential to succeed in most jobs. If you develop good, friendly relations with your close associates, you'll probably have an easier time attending these banquets, parties, and conferences. Think of them as opportunities to talk about what you enjoy most—your work!

You'll probably expect most promotions and advances you receive, and you will usually take a bit more responsibility at a time. Therefore you may become frightened or anxious by a sudden or unexpected promotion. Don't allow yourself to be. Your superiors obviously trust your capabilities, and you should, too! Learn all of what's expected of you and plunge in. You'll soon find that you already know much more than you give yourself credit for.

Your rational outlook will help you realize when you're in a dead-end situation. If your talents are being wasted, you're not rewarded sufficiently, or you just plain hate your work, it's time to move on. Virgos can easily squeeze job interviews into lunch breaks and before or after regular hours. Make sure you're advancing in pay, responsibility, or enjoyment of your work. Then settle down to enjoy a long and productive business relationship.

Do

- Find a secure, stable position.
- Use your keen mind.
- Create the systems and organization to work more efficiently.
- Follow through on future plans.
- Cultivate your imagination.

Don't

- Sell yourself short.
- Overwork.
- Let yourself be taken advantage of.
- Be too critical of yourself or others.
- Get bogged down by too much detail.

LIBRA
September 22 to October 24

"All I had was taste."
—Ralph Lauren,
Celebrity Register

In the Balance

Libra is symbolized by the scales—two pans and a balance, to be more exact. We can still see these being used in old-fashioned nut, grain, and produce shops, but in these computerized times, weighing is more often done in a less poetic, electronic way.

But Librans still use the balancing method! They like to wait and weigh, to carefully take all the evidence into consideration before making a judgment. The scale tips back and forth, first one pan dips and then the next, as Libra takes stock. Once a decision is reached, it will be fair, which is the way Librans like it. Libra is the only astrological sign that's not represented by a human or an animal. The people ruled by this air sign are able to be amazingly objective and uninvolved when exercising their reason.

Perhaps we're most familiar with the scales as a symbol

for justice. Librans are often attracted to establishing justice and balance in all areas of their lives. They are great negotiators, arbitrators, and seekers of truth, and they need to be sure everyone is in harmony. This trait is probably responsible for Libra's need to co-exist in a partnership: You can't weigh with only one pan!

Charming, friendly people, Librans always seek beauty and peace. They are naturally refined, polite, and calm individuals who believe that give and take is necessary to make any relationship work. Picture the scales cast in gold and ivory and you will understand why this sign has such a love for the finer things in life. The exquisite taste exhibited by Librans can be seen in every facet of their lives. Like John Keats (who's actually a Scorpio) they believe that "beauty is truth, truth beauty."

In their need to please everyone and to see all points of view, Librans can be indecisive or procrastinate. This can be a liability, especially in business. But once a real compromise has been reached by Libran logic, you can bet that all will agree it's fair, and the Libran will proceed with the job.

Get to Work! What to Look for in a Career

As you always strive for a sense of harmony and order, it's important that your work atmosphere be pleasant. You should try to find co-workers who are congenial and likable; nice and polite people can help you feel better about your work. You like professionality in yourself and others and will complete all work more efficiently if you feel your co-workers can be relied upon for courteous assistance, objective advice, fair dealing, and an understanding of the needs of all concerned.

You Libras always need to be able to work in cooperation with others. Everyone has special skills, talents, and abilities, and you recognize that the best results can be achieved when these are combined. Working alone for long hours will suppress your natural talents and cause you to feel depressed and unhappy. Make sure there are opportunities for partnership, shared projects, and companionship on the job.

You are sensitive to your environment and you will be spending many hours at your workplace—make sure it meets with your high standards. You would love a gorgeous, luxurious office, but this is not a necessity. What you need is an orderly, clean, and comfortable work environment. It will help if you feel your surroundings are tasteful and attractive as well. Since the look of a company makes a lasting first impression on anyone, and as *you* always make a good business impression, you'd like your work area to do this, too.

Any company with which you're associated should also represent quality. You need to feel that you're contributing to a positive communal effort. As a member and possibly a representative of your firm, you want to be proud of the overall goals, policies, and products of the company as a whole. You must believe that the business strives for quality and is cognizant of the needs of its employees and clients.

You should avoid high-tension work or jobs that require aggressive action in order to be successful. These run counter to your pleasing manner and need for harmony and balance. Similarly, rough, crude, rude, or offensive co-workers will really turn you off. Those who don't strive for politeness in language and behavior will prove difficult for you to work and cooperate with, and they can be detrimental to your own attitude and output.

A Libra businessman was interested in the arts and he joined an off-Broadway theater company. The theater was run on a shoestring budget, and the Libran soon found the offices dirty and depressing. His associates were at times unreliable, and morale tended to be low. After attempting to improve the group for several months, he realized the situation was beyond his ability to improve and he moved on to a more attractive opportunity.

Your choice of vocation is important: You will not be successful if you cannot enjoy what you do. What inspires you to work? What makes you feel as if you have a purpose? What tasks would you like to do, even if there were no demand for their immediate completion or supervisors to push you to finish? It's not necessary to pin down a specific job at first, but it's helpful to zero in on a field, type of situation, or kind of work you'd like to do.

Then proceed to think about where you'd like to work. Your home town? A nearby city? Perhaps a rural area or another business center in the United States or abroad appeals to you more? Visit the areas you're attracted to and see if your previous impressions were accurate. Find out what opportunities are available in your area and field of choice. Think about what you're qualified to do and what training you might need to get the available positions.

You should make a conscious choice about what's right for you. Get to know yourself better in terms of your needs and goals. Be objective and practical. With a definite, more specific idea of what you really want and need, you'll be better prepared to get it.

What's Your Line? Your Vocational Choices

You should use your judgment, good taste, and talent to create a career that you can love and develop. The many different fields relating to the arts are good choices, as are creative fields where self-expression is a prerequisite.

You are wonderful in dealing with people to resolve conflict, and you can make a good negotiator, arbitrator, sales or marketing specialist.

STAR SUCCESS

Johnny Carson has used his Libra charm and grace to create one of the most successful careers in show business. He began as a radio host in the fifties and soon moved into television. Carson joined the *Tonight Show* in 1962 and stayed with it for thirty years of phenomenal success.

He's been so popular on television mainly because he is friendly, likable, and entertaining. Librans know just the right thing to say at any moment, and Carson never needs off-color jokes to get a laugh. Like most Libra people who work best in partnership, Carson has been paired with Ed McMahon for over thirty years. Johnny has sponsored and owned a line of clothing—also a Libran vocation.

Angela Lansbury is a Libra who has succeeded in another Libra-ruled field: the arts. Her graciousness, delicacy, and sense of decorum have helped her develop a career that has spanned more than fifty years. She's been called both a "class act" and the "nicest star in Hollywood," both testimony to her Libra friendliness.

Libras have many talents. For twenty years Angela acted mostly in supporting roles in such films as *National Velvet* and *The Manchurian Candidate*. In the sixties and seventies she branched out to live musical theater. Audiences were captivated by her Libran singing and dancing talents in *Gypsy* and *Sweeney Todd*. In the eighties Lansbury moved on to television, starring in *Murder She Wrote*, one of the top-rated shows of the decade. Most recently, she lent her vocal talent to Disney's *Beauty and the Beast*, singing the title song as the ever-gracious Mrs. Potts. Lansbury's success has shown that, like a true Libra, she is ambitious and able to balance her talents to fit any type of role.

Ralph Lauren has used his Libra style, sales, and marketing ability to develop a business that grosses nearly a billion dollars a year. Growing up poor in the Bronx, he literally created himself and his career through projecting an image. Starting as a salesman for Brooks

Brothers and Bloomingdales, he cultivated the look of success. With no experience or training, a manufacturer soon let him design neckties.

Ralph Lauren founded Polo Fashions for men in 1967. The line is a typically Libran creation of quality and elegance. Lauren's apparel is understated and never trendy. Keeping this basic principle in mind, the designer expanded to womenswear, fragrances, and accessories. In typically Libran fashion, Lauren utilizes the best of the past and present to create classic looks that never go out of style.

Put a checkmark next to each question that you'd answer with a "yes." If there are several checks for a few career groups, review these first and think about the career suggestions we've listed. If you believe that one of these areas is right for you, investigate your selections further or those closely related to them. Also, take a look at the rest of our suggestions for other possibilities.

___ Do you have creative talent and superior taste?

___ Can you express yourself well?

___ Would you like a creative job?

___ Can you market yourself to the public?

___ Do you feel a need to create a refined atmosphere in some way?

You are an Artistic Libra. You can succeed by applying your talents to make the world a more beautiful place. A career in the performing arts may be right for you, including work as a musician, singer, dancer, or actor. Other artistic vocations you might enjoy are illustrator, composer, fashion model, poet, writer, and graphic or fine artist.

Being a milliner, lace maker, embroiderer, tailor,

dressmaker, or apparel manufacturer may appeal to you. There are many other diverse ways in which you can bank on your talents, including positions as a photographer, picture mounter or framer, painting or photo restorer, draftsman, cosmetologist, makeup artist, perfume manufacturer, gem polisher, engraver, paper hanger, house painter, confection or pastry chef, candy or chocolate manufacturer or dealer. Some down-to-earth jobs in this category include sculptor, beekeeper, fruit grower or preserver, gardener, metallurgist, or landscaper. You would also enjoy any handicraft, including work with wood, wicker, knickknacks, or other keepsakes.

___ Do you have a discerning taste or a sensibility for the classic?

___ Can you recognize current trends and styles?

___ Do you appreciate things of great worth?

___ Would you feel comfortable handling valuable objects?

___ Would you like to help others beautify the world?

You are a Luxury Libra. You'd enjoy work in any high-quality trade. This includes positions as a designer, buyer, consultant, or dealer of jewelry, clothing, lingerie, furs, art, or fine-quality foods. You may choose work as a florist, interior designer, interior decorator, horticulturist, botanist, or wine merchant. Some business and management-oriented jobs in this category include agent, art gallery manager, architect, or museum curator.

___ Can you express yourself succinctly?

___ Do you enjoy smoothing ruffled feathers or helping relationships work?

___ Do you understand the fine art of compromise?

___ Can you be fair and impartial?

___ Would you enjoy dealing with the public?

You are a Mediating Libra. Your great talent is to act as a counselor to help others solve their relationship problems for the benefit of all. Positions in the legal or justice system can appeal to you, such as judge, attorney, justice of the peace, legal advisor, paralegal, arbitrator, politician, political aide, or lobbyist. In the private sector, you can utilize your talents to succeed as an agent, adjuster, negotiator, intermediary, public-relations representative, personnel director, labor relations specialist, customer service representative, or wage-hour compliance inspector. You might enjoy work in a dating service or in the Peace Corps. Other rewarding jobs in this category include being a minister, a marriage counselor, or family counselor.

___ Do you like to talk?

___ Do you enjoy sharing with others?

___ Would you like to work with or for the public in some way?

___ Do people and ideas stimulate you?

___ Do you have the power of persuasion?

You are a Communications Libra. You should use your talents and enjoyment of ideas to help others. Many diverse positions in sales, marketing, and advertising are open to you. You could succeed as a correspondent, telecommunications specialist, telephone operator, market researcher, or pollster. You may want to try work as a social secretary, gossip columnist, receptionist, flight attendant, cashier, teller, or host/hostess of an elegant club or restaurant where your charm and savoir faire can be a big plus. Other areas in which you'd be suited include work in publishing or a position as a vocational counselor or teacher of any of the subjects in this group.

___ Do you want a stable position in the business world?

___ Do you aspire to a responsible position?

___ Would you like to work with people helping others?

___ Could you help make people's lives easier or more pleasant?

___ Can you see the beauty of practical, efficient, or labor-saving goods and devices?

You are a Professional Libra. You have the ability to work your way up to an ideal position that can utilize your interpersonal skills. Some of the many Libra-ruled businesses you can choose from are furniture manufacturing, department stores, and hotels (on the managerial or executive level). You may enjoy work with electronic and computing machines, typewriters, duplicators, and other office-related machinery. You can work successfully in the sales, marketing, public relations, advertising, or legal department of any large business or corporation. Financial positions that you might like include work as a financier, financial analyst, stockbroker, credit manager, claims representative, purchasing agent, appraiser, or comparison shopper.

Libras can also succeed in the medical field. You might be successful specializing as a plastic surgeon, dermatologist, hematologist, or urologist.

___ Do you have the ambition and single-mindedness to make it on your own?

___ Are you unmatched in your field for artistic taste?

___ Do you feel you understand what the public wants?

___ Can you market yourself to the public at large?

___ Do you need to work in an atmosphere you've created for yourself?

You are an Entrepreneurial Libra. You should own your own business. Libras do especially well in partnerships, and you should consider working with someone whose strengths can balance your business weaknesses and vice versa. Look over the above categories for a field and make sure you choose something that will be rewarding, profitable, and reflect the "real you"!

Happy Hunting! How to Get That Job

Before you begin your job search, you should have already made some general choices regarding what field and what type of job you feel you're best suited for. Don't waste your time by trying all kinds of different positions or following up on offers of jobs that will not be right for you. Remember to consciously seek the golden mean, whether it be between satisfaction and pay, distance to and from the workplace, co-workers and supervisors, or pleasure and responsibility.

It will help you to work with others in order to find the best position. If you have a friend seeking work, you can find strength, encouragement, and good ideas in that person. Sharing your own thoughts with others can help solidify them and give you some objective insight.

Working with an employment agency or placement service can also be to your liking. You won't have to "get your hands dirty" by negotiating for your own salary, benefits, or title. Find a good agency by getting recommendations from individuals you know, or interview a few companies yourself. Get names of several agencies that place workers in your field from newspaper advertisements and drop by to find out what they can do for you. What kind of listings do they have available? How many jobs can they send you to this week? Don't settle for what these people would like to do for you but insist on interviews that *you* would like. You'll eventually find an agency with the right opportunities for you.

You do best dealing with people in a direct manner. While the Libran letter-writing style can be exquisite, your personality on the phone or in person is even better. Try to show yourself to your best advantage, as your refined personality is a plus in any interview. You put others at ease with your intelligence and tact while commanding respect with your dignified demeanor.

Most interviewers will respond to your politeness. Particular attention to dress is always regarded as a positive asset in an interview, and it is one that you possess. Find some tasteful and businesslike thank-you notes to send afterward with your personal thoughts. These will reinforce your interest, and you can also refer to any qualifications you forgot to mention earlier.

But Librans can be procrastinators; you like to have a long time to make important decisions. If you've gotten a job offer quickly, you may not have the luxury to mull over whether you want it or not. Remember that there are probably a lot of other well-qualified persons out there just waiting for such an opportunity. Don't wait too long. If you've been through a long interviewing process with a certain firm, it's best not to take more than a few days to let them know if you'll accept their offer.

If you're really in a quandary, it may help to go in for another interview. Try to speak with some of the people who'll be your co-workers, and get a sense if the atmosphere of the place is right for you. As many interviews are done away from the actual job site, it's always a good idea for you to see as much of the company as possible.

If you're deciding between two offers, be as objective as possible. Make a list of the pros and cons of each and weigh the relative importance to you of salary, prestige, environment, promotability, and any other crucial factors.

Sometimes you'll get an offer during a second interview. Don't balk in responding—say "yes" right away. You can always change your mind later, and you might lose out if you don't jump right in. You may add that you just need to discuss your decision with your family or spouse as an "out." Don't let yourself feel that you're acting unfairly in this situation. One individual seeking employment is at a disadvantage against any firm. You must act in your own self-interest!

Getting Ahead: How to Do Your Best on the Job

As an air sign, Libra's mental qualities are emphasized. Yours is a balanced mind, with excellent intellectual and logical capacities.

You can weigh many diverse factors, situations, and personalities in order to come to a well-reasoned conclusion of how and when to act. You will utilize people, written records, and anything else available to you in order to insure that a decision *will* work in practice. While you respect the tried and true, you are also not afraid of innovation if a plan makes sense to you. Thus you can make large decisions and will not often misjudge a situation.

Working with language is enjoyable to you. You express yourself beautifully in speech and writing, knowing exactly the right thing to say at the right time. You can use these talents effectively in any communications on the job, but especially in correspondence, reports, and meetings. You are equally comfortable with figures and understand financial and business matters well.

If you love and enjoy your work, you will be an efficient, careful, and thoughtful worker who plans ahead. Your attention to *all* contingencies will keep you from making careless mistakes. Typically fair and honest in business dealings, you can be relied on to keep appointments and to live up to your responsibilities.

The Libra character has a core of strength. You are not wishy-washy, although you may at times appear to be so. You can be shrewd and usually know how you want things done. You also have the ability to get what you want without rocking the boat.

Libra's greatest talent lies in the ability to be democratic. You enjoy dealing with people and try to be pleasant regardless of the circumstances. You understand that "business" is simply getting things done for other people.

You instinctively know how to pull together with others to make a stronger whole. Everyone has talents, and you have the ability to blend your skills with those of others to get results. You find the natural group environment of a company or firm well suited to your work style and therefore are an effective businessperson.

You seek out harmony and can use this to your advantage. People naturally like you and gravitate toward you. You make people feel that attention is paid them and their needs are met. For example, a Libra psychic we know understands her clients' needs and talks realistically about their lives. People are attracted and drawn to her, not only because of her extrasensory talents and objective advice, but also because she is easy to be with and talk to.

Because you so easily understand others' points of view, you can have good marketing and advertising ideas. You can play devil's advocate in discussions and can anticipate clients' or co-workers' concerns. You have an excellent head for debate or brainstorming.

You are usually well dressed, as your outer appearance

is an extension of your inner refinement. You should cultivate a style that can help you get ahead.

You have the ability to plan ahead and to follow through to reach your goals. You are realistic about what you can accomplish. Yet you will not rest once certain objectives have been met but will create new ones.

Your thoroughness promises success and recognition. Your excellent sense of timing tells you just when you should ask for a raise, promotion, or your own office. As you are so well-mannered in requests, it's easy for others to give you what you want!

An inharmonious or discordant situation can cause you to neglect your work. You may retreat from reality by concentrating on your personal life. Avoid this tendency by getting a job where professionalism and congeniality are the rule.

Librans operate on the pleasure principle. You don't like to do anything that doesn't please, stimulate, or relax you. Remember that in the business world, there will be things that you must do that you don't particularly like. Only about one percent of working people get others to do *everything* that's distasteful to them. Don't leave a position because of small problems—don't hop from job to job because of personality conflicts or the occasional distasteful situation. It's best if you can smooth things out—your career will not grow if you continually avoid your problems. And don't regularly make co-workers do the dirty work. If you find someone to swap duties with you or who enjoys what you dislike, that's great. But in an office where everyone has their turn to take out the garbage—make sure you do so on your day. It's only fair.

You Libras need to realize that you will never find your ideal on this earth. You will benefit from being more pragmatic and accepting some of the harsh realities of the working world in order to survive. There are many aggressive, obnoxious individuals in the business world who have succeeded by following the mottos "Might is right" and "Money is power." You cannot operate in this manner, but you may have to deal with individuals who do, no matter what field you're in. Remember to be fair and don't avoid difficult people. Try to learn what these people need and deal with them quickly and efficiently.

It's important to listen to *what* someone is saying, rather than *how*, especially if you have a cantankerous boss. Many people have trouble expressing themselves or have abrasive personalities. While you may dislike the way these people put themselves across, try to see what's behind their mannerisms. Often you will find that there is an essentially cooperative, businesslike individual hidden under a difficult exterior.

To avoid difficult situations, you may let more assertive individuals make decisions for you, but you'll be short-changing yourself. In small matters this practice can be acceptable, but if you really want to get somewhere in your career, you must make your own choices and take responsibility for them.

Since you always try to please others, you can frustrate yourself. The old adage about not being able to please all of the people all of the time should be learned by all Librans! Especially in business, some people are going to be happy with the way you do things and others will be upset. While you should be able to have pleasant relationships with those around you, don't push yourself too hard by worrying about what others may think.

Perhaps the biggest problem for Libra people is indecisiveness. Many work situations force you to act quickly, but you can get hung up on the small things. For example, if you do not know whom to call first, just make *a* call—any call. You may have to call back your first customer after talking to the boss, but you may not have been able to avoid this in the first place. Remember that decisions aren't written in stone. Things come up later that will change the way you see a situation and the way in which you'll act. If you *are* pushed into acting too soon, don't worry about having to do things over later. This is what the business world is all about!

One thing you can control is procrastination. Some Librans get caught up in constantly thinking about new possibilities. Don't let yourself think so much that you end up getting little accomplished.

If you find your co-workers disruptive, your work unfulfilling or repulsive, or if you cannot condone the actions of the company, it is best that you make plans to go elsewhere. With your excellent interpersonal skills, you'll have no problem leaving graciously. Just don't debate too long about it! Attempt to find another position while you're still employed, but try to arrange for some time off in between to relax and prepare yourself for the more rewarding position waiting for you!

Do

- Use grace and charm to your advantage.
- Find a job you can love.
- Work effectively with others.
- Be fair when it comes to doing unpleasant tasks.
- Cultivate firmness and decisiveness.

Don't

- Worry about what others think.
- Procrastinate.
- Misjudge others by their outer appearance.
- Avoid tough issues.
- Be too idealistic.

SCORPIO

October 23 to November 23

"Just go out there planning to win
and make sure you do."
—Ted Turner,
*Lead, Follow
or Get Out of the Way*

Arachnid

Scorpio is represented by the Scorpion, a rather unique creature. Emotionally intense and strongly determined, Scorpios can do almost anything when properly motivated.

The common scorpion lives in desert and tropical areas such as Mexico and Texas. Its small size (from two to six inches) belies its powerful sting. While the scorpion's sting is painful, it is seldom fatal to man. People born under the sign Scorpio can withstand difficult circumstances to get what they want. While their quiet demeanor and often compact physique make them appear weaker than many, they are physically and emotionally one of the strongest signs of the zodiac. Many Scorpios are fierce business people, and some can be deceitful and underhanded. However, these negative types of Scorpio more often end up doing more damage to themselves than those they seek to destroy.

The scorpion comes out at night and spends the day in dark hiding places under stones and plants. Likewise, its human counterparts are retiring by nature. Many of them prefer a private atmosphere. They'll close doors, pull down blinds, and take other precautions to insure that they're not easily interrupted. Some desert scorpions can have up to twelve eyes, and Scorpios are very attentive to the outside world as well. Nothing misses their sharp, penetrating, and sensitive scrutiny.

One of the most amazing things about scorpions is that the females carry their very young on their backs. Scorpios are likewise committed to those they love and care for. They are loyal and emotionally supportive. Yet only a few people earn this caring treatment! The constellation Scorpio contains the bright red star Antares at its center. From this, we can see Scorpios to be passionate and intense at heart.

Scorpios need intense experiences in order to be happy in their careers. When their energies are channeled into projects, these people can succeed through dedication and strength of will alone.

Get to Work! What to Look for in a Career

You need a job that challenges you in some way, one that draws on your inner resources, whether they be physical, emotional, or intellectual. You are self-governed, meeting challenges head-on and thriving on solving problems.

You do your best work without any assistance. You should have a position where you are in charge of your own work or can at least make some decisions. You can function well as a consultant or specialist and can invest your money to good financial advantage. While this sign can respond to discipline, direct control by others will not be conducive to your career growth. You should seek instead a position of more self-sufficiency.

You need emotional satisfaction and financial security from work, and if these are present, you will keep your job for a great length of time. Once you feel that your abilities are not being utilized to their full extent, however, you try to move on, planning your next opportunity in a systematic way.

You will be most happy if you find you are getting something "real" accomplished in your position. Pushing papers will not be stimulating for you, as you don't see the value in this. You can, however, commit yourself to even the most routine or mundane task if you feel you are doing the work well, and if you believe it can be a steppingstone to your ultimate objectives. You are quite goal oriented, and you'd like to eventually have the power to command or to do things your own way. You should also seek a working environment that will provide you with at least some quiet and solitude. You would appreciate a cozy and comfortable retreat in which you can be alone and undisturbed when necessary.

What's Your Line? Your Vocational Choices

Investigative and financial work are both excellent for Scorpios. As you are interested in the mysteries of life and death, fields related to these subjects may appeal to you. The restoration of people or things is also stressed, and many Scorpios can give new life to failing businesses.

Jonas Salk succeeded in scientifically researching the polio virus, which causes paralysis and often death. A typically dedicated Scorpio, he worked sixteen hours a day, six days a week, to develop a vaccine, which was first administered to children nationwide in 1954. Salk's vaccine was almost 90 percent effective in preventing polio, and it is considered a significant medical breakthrough. As Scorpios usually seek greater control over their work and often work well with outside funding, Salk opened the Salk Institute for Biological Studies in La Jolla, California, in 1963. Many of the top scientists of our day have worked there with Salk himself, attempting to find cures for multiple sclerosis and cancer. In the late 1980s and 1990s, Salk set to work on a kind of vaccine to halt the development of AIDS in those infected with the HIV virus.

Many Scorpios are shrewd business people and Christie Hefner is no exception. As the daughter of Hugh Hefner and president of Playboy Enterprises since 1982, the additional Scorpio themes of family inheritance and human sexuality also play a part in her career. She handles the business side while her dad sticks to directing editorial content.

Like many Scorpios, Christie was able to turn the fortunes of her father's business around by streamlining the corporation to make it more profitable. She has also been responsible for Playboy's successful cable-TV channel. While Christie Hefner has gotten criticism from some feminist groups who regard *Playboy* magazine as pornographic, true to her Sun sign, she is quite adamant about the publication's excellent treatment of its models, philosophic support of feminist policies, and overall record of hiring and promoting women. And Hefner, as a member of the board of directors, has given grants for such Scorpio-related causes as gun control, aid to rape and incest victims, gay rights, and relief to Vietnam veterans.

Scorpios often enjoy tough emotional challenges, and Scorpio Jodie Foster has thrived on these in her work as an actress. Beginning in commercials, she has spent much of her life in the emotionally charged world of film. At thirteen, Foster was nominated for a best supporting actress Oscar for her work as a prostitute in *Taxi Driver*. Other demanding roles have included the murderess in

The Little Girl Who Lived Down the Lane and a dying heart patient in *Echoes of Summer*. Most notable, of course, were Foster's Oscar-winning performances as rape victim Sarah Tobias in *The Accused* and FBI agent Clarice Starling in *The Silence of the Lambs*. In all of these roles she's used her Scorpio emotional intensity and conviction to bring gut-wrenching characters to life.

But the Scorpio flair for business and finances is also obvious in Foster's career. She has virtually supported her family since childhood and is producing and directing films, realizing more of what Scorpios love most —control. Her 1991 directing debut, *Little Man Tate* (a film in which she also starred), was greeted with rave reviews.

Put a checkmark next to each question that you'd answer with a "yes." If there are several checks for a few career groups, review these first and think about the career suggestions we've listed. If you believe that one of these areas is right for you, investigate your selections further or those closely related to them. Also, take a look at the rest of our suggestions for other possibilities.

___ Do you intuitively understand how investments are made?

___ Does trading excite you?

___ Are you stimulated by helping others with their financial needs?

___ Do you like negotiating or using your knowledge effectively while earning money yourself?

___ Does the idea of increasing your income by commission attract you?

You are a Financial Scorpio. Scorpios are natural money makers, and the financial field is great for you.

Any job that earns commissions is good, but work in the stock market and with taxes are both ideal choices. The law is also an area where Scorpios can succeed. You could become an attorney or paralegal specializing in finance, negligence, insurance, taxes, bankruptcy, or inheritance, or an estate executor. You could enjoy working as an insurance investigator, insurance salesperson, policy checker, financial advisor, estate buyer, stock and commodities trader, bond broker, financial analyst, I.R.S. agent, tax consultant, bank employee (teller through executive), loan officer, mortgage and customs broker, claims adjuster, money lender, pawn broker, collector, accountant, actuary, bail bondsman, bookmaker, or agent.

___ Do you feel a need to help the human race survive?

___ Are you interested in the transformative powers of nature?

___ Do you think you can use your powers to help others?

___ Do you like to delve into the unknown?

___ Are you stimulated by human needs and emotions?

You are a Transformative Scorpio. You can succeed as a general, reconstructive, or exploratory surgeon; periodontist; obstetrician or gynecologist; endocrinologist; obstetrical or surgical nurse; medical, chemical, or biological researcher; epidemiologist; pathologist; biologist; chemist; drug or atomic researcher; energy transformer; biological or chemical microscopist; nuclear-medical technician; X-ray or radiology technician; psychoanalyst; psychiatrist; sex therapist; hypnotherapist; hypnotist; fertility clinic employee; pharmacist; hospital safety officer; medical records technician; or statistical or technical manuscript typist.

Some areas that may not be chosen by others will be ideal for you. As you are interested in the forces of nature, fields related to death and dying, metaphysics, and the disposal of waste are all suitable. You could enjoy work as a death therapist, past-life therapist, psychic researcher, metaphysical advisor, funeral director, embalmer, coroner, forensic detective, cryonics technician, environmental conservationist, recycling plant or sewage disposal operator, or sanitary inspection engineer. Other areas include pest or insect controller or entomologist; manufacturer, distributor, dealer, or salesperson of pesticides, fertilizers, sprays, and pest killers, or waste-to-energy plant worker.

___ Do you like to get to the bottom of things?

___ Do taboo subjects or hidden motives attract you?

___ Do other people's secrets intrigue you?

___ Do you like to work alone, using your instincts as a guide?

___ Would you like to work for an organization associated with power in some way?

You are an Investigative Scorpio, and this aptitude can take you into detective work, historical research, or even psychology. Your secretive nature makes you suitable for undercover police work, and your probing abilities can be put to good use in archaeology, decoding, or library science. You might enjoy work as a secret service agent, undercover agent, police detective, private detective, criminologist, fingerprint expert, polygraph operator, corrections officer, investigative or crime reporter, true crime or mystery writer, atomic researcher, sexual science investigator, or censor.

___ Do you like to deal with the basics?

___ Does getting down to the very essence of things stimulate you?

___ Do the rules of elemental nature attract you?

___ Do you like the process of transforming raw materials into something useful?

___ Would you like a secure position?

You are an Elemental Scorpio. Scorpio is often attracted to dangerous work with metals, chemicals, or heavy construction. Your workplace can be underground, underwater, or in some other hidden location. You could be interested in mining or working in a public utility (such as gas, water, or electric) or power plant. You may want to look into the iron and steel industry as a processor, dealer, or distributor; or as a manufacturer of cars, hardware, tools, cutlery, surgical instruments, refrigerators, or washing machines. You could become a foundry worker, machinist, smith, pipe fitter, plumber, smeltery operator, locksmith, or lumberjack. The manufacture, distribution, or sale of guns, armaments, explosives, or fireworks could interest you, or you could own or manage a shooting gallery. Becoming a demolition expert, bomb diffuser, firefighter, excavator, boxer, wrestler, or martial arts expert could also attract you. Constructional engineers with naval or marine interests such as submarines, hydraulics, and diesels, or mining engineers and excavators are often Scorpios. The mining of iron or precious stones may interest you, as would the manufacture of jewelry.

___ Do you want to create, change, or develop items into something better?

___ Would you like to see the tangible results of your work?

___ Do you want to help the world improve, at
least on some small level?

___ Do you want a field of specialization that
offers variety and continuous challenges?

___ Do you have the strength to be committed to
your work?

You are a Creative Scorpio. Bringing things back to life is often stressed, and Scorpios can do wonderful renovation work on buildings, furniture, photographs, or clothing, and also give new life to failing businesses. You may enjoy working as a carpenter, archaeologist, actor, composer, writer, rock musician, photo developer, or restorer of old manuscripts and books. You might love working with antiquated homes, buildings, clothing, and jewelry; selling used cars, furniture, or clothing; manufacturing ice cream or soft drinks; brewing beer and wine; managing a hotel, cafe, bar, ice-cream parlor, restaurant, or butcher shop; breeding or raising livestock; harvesting lobsters, oysters, or clams; or managing an aquatic museum or aquarium.

___ Do you resent authority?

___ Are you willing to take financial risks to
realize your independence?

___ Do you have good business sense?

___ Would you like to be in sole control of a
venture?

___ Do you feel you can survive tough economic
times?

You are an Entrepreneurial Scorpio and should own your own business. Most Scorpios like to work on their own, and this can be a great asset in beginning a new venture. Your business acumen and shrewd judgment are important abilities that will help you succeed. Go over the lists above to help you find a uniquely Scorpio vocation.

Happy Hunting! How to Get That Job

Scorpios are realistic, resourceful, and independent. You probably have a good idea of what you want and how to go about getting it. Use these characteristics to help you find an ideal position.

One of your best bets in seeking employment is to find a good employment agency. If you can get a personal reference, so much the better. If you're a recent graduate of a training program or college, these institutions often have placement services. If not, consult the want ads in a major newspaper serving the area of your choice. Many agencies will advertise, especially on a Sunday, and you can get to know what types of position they fill. See if they place people in the areas of work that interest you, and check what's being paid for specific positions that you feel you could fill. Remember, though, that these agency ads are lures to get you to come through the door and are often exaggerations or samples of positions they fill. Yes, they can be falsifications, and it's best not to expect to land a specific position from agency ads. Rather, use them as guidelines to compare agencies and help you determine what their specialties are.

Once you've selected a few employment agencies and have visited them, evaluate what the agents can actually do for you. Agencies have many listings and will try to get you to fill one that they have available—make sure you are interested in the positions they suggest. Take your time and make it perfectly clear what you'll settle for.

Most employment agencies will of course try to get you the highest salary possible because their commission will be higher, so they will send you on the highest-paying interviews first. They're serving both you and them at the same time. Yet one employer may have a tremendous benefits package at the same salary as another who doesn't. Keep this in mind, as agencies don't often concentrate on these and other bonuses.

Follow up with your agent, if you feel he or she is good and is really trying to help you. Agents get new opportunities on a regular basis. As they ordinarily try to place people quickly, it's to your advantage to stick with them. Take your time in making a final decision as well. You'll probably want a long-term, permanent position, so see as many employers as you comfortably can and carefully think through the pros and cons of each offer you receive.

For your interview with the employer, try to be as pleasant and likable as possible. You are generally self-assured and confident, but guard against appearing overly assertive. These are superficial attributes, of course, but first impressions are lasting ones. Let interviewers do their job on the initial occasion. They want to feel that they're in control and will have many questions about your previous work experience, education, and background.

Don't be cagey or evasive whenever you can avoid it. Be tactful and keep your opinions to yourself. Concentrate on the facts. Decide beforehand exactly what you want to reveal and discuss, and anticipate such questions as "What do you hope to be doing five years from now?", "Why did you leave your last position?", and "How well do you feel you work with others?" If the interviewer gets the impression you're not being candid, it'll be held against you.

When the questions are finished, bring up whatever has crossed your mind. Personnel people are usually quite knowledgeable and friendly. Ask what benefits the company offers, if you haven't been told already. Find out about their health-care package, vacation schedule, and overtime pay. Many larger corporations also have discounted cafeterias, pension plans, and a certain amount of job security. Although these don't give you extra cash, they do have value and are certainly not taxable amenities. Your final decision should be based on both the salary and benefits package.

The employment agency will want to speak to you after your interview. If you feel you should be paid more than the firm's offer, mention it to your agent, who may be able to negotiate a higher compensation for you. The agent will also get an idea of when the employer will make a decision and whether you're in the running for the position. At this point, just wait, decide what you'll do if you get an offer, and go on to the next interview!

Getting Ahead: How to Do Your Best on the Job

Once you've settled down in a position that you feel is rewarding, you'll probably want it to last. You get a great sense of security and confidence from knowing your job, your associates, and your daily routine. When you become familiar with what's expected of you and what you can expect of others, you will handle your tasks effectively. You are dependable and reliable, and those in charge will soon realize this as a great asset and will want to hang on to you too.

You have a strong will, and once you have made up your mind to do something, you'll do it. Your strength of will and commitment to goals are a few of the characteristics that can contribute to success in the workplace. You Scorpios are forceful individuals; when your energies are well directed, you are virtually unbeatable.

You'll be extremely patient in overcoming any obstacles and will not swerve from a committed path. You are quite loyal to co-workers who treat you well and will be protective of close associates. You'll often act on a point of honor in even the simplest business discussions.

You are self-sufficient and take intense pride in your work. You'll make your own decisions regardless of what others think and will not be intimidated or influenced by the opinions of others. Scorpios are realists by nature, but you can make judgments on instinct. These feelings are often quite reliable.

You are a naturally effective business person. In control of your own actions, you are disciplined, and you plan well in advance. Preparation is always quite thorough and most often well organized. Of all the twelve signs, Scorpio has the greatest ability to probe a subject in depth. Skeptical until proven wrong, nothing will escape your intense scrutiny. And you'll ordinarily have a long list of reliable data to back up any conclusions you reach.

Scorpio's courage and leadership ability can make you rise through the ranks to positions of authority. You love power, wealth, and privilege, but you can resent society at large for being oppressive to the individual.

Your capacity for hard work and your ability to commit yourself exclusively to one task at a time are great attributes for any type of work. You can tune out other people and distracting influences, as you get totally involved in what you are doing. You are thorough and can often be painstaking in your undivided attention to the details of your work, as you like to understand the complete workings of things. If your position involves research of any kind, you'll probably be content. However, this type of task is often an independent one, which can be incorporated by you into many jobs. Your supervisors will be pleased when they find how completely you've gotten to know your subject.

Whether you are more ambitious or security conscious doesn't matter in the least. Once you have set a goal for yourself, you slowly but steadily pursue it. Each step you take up the corporate or business ladder is one that represents your solid background and hard work. You are willing to wait a long time for rewards, and you can outlast many less committed co-workers through sheer persistence alone.

You have a quiet strength and great personal magnetism when you are operating in a positive frame of mind. These can help when working with others. But you may not be conscious of how strongly you come across to others on an emotional level. You are generally quite subjective and can benefit from trying to understand the other person's point of view. Although you don't often find the need for counsel from associates, you can also benefit from seeing a broader picture by finding out what others think.

Always try to be tactful and avoid sarcasm—some people just don't *get* it! Many other signs, like Aries, Taurus, and Sagittarius, are more direct and take things on face value. Try to see their way of looking at things. This is very difficult to do, but if you understand others better, it will go a long way in helping you work with them.

You become personally involved with everything about you, and this is one reason you take great pride in your work. Yet you must realize that you will come into contact with many people on the job on a day-to-day basis. Their behavior can often be upsetting to you. Cultivate a distance or temper your natural sensitivity in dealing with difficult personalities. Don't take personally any slights you may feel from others. Your co-workers may be tired, stressed out, or just angry about their own jobs.

While sensitive to other people's conduct toward you, you may at times be unconscious of others' needs. Again, a more objective view can help you. Don't assume that just because someone has a tough exterior they can take everything that you dish out. Tolerance of others' shortcomings and recognition of their feelings will always help on the job. Try to treat others not as they treat you but as you'd like to be treated.

It's sometimes difficult for you to take direct orders or listen to a boss that you don't like or feel is incompetent. However much you may at times resent the powers that be, realize that everything will eventually change. People can change their attitudes, policies, and even jobs, and we live in a world where things are constantly in a state of flux. Know that if you do your job well, the power structure will one day include you if you want it to. In the meantime, be polite and businesslike and make suggestions when you can. If none of this works, grit your teeth and bear it, or seek a transfer.

One of your greatest assets is your ability to be realistic about what you can accomplish in terms of schedule as well as advancement. But try not to take advantage of others and don't get too involved or caught up in office politics. Your hard work and commitment will always win out. If someone on the job has really hurt you personally, realize that their behavior will hurt their own career in the long run. Scheming or trying to give them their due will only hurt *your* career—avoid it at all costs. Most people who work together on a regular basis know how their associates behave and what their character flaws and problems are. If a co-worker has treated you unfairly, let the system handle it—a person with a negative attitude will soon be known to all for what he or she is.

Because you are a very private person, it's important for you to recognize the difference between your workplace and your home. For example, remember that your personal desk is really company property. So be on guard against what you may view as an invasion of privacy. If you keep papers you don't want others to see or personal valuables at the office, make sure that they're carefully locked away in a sturdy drawer or locker. You should also make an extra effort to enjoy the company of those about you. Some Scorpios can have a tendency to withdraw, and this is not productive to developing good working relationships.

If you find your position is not working out, evaluate it. Does it offer the financial rewards you need and want? Does it give you a sense of stability and security? Are there opportunities for advancement? If these basic needs are being met, you can do a lot to improve your situation because, of all the signs, Scorpio has the greatest transformational ability. Others will respond to an improved attitude (even if it's put on!), and you can work to develop what you do into something more fulfilling.

You usually wait a long time and exhaust all possibilities before making a decision, but once it's been made you need to act. If you're increasingly feeling angry or unhappy with your current position, begin a job search at once, while still employed—you can study what's out there in your free time and interview on a lunch hour or on time off. Compare and contrast—you may find that you prefer the known to the unknown. If you keep up your search, however, you're sure to find a position that offers an improvement.

A Scorpio woman we know was successful in her job as a banker and enjoyed a regular paycheck as well as generous employee benefits. Eventually, she wanted to find a job that was more emotionally rewarding and requested a transfer, but no positions were open. However, because of her request, she was laid off and received severance pay and unemployment benefits. While taking classes to improve her skills, she began her own home-based business.

Try to use your imagination whenever possible: This can be a great asset in directing your tremendous energies properly. Don't dwell on things that bother you. Instead, concentrate on those tasks and people that nurture and support you. Your steady climb to the top will be met with satisfaction. Once you've found your niche working for others, you may even want to try and work for yourself, too!

Do

- Try to have control over some aspect of your work.
- Be more pleasant and socially adept, and try to compromise.

STAR SUCCESS

- Channel your energy effectively.
- Get a job that offers emotional rewards.
- Listen to your boss.

Don't

- Let your desire for power and control cause you to be insensitive to the needs of others.
- Scheme at the workplace.
- Be overly sensitive to co-workers.
- Be intolerant or give others a tough time.
- Act in a secretive manner or be overly suspicious of co-workers.

SAGITTARIUS
November 22 to December 22

"If I believe in the pot at the end of the rainbow, it really doesn't matter if I ever get there; the fun of chasing it is reward enough for me."
—Douglas Fairbanks, Jr., *Knight Errant*

Ready, Aim, Fire!

Sagittarius is represented by the archer, poised with bow and arrow, ready to shoot. In the constellation Sagittarius, the tip of the archer's arrow falls right in the middle of our galaxy. Perhaps this is why natives of the sign aspire to higher realms of thought and study such complex subjects and philosophies. Faith is important in their lives; beliefs and values are always the basis for their actions. They like to reason and discuss, share and argue ideas and ideals. The Sagittarian cares deeply for the welfare of others.

The arrow symbolizes Sagittarius' direct and open nature and often barbed wit. Sagittarians speak their minds—sometimes too much so! They possess a great deal of energy and enthusiasm. While Sagittarians have the confidence to undertake any task, once their attention is diverted, these people often find it difficult to resume a project. One line of thought and energy is followed at a time. It's also difficult for them to follow the advice of others. They must act on their own initiative. Yet in the glee of accomplishing a task, they may also overlook important details.

The archer is not actually a man. He's a centaur—half man and half horse! Up in the sky at night, he looks as if he's about to go galloping off to explore the entire Milky Way. Above all, Sagittarians love freedom and independence, and they see this as a value to be cherished. They need to travel, especially in the great outdoors. The down-side of this expansive nature is that it always needs somewhere else to go! The archer resents restrictions. Sagittarians can prove too restless for most office jobs or those requiring sitting for long periods of time. Their minds, too, need to work freely, and too much control from superiors will squelch this sign's natural talents and cause them to rebel.

Perhaps because part of the archer is a trusting animal, Sagittarius is the most genial and good-natured sign of the zodiac. Full of an innate optimism, there is a complete lack of suspicion of others. They love people and are eager to get to know them all! Often they can simply "luck into" good positions because they believe it can happen.

Get to Work! What to Look for in a Career

Your natural enthusiasm and self-confidence are the most important traits to use toward a career. Sagittarius is a fire sign, and you have so much vitality that you can quickly seize opportunities and challenges. This high-spirited, spontaneous nature can be expressed in whatever area you choose, especially positions that require thinking on your feet or adaptability to ever-changing situations.

Most important for any Sagittarian is the need to have a position that offers some kind of freedom. This can take the form of making your own decisions or acting alone, or it could even include the ability to physically move about. If you live in a big city and find it necessary to secure an office job, be sure that there are large windows and an opportunity to see others in the company or go out for errands or meetings. Anything that breaks up the routine is welcome to you; you desire change, excitement, and variety. If you feel trapped and bottled up, you won't be utilizing your talents to their best advantage.

A Sagittarian man works as director of marketing for a promotions firm. He has much variety in his work, as he oversees a staff that works with little interference from other departments. He has contact with other people and corporations and also enjoys a lot of foreign and domestic travel as part of his position.

Above all, you need to tap your energy. You most enjoy working directly with others, and indeed, you need human companionship in order to enjoy your work. You should deal with people and be able to interact as part of your job. Your positive attitude can be put to great use in sales, marketing, committee work, or in the entertainment field.

You should be able to continually meet new challenges and must believe in your work. In the best situation, your position will involve working for a cause or have some degree of helpfulness involved. At the least, your job must seem to be important to someone or some goal. Sagittarians are often drawn to spiritual or church work or other public concerns. They can be ardent political activists or grass-roots crusaders.

What's Your Line? Your Vocational Choices

Sagittarians like to do things in a big way, whether it be to travel far, touch lofty subjects, improve the world situation, or succeed in large enterprises. Your enthusiasm can take you wherever the imagination aspires.

Sagittarians live in a world of ideas and ideals, and William F. Buckley, Jr., is a good example of a Sagittarius who has used these attributes to create a successful career.

Many Sagittarians succeed as writers, and Buckley, whose first literary success was the controversial bestseller *God and Man at Yale,* founded the *National Review* after several years' work as a typically Sagittarian freelancer. The *National Review* now has a circulation of well over 100,000, and it is credited with solidifying the current conservative movement in this country.

Demonstrating the Sagittarian love of variety, Buckley has written a syndicated column for over thirty years and has published many books of his political commentary. He's the author of a spy series in the Sagittarian adventure-thriller mode and has contributed articles to many noteworthy magazines. Perhaps best known for his long-running PBS series, "Firing Line," Buckley, like many of his sign, delights in debate.

Cathy Rigby is a Sagittarius who first succeeded in a sports-related career, another popular outlet for that amazing energy. Beginning gymnastic training as a young girl, she often traveled to distant locations to compete. Rigby participated in the 1972 Olympics in Munich, Germany, and became a sports commentator on ABC for many years afterward.

Cathy Rigby's most recent success has come in her revival of *Peter Pan.* In it she acts, sings, dances, and uses her athletic ability to fly (via a wire, of course) across the stage. She probably enjoyed playing Peter because of the

Sagittarian-like qualities the character possesses: intense convictions, idealism, and a childlike love of life.

Singer Tina Turner can be seen as the embodiment of Sagittarian energy in her record albums, stage shows, and concert tours. Her feisty spirit endows all of her performances with great fervor. Turner grew up in a small town in rural Tennessee and, like most Sagittarians, yearned to travel to a bigger and better place. She soon moved to St. Louis and occasionally sang with Ike and the Kings of Rhythm; with this group Tina would record fifteen hit albums over the next ten years.

Ike and Tina Turner's first success came in Great Britain. They opened for the Rolling Stones in a concert tour in 1966 and later returned to the United States to popular and critical acclaim. Tina Turner's bold, almost revivalist style of performance was the hallmark of the Ike and Tina Turner Revue, but most Sagittarians prefer to have independent careers. She released four solo albums in the seventies, before again touring with the Rolling Stones in 1981. She revitalized her career at this time and has gone on to record the smash-hit album *Private Dancer* and others. All Sagittarians have strong beliefs, and Turner credits her success in part to a balanced life that includes study and meditation.

Put a checkmark next to each question that you'd answer with a "yes." If there are several checks for a few career groups, review these first and think about the career suggestions we've listed. If you believe that one of these areas is right for you, investigate your selections further or those closely related to them. Also, take a look at the rest of our suggestions for other possibilities.

___ Would you like to deal with new people and things?

___ Are you stimulated by the challenge of the unexpected?

___ Do you like to start new projects and lead others?

___ Does using your personality on the job appeal to you?

___ Do you enjoy travel?

You are an Explorer Sagittarius. You'd enjoy any job that expands your horizons. Try roving as a troubleshooter, advance agent, explorer, forester, surveyor, or prospector for oil deposits, gold, and other precious metals and minerals. Jobs in the travel industry such as pilot, air-safety inspector, immigration officer, customs inspector, flight attendant, balloonist, international air courier, ticket agent, ground-crew worker, air-traffic controller, airport VIP host, tour guide, or traveling salesperson can all be good positions for your restless spirit.

___ Are you excited by dealing with other people?

___ Are you attracted to foreign cultures?

___ Do you speak a foreign language well?

___ Would you enjoy travel as a part of your job?

___ Does the international political situation attract you?

You are an International Sagittarius. Perhaps of greatest interest to Sagittarians are those careers involving travel and foreign cultures. Many positions in these fields are appropriate, including ones that call for facility in languages and the ability to understand other cultures. You'd enjoy work with the foreign service or for international agencies. Consider becoming an ambassador, foreign emissary, diplomat, consular service worker, importer-exporter, foreign trader, foreign legion member, travel correspondent, linguistic anthropologist, translator of ancient manuscripts and languages, interpreter, simultaneous translator, or bilingual secretary.

___ Do you have high ideals about certain issues that affect us all?

___ Would you like to try to make a difference with your job?

___ Do you enjoy sharing your views with others?

___ Do you believe in the democratic system?

___ Would you like a position that makes you feel you're doing something for your country?

You are a Political Sagittarius. You'd love becoming involved with the local, city, or federal government in an administrative position, or consider becoming a politician, assembly person, political ethicist, senator, representative, alderman, judge, lawyer, paralegal, law court attaché, law enforcement officer, court clerk, court reporter, legal investigator, military officer, activist, or lobbyist.

___ Are you committed to God, the law, or another belief system?

___ Do you want to help others?

___ Are you fluent and confident in expressing your views to inspire and help others?

___ Do you believe in higher education as a positive force?

___ Would you like to stimulate others with the power of your thoughts?

You are an Educational Sagittarius. Your abilities can be utilized to lead, teach, and inspire others. Think about becoming a minister, clergyman, priest, rabbi, evangelist, ecclesiastical dignitary, doctor of divinity, philosopher, jurisprudence writer, Sunday-school teacher, sexton, monk, nun, or other church-related position. You might like the position of professor or teacher, particularly on the subjects of law or ethics. If you have an interest in critical writing or thinking, you should try being a lecturer, inspirational speaker, political correspondent, cultural anthropologist, human rights activist, university or religious institution administrator, think-tank member, librarian, or book-store manager.

___ Do you enjoy books, writing, or the publishing field?

___ Would you like to "spread the word" to others on a large scale?

___ Are you an independent thinker and worker?

___ Do you enjoy doing things in a big way?

___ Are you capable of visualizing and creating original concepts?

You are a Large Scale Sagittarius and would enjoy work as a big business executive or entrepreneur. Your expansive nature turns any project into an adventure, but you'd especially like to work as a publisher, book manufacturer, novelist, or writer specializing in foreign cultures, countries, and people. You might also consider becoming a dramatist, advertising or promotion executive, fundraiser, philanthropist, wholesale grocer, clothier, or dealer in essential commodities. Your big ideas can help you succeed in any large-scale endeavor in the business world, or as an accountant, actuary, or stockbroker. Most Sagittarians aspire to executive positions and are able to grasp the big picture in order to make sound business decisions.

____ Do you like to work with groups?

____ Would you like to make your love of animals a career?

____ Would you enjoy an exciting position dealing with the physical world?

____ Are you stimulated by the power of the natural world?

____ Do you feel society should return to a simpler time?

You are a Natural Sagittarian. The ultimate extension of Sagittarian tendencies is a career involving the out-of-doors. It is not Mother Earth or nature, per se, that attracts you, but the wide perspective and unlimited possibilities that the wilderness presents. It's likely that a lot of immigrants founding the New World were Sagittarians who loved adventure, exploration, challenging the elements, and breathing untouched air.

You are natural sportsmen and can find work in such team sports as baseball, football, hockey, soccer, polo, archery, and skeet shooting. You could become a sportswriter or broadcaster, sports manager, umpire, referee, recruiter, hiking guide, white-water rapids guide, or aerialist. Sporting-goods manufacturer or dealer can also be appropriate.

Because you love animals (typically horses and large dogs are your favorites), careers involving cattle or sheep herding, animal breeding, racing, owning, or caretaking can bring you great satisfaction. Other choices will appeal to your fundamental interest in the natural world, such as astronomer, conservation scientist, metallurgist, meteorologist, sociologist, civil engineer, veterinarian, game warden, animal rights activist, zookeeper, or zoologist. You would also enjoy managing or working in an animal hospital or pet store or grooming parlor. You could be a stable or dude ranch manager, trainer, jockey, hunter, safari guide, boating guide, forest ranger, mountain climber, rodeo performer, or circus performer. You may enjoy work with trees and plants as a forester, landscape architect, environmentalist, or crop duster.

___ Do you resent the confines of working for others?

___ Would you find excitement in working independently?

___ Do you have big ideas and visions that you want to try out?

___ Would you prefer coming and going as you please?

___ Are you stimulated by the challenge of the unexpected?

You are an Entrepreneurial Sagittarius. You will probably only be satisfied if you can own and operate your own business. Many Sagittarians also succeed in freelance work. Look over our other quizzes to help you come up with a unique business that only you can handle.

Happy Hunting: How to Get That Job

An education often pays off in a big way for Sagittarians, so your college degree or advanced training should be used as a stepping-stone to your career goals. Most employers feel that a degree guarantees a certain amount of intelligence, competence, and independence. In your case, they'll be correct.

If you have no formal education beyond high school, let your life experience show your strengths. The summer you spent painting sets at the local theater company is genuine work experience, whether you were paid or not. And your trip to Mexico with your family taught you a lot about dealing with a different culture. You really know much more than you think you do when you start to add up your experiences in this way.

If you have attended college or taken a specialized training course of any kind, these institutions will generally offer career-guidance centers as well as placement services. Utilize their resources as fully as you can. Your school has the inside track on the jobs in your field, and it may provide interviews with prospective employers who visit the campus. Most will even let you return for their services in the years following graduation.

Advertising is also a great way for Sagittarians to look for a position, and the want ads are a good place to start. You can also place situation-wanted ads in most newspapers and reach hundreds of prospective employers. Sell yourself! Mention your education, experience, or other cogent information, especially what type of position you're looking for, as well as those personal characteristics that will make you a good employee. If you're interested in a specific field that has a publication dedicated to your special interest, look or advertise there. While many readers will not be employers, those who will might offer ideal opportunities for you.

Finally, tell everyone you know that you're looking for a job. Word of mouth goes a long way with Sagittarians! The more people you reach in this manner, the more opportunities you'll find open to you.

Once you've landed a job interview, use your amiability and easy manner. Interviewers like people who seem confident, collected, and relaxed, and you're naturally so. But don't overdo—don't gush or monopolize the conversation. It's just an interview, not an opportunity to tell your life story or share your deepest religious beliefs!

You can be too frank, so try not to "tell all" when asked about previous positions. "My employer could not help me reach my goals" is far superior to "My manager never really knew how to use my skills, and we'd have so many arguments that I finally just had to quit." No one needs to know *all* the excruciating details of your every past job experience. Sum them up in an overview, and you'll be safe.

If you're up for a position that you've had no experience with but feel you can handle competently, just say so and don't be afraid to sell yourself. Your winning personality can again help you here, but try not to exaggerate. If your only job experience is opening envelopes for the Publisher's Clearing House sweepstakes one summer, don't try to convince personnel that this qualifies you to run a major marketing project for a successful magazine. Unless, of course, your specific examples can back you up, such as "I'm completely familiar with the organization needed to set up such a project," and "I had a lot of better ideas on how to run the place, such as . . ."

You will impress people with your intelligence, spirit, and integrity. If the job requires these, you're perfectly justified to mention your academic awards. Even your personal ethics can be discussed if the position requires someone absolutely trustworthy to handle cash or valuables. But again, don't overdo! No matter your candor, saying "I'm completely trustworthy" too much may cause doubts in anyone. Be yourself, tell the truth (an abridged version), and have a good time during the interview.

Getting Ahead: How to Do Your Best on the Job

All Sagittarians are able to see the larger picture, or see the forest despite the trees. Because of this, you are able to reduce situations to their basic elements and handle them as such. You have the ability to eliminate unnecessary detail and cut through needless red tape to get to the heart of any matter. Executive ability and good judgment naturally follow, as well as the capacity for large enterprise.

You are able to see the broader perspective but can use help with the details. If you're able to, make sure you have a good assistant or secretary! This can be invaluable to you in helping with routine tasks and involved follow-up work. If you're on your own, build up these skills. You are not ideally suited to them, it's true, but if you prove yourself now, later you'll be able to advance to a position which corresponds more to your talents.

Many entry-level jobs involve routine work. If you believe in your heart that you cannot succeed at this, set about finding a position that utilizes your positive skills. Your educational background or school connections may help you bypass lower-level positions and jump directly to something less detail-oriented.

Sagittarians are well-known for utilizing their inspiration to good advantage. You have a strong intuition, and you often make your best decisions in action, not needing or wanting a lot of lengthy thought. Learn how to use and trust your hunches and pay attention to the types of decisions you are able to make work positively for you. In this way you'll develop more conscious control of a typically unconscious process.

You Sagittarians are idealistic and really do believe in truth, justice, and the American way, not to mention the goodness of God and all His peoples. Because of these traits, prejudice is never a part of your nature. You are adaptable to the needs of others and have the knack for making the best of any situation you happen to find yourself in. You laugh easily, enjoy life in general, and like having fun.

You will find it easy to develop casual relationships with most people about you. This gives you enjoyment and camaraderie, while at the same time insuring that you have human resources around you when you need help in a hurry. You Sagittarians can learn much about the job situation, other companies, or corporate organizations, just by talking to people. Your genial manner guarantees that others will repay your kindness. When on the job, knowing the right people and facts can help to get things done quicker, easier, and more pleasantly. If you have the opportunity to see someone in person rather than use the phone or fax, do so by all means. In this way you can get to know your associates even better.

But don't talk too much! Be aware that work is not a social situation, and while you may be happily chatting away, your co-worker has a deadline. Your frankness and candor are some of your best attributes, but when you say "You're getting fat" or "Your dark roots are showing," remember that others may be sensitive to their outward appearances and shortcomings. Try to become aware of which co-workers really share your sense of humor or can take your uninhibited comments in the constructive way in which they were intended.

You are generous to a fault and will offer any assistance to help others. Again, remember that you are at work and have your own work to do. Before you make promises, think about what you really can accomplish. If you *are* willing to do something for a co-worker, write it down. In this way your quick-moving mind won't forget! Keep a pen and pad on your person at all times. You can jot down facts and figures, tasks the boss wants you to do, and any added obligations. A good habit to get into will be reviewing your notes several times a day. Writing is a strength, and if you can put together a memo, you'll be more inclined to take the time to include everything you need to say. Don't send anything out immediately, but review your work quickly several hours later to be sure you've said what you had in mind and said it with brevity and finesse.

Your need for movement and adventure can lead you to change jobs more frequently than most. This tendency, though, is not the most productive for advancement in your career. Most employers like to hire and train people that they feel will make a lasting contribution to their company. If your resume shows several positions in the last three years, your prospective boss will rightly wonder how long you will stay with the firm. It's much better for your long-range future to try to change positions within one organization when at all possible. Or seek a position that, of its very nature, will provide you with change and variety.

Your career advancement depends on you alone. You will do as well as you imagine you can, and for most Sagittarians the sky's the limit. You can always benefit from having a lot of irons in the fire; there'll be a greater chance that one of many opportunities will work out for you.

If you currently have a job that doesn't give you much freedom, you can easily find ways to change things. Volunteering for outside tasks or special projects is one sure way to get out of your rut. You always have good ideas, and your boss may like your suggestions well enough to have the confidence in you to allow you to run with the ball. Remember that the telephone can be your best friend, taking you across country with just the touch of a few buttons. You can get a lot accomplished by telephone networking and will probably develop some good friendships in the process. At the same time, you'll also enjoy the stimulation of many people and places without leaving your desk.

Eventually, however, you may realize that you want to be more self-governed. Positions such as consultant or freelancer can provide you with new and stimulating jobs on a regular basis, and it's commonly known that most can last from as little as three months to a year. Temporary agencies can also be good employers, sending you out to work when and where you choose. How long you stay is always an option, and you may find an ideal position. Many permanent employees were first introduced to their employers through temporary services.

A Sagittarian computer graphics artist we know even-

STAR SUCCESS

tually found that she preferred freelance work. She likes the independence and variety that this type of work offers. This Sagittarian is successful because she enjoys keeping in touch with her many contacts and isn't afraid of calling or writing if she hasn't heard from them in a while.

When you decide to leave a job, you'll probably make a firm decision and will want to walk away as quickly as possible. Try to give at least two weeks' notice. This short period may be the most difficult for you to get through after you've made a decision, but if you want to leave on good terms it's really essential for you to tie up loose ends and let the company have adequate time to replace you.

It's also a good idea to get a letter of reference from one of your superiors or from personnel to submit along with your resume or applications for a new position. You'll be off soon enough on a new career adventure! Consider yourself fortunate that you have all that Sagittarian luck, inspiration, and boundless energy. Something's sure to turn up!

Do

- Cultivate fixidity of purpose and keep your vision focused on one goal until it's reached.
- Work with people.
- Use and trust your intuition and insight.
- Find a position that offers freedom.
- Control your restlessness and wanderlust.
- Exercise tact and diplomacy at all times and keep your promises.

Don't

- Take a job you can't believe in.
- Be distracted by co-workers or scatter your time and energy.

- Get hung up on red tape and detail.
- Be undependable, careless, or inaccurate in your work.
- Be impatient and impulsive.
- Be in too great a rush to move on to greener pastures.

CAPRICORN

December 21 to January 21

"Set a goal and energize yourself to achieve it."
—John Opel, *The Computer Establishment*

Mountain Climber

The sign Capricorn is depicted by the goat, actually a "horned goat" if we translate the original Latin word. Goats are considered skinny animals, but they are known to be tough—their hide is sometimes used for leather. This small animal is cut out for survival, and it's no coincidence that Capricorns are, too. They understand only too well the rigors of the world and are careful that they be prepared for the catastrophe that they believe can happen at any moment.

The myth about goats eating cans and glass isn't true, but it's quite evocative of what Capricorns are really like. The goat does a good job of finding food for himself, whether or not it's easily available. He can subsist on next to nothing. Similarly, Capricorn people can get by with very little cash. They don't need a lot and can thus survive in tough times. They just pull in their belts, streamline their lifestyle, and watch all of their fat competition jump out the window.

Many wild goats are found in the mountains, as they can climb higher than any other animal. Their surefootedness is legendary. In the same manner, Capricorn people will work their way to the top—careful only to step on the sure and solid rock and instinctively knowing when a situation is precarious. Slowly but surely, the Capricorn builds up a security system through cautiousness, frugality, and hard work.

An Earth sign, some Capricorns can get a little *too* involved in the material world, craving only possessions and status symbols. They have fine taste and a discerning eye. Did you realize that both angora and cashmere wool can come from goats? This sign is a lot more than just business.

The goat is also known to be intelligent and playful and can even make a good pet. Capricorn people have organized minds, and many have a somewhat dry or cynical wit and humor. While they know that life is a serious business, they can laugh at it, too.

Notice that little beard on that goat? Capricorn people usually live very long, productive lives, often well into old age. And they just don't get older, they get better!

Get to Work! What to Look for in a Career

So you're a Capricorn? You'll probably work harder, play less, and move ahead more steadily than any other sign of the zodiac. Capricorn is the careerist extraordinaire: In the business world your down-to-earth instincts will lead you in the right direction for success. However, you do need a few necessities in order to feel comfortable and secure in the work-a-day world.

You should seek a position in a businesslike environment, with a consistent schedule and clearly assigned duties. You should not be constantly thrown by unexpected circumstances. You are a steady, reliable worker in set circumstances, and you feel most secure in a position that you can stay with for a long period of time.

You also like your associates to be organized, reliable, and businesslike. You will function most effectively when you feel you can rely on co-workers for support when you need them. Traditional businesses like accounting, manufacturing, and banking attract many Capricorns because of their conservative and predictable nature and their appeal to like-minded individuals.

You need to be able to move ahead, and whether you choose to work for a small business or large corporation, you must have the opportunity to advance. A dead-end situation is not for you, and you will quickly be frustrated by a boss who doesn't recognize and reward your efforts. You'll be happiest when you can reach a position of respect and prominence.

If you know you cannot move ahead in a particular situation, you should at least be learning new skills. You will be thus moving ahead intellectually and emotionally in terms of self-esteem and experience.

Money is another concern to Capricorns. While you can make a little go a long way and will compromise on salary in order to get a better position in the long run, you need to be earning a steady income. As you are such a responsible and reliable worker, you'll also expect increased pay commensurate with your efforts. While you can wait a long time for what you're due, you must get regular pay raises in order to feel satisfied.

Most Capricorns are somewhat reserved, and you'd probably enjoy having your own private area in which to work. An office is ideal, a cubicle or corner almost as good, and a desk in a quiet area will also do. You simply need privacy and quiet in order to collect your thoughts and do your best.

In planning for a career, just think ahead (most of you

will be doing this already!) and make sure your education is geared toward a goal you have in mind. A trade school satisfies this need well. If you plan on attending college, decide what you'll be studying as early as possible and gear your studies toward what you intend to be doing later. If you haven't yet "found yourself," at least try to narrow down your choices to a specific field or two. In this way all your efforts will be directed to some practical result.

Your local library probably has a few job-outlook books available in the reference section. Study these as part of deciding on a career choice. They'll provide information about future growth in a field you may be considering. Make sure that your ideal job will still be around when you're ready for it!

What's Your Line? Your Vocational Choices

Capricorn rules business, and thus you probably have organizational, managerial, and administrative talents that can be applied in many different industries. You like more conservative or traditional positions, preferring the tried-and-true professions to wild, innovative, or unpredictable ones.

The quintessential Capricorn, John R. Opel spent his entire career at IBM. After earning an MBA, he joined the corporation as a sales representative. In true Capricornian form, he worked his way through the ranks over the next decades: executive assistant to the president, corporate vice president, vice president of corporate finance and planning, and senior vice president.

Elected president of IBM in 1974, Opel contributed much to the company's period of phenomenal growth as IBM developed a line of compatible computers and PCs that would become the industry's standard by 1981. Opel went on to become chief executive officer and chairman of the board. His typically Capricornian ideas centered around creating the lowest-cost products on the market. True to his sign, John Opel was known to work long, hard hours, encouraged promotion from within, and stuck to wearing business suits when the company abandoned its strict dress code. After retirement, he continued to serve as chairman of IBM's executive committee.

Dolly Parton may not seem like a hard-core business person, but as a Capricorn she certainly is. Her story is typical of this ambitious sign: She is a self-made woman. Born in a wooden shack in Tennessee as the fourth child in a family of twelve, she helped raise her younger siblings. Dolly left for Nashville right after her high-school graduation.

Dolly Parton has succeeded because of her Capricornian hard work and business acumen. As head of Dolly Parton Enterprises, her career proceeded slowly but surely. She sang for many years at the Grand Ole Opry, wrote and recorded her own songs, and went on to become a featured performer on television. Concerts and solo albums followed, as well as roles in films, such as *9 to 5*, *The Best Little Whorehouse in Texas*, and *Steel Magnolias*.

Like most Capricorns, Dolly is down-to-earth and makes all business and investment decisions on her own. She has built up her empire by cofounding a publishing company and running her own theme park.

Capricorns can utilize managerial talents in virtually any field. Brandon Tartikoff is just one example. Head of comedy programming at NBC, he worked with Grant Tinker (yet another Capricorn!), and the two were committed to a Capricornian idea—giving a new TV series enough time and exposure to catch on. Such series as "Cheers" and "St. Elsewhere" began with low ratings but succeeded over time. The two also introduced one of the most popular series of the 1980s: "The Cosby Show."

Tartikoff, like most Capricorns, is noted for his serious

outlook and motivation to move ahead. He went on to become chairman of NBC Entertainment and later went to Paramount Pictures.

Put a checkmark next to each question that you'd answer with a "yes." If there are several checks for a few career groups, review these first and think about the career suggestions we've listed. If you believe that one of these areas is right for you, investigate your selections further or those closely related to them. Also, take a look at the rest of our suggestions for other possibilities.

___ Do you handle money well?

___ Can you help others organize their affairs?

___ Are you good with detail work?

___ Would you like a steady position offering advancement?

___ Can you adapt your knowledge and skills to a fluctuating market and client demands?

You are a Financial Capricorn. There are many positions in business and industry where you could utilize your money skills to help others, as well as provide yourself with a nice regular paycheck. Such positions as securities broker, bank officer, credit manager, bookkeeper, actuary, statistician, accountant, or accounting clerk would all be good choices for you. For those who'd like a more high-powered position, becoming a financial planner or analyst, management consultant, market analyst, economist, underwriter, financier, corporate or business attorney, business planner or teacher, goods manager, or real-estate dealer might be right for you.

___ Would you like to be in control?

___ Do you have good organizational and administrative skills?

___ Would you like a position in the business world?

___ Can you supervise others?

___ Do you want to have a job that promises advancement?

You are a Managerial Capricorn. You can utilize your administrative, managerial, and organizational skills to run or manage a small or large enterprise. Managers, directors, executives, administrators, and their assistants are often Capricorns, especially in manufacturing, distribution, and corporate offices. Efficiency experts, management consultants, inventory-control managers, office and business inspectors, production coordinators, and theatrical producers are also part of this category, as are career planners and counselors and apartment or condo managers.

___ Would you like to see the tangible results of your work?

___ Do you enjoy work with your hands?

___ Would you like your work to stick with basics?

___ Can you deal with work that may be seasonal or fluctuating?

___ Would you like to practice a skill or trade that will be of importance to others in their daily lives?

You are a Craftsman Capricorn. You'd like to work with raw materials, creating things of beauty or of lasting use to others. The building and construction trades might be perfect for you, specifically using, constructing, or installing brick, cement, stone, slate, sand, gravel, tile, coal, or ice. Other possibilities include working in demolition or with leather goods. Work as a terrazzo layer, tile setter, potter, mason, plasterer, bricklayer, drywell worker, insulation installer, roofer, carpenter, grain dealer, mountain-climbing guide, tanner, leather-goods manufacturer, precision assembler, upholsterer, bookbinder, printer, engraver, or cargo handler could also give you satisfaction and a sense of doing an important job.

___ Do you have an eye for detail work?

___ Do you have good organizational and administrative skills?

___ Are you interested in government?

___ Would you like a position offering prestige and status?

___ Can you function as a manager in a large-scale operation?

You are a Government Capricorn. Your ability to function within large structures and legal systems can help you rise ahead in the political arena. All government positions, from the local to the federal level, including election worker, assemblyperson, mayor of a small or large city, or political appointee, should be considered. Some examples of the many jobs in this category are diplomatic appointee, regulatory inspector, public safety and construction inspector, census taker, pollster, labor organizer, union official, municipal or civic employee, military strategist, and corrections official. Other related positions include political scientist, writer, historian, or geographer.

___ Do you have an organized mind?

___ Are you interested in the natural world?

___ Would you like to work alone, at least part of the time?

___ Does the Earth or its history interest you?

___ Do you have an interest in the past or enjoy planning for the future?

You are a Natural Science Capricorn. You would enjoy earth sciences or those dealing with accomplishing practical tasks. You may enjoy a career as a geologist, archaeologist, mining inspector or engineer, classicist, anthropologist, archivist, antiques dealer, or museum curator. Modern jobs for you that are future-oriented include architect, draftsman, urban planner, landscape architect, and land surveyor. Other Earth-oriented positions that you might enjoy are astronomer, meteorologist, environmentalist, chemist, soil conservationist, navigator, and agricultural or biological scientist, engineer, or technician.

If you are service-oriented and have an interest in medicine, you may work as a chiropractor, orthopedist, bone specialist, dentist, dental assistant, or lab technician. You could also consider teaching these subjects.

___ Are you more organized than others?

___ Do you want to create a career through your own initiative and hard work?

___ Would you feel secure enough to strike out on your own?

___ Are you hard-working, efficient, and realistic?

___ Do you have practical goals and a program for success?

You are an Entrepreneurial Capricorn. Your drive, dedication, and sense of responsibility can make you a successful business owner. Look over our quizzes for an area of specialization, or come up with your own ideas to create a solid, practical business that fills a real need. If you plan well, you'll have a successful and rewarding enterprise in time.

Happy Hunting! How to Get That Job

The traditional path is always best for you, as it represents the tried and true. Standard, accepted practices that lead to jobs are the ones in which you'll place your confidence. Whether you use a school placement service, employment agency, or newspaper advertisements is up to you. If you are highly trained, professional journals are also there for you, with help-wanted sections in your field.

What works for you Capricorns is making a greater effort than anyone else. Your job search could take up to six months, so be prepared. Still, you should use as much time as you can on a regular basis to look for work. You are naturally able to concentrate your efforts for a desired result, and job-hunting is certainly no exception. Have a plan and execute it in an organized, efficient manner.

Adopt a job-hunting routine. This may include picking up a city paper on Sunday, a local one during the week, and visiting an employment agency on a certain day. Plan to spend at least some time every day or a set number of hours a week looking for work. You can do business research at a library or personnel office, write follow-up letters, or place phone calls.

Don't let any stone go unturned—pursue as many opportunities as possible. If you didn't get a particular job with a certain company, keep in touch regarding any future possibilities. It's quite possible that a recently hired employee may not work out. If you've shown enough interest and enthusiasm, you could be the first alternate candidate they contact.

Remember to be more assertive than you feel is necessary. Capricorns have a tendency to hold back for fear of being too aggressive. The more forceful Capricorn will learn more and find more opportunities. If you want to call and follow up on a job opening but feel insecure, *do it anyway.* You'll find it's not that big a deal, and you'll learn more about how to go about landing a position. What's the worst that could happen? Someone can either hang up or be rude, and you can handle both. Afraid you'll jeopardize an opportunity? Then don't identify yourself!

Capricorns are always able to work their way up the corporate ladder. If you're not finding your dream job, take a lesser one that offers promotability. A part-time position can also lead to a career opportunity once people get to know you. You may not give off flashiness or optimism, but once an employer realizes what a capable and dedicated worker you are, you'll be kept on board. Increased responsibility will naturally follow.

You Capricorns are generally punctual, well dressed, and well-prepared. These are some of the required basics for interviewing prospective employees. So you've already got a lot going for you. Your resume will be clear and to the point about previous experience. But personality wins the job.

Cultivate your social graces for these occasions. Don't allow yourself to "clam up" because you're nervous. It can't hurt to have a few pleasantries prepared for awkward moments. Or think about what you could've said at the last interview and use it for the next one. You can be too humble and quiet at times, so concentrate on being up-beat, enthusiastic, and charming. Many people are too busy to look beyond a personality for experience and depth. Don't lose a job that should've been yours just because you didn't smile.

Finally, ask for more money than you think you deserve because Capricorns often underestimate their worth. Most employers will also try to talk you down a bit, so this technique works on both counts. Don't feel that you'll blow the deal—an employer who's interested will negotiate. You'll also soon be frustrated if the pay isn't what you think you're really worth.

Getting Ahead: How to Do Your Best on the Job

You have a lot of intelligence, and although you do not usually learn quickly, whatever you do learn you do thoroughly and well. You have the ability to concentrate and can get much accomplished despite distractions or difficulties. You pay attention to all details while remaining aware of the larger picture.

In making any decision, you always take your time. You are especially serious in any business situation, realizing how the results of your actions will affect the progress of your project. You are able to project your concerns into the future and can thus anticipate problems, solutions, and the safest way to proceed. Your judgment is cautious but sound.

You feel a sense of accomplishment and satisfaction in doing something to the best of your ability. You are self-guided, self-disciplined, and a diligent worker. You will not require supervision, as you aren't someone who likes to goof off or socialize while on the job. Employers will get more for their money from you than most other signs of the zodiac. A bit insecure, you are afraid that at any moment you could be caught not doing your best!

You can be counted on to accomplish work given to you. You are conscientious about your own work, and co-workers know they can rely on you at all times. Capricorn rules time, and you are someone who is aware that getting things done properly can take time. You are patient and methodical and have a great deal of endurance. While someone else may be bored with a task, you will keep at it until you finish. Even tasks you may dislike are accomplished with the same businesslike attitude. Your career advancement also benefits from this outlook.

Capricorns are highly organized. You easily come up with systems and structures that can make doing the job easier and more efficient. You know where things are because you have the ability to categorize and put things into order. "A place for everything and everything in its place" is a good motto for all Capricorns on the job. A Capricorn office manager we know was asked to open the new branch of her company. This she did with relish, making certain all files and procedures would be sound, and the work spaces were comfortable and functional.

One of the things that you can organize best is money. Your good sense coupled with a cautious outlook make you someone who is well suited to handling finances. When in charge of funds, you will be frugal and resourceful. You can save an employer lots of money! You will also make a little go a long way and will plan purchases well in advance. These aptitudes are necessary for most executive positions, which are the ones you usually aim for.

You are able to work within existing business structures, and obstacles do not intimidate or frighten you. You take set-backs and frustrations in stride. You'll probably be able to outwait many troublesome people or situations. You realize that paperwork and even red tape have their place, and you are able to work with them in order to get your job done.

Capricorns make slow, steady progress. You won't be tempted to take shortcuts that can backfire, but will build up a solid reputation over time. You set high goals, anticipate what you'll need to do, and set out realistically to reach the highest peak. Your ability to act on short- and long-term objectives will insure your success. You are constantly aiming for the future but will reevaluate your plans according to opportunity. This practical adaptation to circumstances helps you utilize all opportunities that are presented to you, while keeping an eye on your ultimate goal.

You are ambitious but in a quiet, unostentatious way. You recognize opportunities when they present themselves and are able to seize them for all they are worth. Regardless of your education, you will learn more from trial and error than anything else.

Although unassuming, you are a natural leader. You have the ability to organize group activity, supervise work, and evaluate performance. Because you know how to take charge, you can attain positions of authority and respect.

All of you Capricorns can benefit from relaxing and enjoying your work more. Take lunches and breaks with co-workers, and if you must discuss work on these occasions, at least bring your good sense of humor. Remember that the word "caprice" comes from the same root as "Capricorn"! When you make the effort (and you should make the effort!), you can be companionable and supportive toward all of your co-workers. The only ones you won't tolerate are those people who don't try their best or who won't take responsibility for their own actions.

Plan breaks ahead of time and take them. No matter how much you enjoy your work, you will be more efficient when relaxed. Play some music or stroll around outside. If you can't see yourself doing something unproductive, find a hobby that is enjoyable for you but that benefits your work as well. An executive may take a Roman history course, learning how business and industry were managed ages ago. Or a construction worker or architect could visit various urban areas across the country and enjoy learning more about buildings in other places.

You will do your best when not overwhelmed with work. If you have much to accomplish, organize the work by task, break it up into small pieces, and budget and schedule your time. Each day you will have totally finished a portion of your work and will have a sense of accomplishment.

But Capricorns can take on too much. Learn when to say no to overtime, extra work, and favors for the boss. A Capricorn administrator was so reliable and efficient that his boss kept giving him more responsibility. The Capricorn assumed many of the boss's problems and eventually felt overwhelmed. At raise time he was not offered much of an increase. Finding a new position took months of patience, but the Capricorn eventually found a less stressful job that paid quite a bit more.

Anxiety is another problem for Capricorns because you may find yourself worrying too much today about tomorrow's challenges. It's not only debilitating, it's unproductive! Careful planning can eliminate your need for worry, but using mental discipline is the only way to alleviate it altogether. Concentrate fully on the work at hand or distract yourself in any way you know how. Chronic anxiety is more a habit than anything else, and you can break that habit once you become aware of it.

You may have a tendency to be too cautious and pessimistic about making decisions or changes. As a rule, you don't like change, but in business it's often necessary and beneficial. You will go only as far as your imagination takes you; if you dwell on the negative you'll get nowhere. Try to see the good instead of instinctively seeing the bad. Look on the bright side of changes that may be forced on you.

Attitude is everything. You will do much better if you welcome each day in an up-beat manner. See each work day as another opportunity to prove yourself rather than putting your nose to the grindstone. Talk to people more. Your tendency to work alone to the exclusion of all else can eventually lead to self-obsession and depression. Check these negative traits by sharing yourself and your feelings with others on the job and looking on the bright side of things.

Remember that everyone can help you get ahead.

Some Capricorns may flatter the boss while stepping on associates. Don't you be one of those. You will create discontent if you simply order others about. All of your co-workers will be more willing to help someone likable and pleasant. While many other signs may not be as sensitive as you, everyone has feelings and responds to care and encouragement.

Finally, try to be more tolerant of others' opinions, instincts, and work habits. In the co-worker section of this book, you'll see that most people are not workaholics like you. Understanding that as a given can help you get along better with others. You should also try considering all advice as constructive rather than critical. You can utilize *all* that people offer if you try.

Once you have found your niche, you will remain content to stay with one employer for many, many years. But when you've reached the top position, you may eventually yearn for something more; at this point many Capricorns become involved with starting their own businesses or begin community or political work.

Father Time is a strong Capricorn image, and you will always learn more as he progresses. Many Capricorns don't come into their own until after the age of thirty or middle age. Time is truly on your side. No matter how old you are right now, you can look ahead to a rewarding career. Many Capricorns also look much younger than their years, so this will help you youthful senior citizens to be hired. Think about Capricorns Benjamin Franklin, Carl Sandburg, Marlene Dietrich, and George Burns—all continued their active working lives well into old age.

When that big break comes, don't let uncertainty, insecurity, or disbelief cause you to worry. You'll soon see that you were just perfect for the job all along. Even Capricorns get lucky breaks—make them work for you instead of distrusting your luck. And don't let yourself be conned into thinking that no job is enjoyable. You *can* find something you really like if you make opportunities for yourself.

STAR SUCCESS

If you need to move on to a new job, you will do it with care and patience. Don't settle for second best. If you keep at it, you *will* find that ideal job. You can turn your dreams into reality through ambition, persistence, and hard work.

Do

- Use persistence and determination.
- Make use of your great energy and ability to work hard.
- Be cautious and patient.
- Keep an eye on a definite goal.
- Cultivate sociability, buoyancy, and effective self-expression.

Don't

- Let pessimism and insecurity keep you from succeeding.
- Cling to passé methods.
- Dwell on the negative.
- Ignore good advice.
- Be too conservative.

AQUARIUS
January 20 to February 19

*"The process was the goal and
I've taken great joy in the process."*
—Oprah Winfrey, *Ms. Magazine*

Footloose

Aquarius is represented by the water-bearer. We really don't have too many water-bearers around in our part of the world, but they probably still exist in the Middle East. Consider Gunga Din, as portrayed in the Kipling poem and the movie. Din carries around a big bag of water and supplies anyone who asks. He's all over the place! Din also must adjust, as he is thrown in with the crowd and never discriminates about who gets the goods. He will happily pour you the stuff of life into a cup, a glass, or directly in the mouth!

Aquarians, though, sprinkle the waters of knowledge on all of humanity. This is a logical air sign whose members like to examine all available information and come to independent conclusions. Symbolic of the necessary interchange of ideas, water is needed by *all* in order to survive. Idealistic at heart, the Aquarian sees all people as brothers, sensing that we are all cut from a piece of the same cloth and deserve the same consideration.

Gunga Din goes his own way, at his own pace and makes his own judgments. Similarly, all Aquarians like to interact but enjoy the freedom of nonrestrictive positions. The footloose nature of the sign prompts many to choose careers where they can have variety and intellectual latitude.

As Aquarians hate limitations of any kind, they excel in casting off old thoughts, ideas, and conventions. They feel change has a value in and of itself. They are drawn to nontraditional concepts and have eclectic tastes. They are curious to explore almost any area of thought, especially if it's unusual. Yes, Aquarians can be rebels, but only because they like to move into the future and resent the restrictions of the past.

Aquarians will liberate others as well. They are tolerant of various beliefs and goals. Part of the Aquarian principle is to happily agree to disagree. Diversity just makes life more interesting to the water-bearer. And like Gunga Din, he'll just keep pouring out that all-important H_2O (or information) to encourage others to get on with their lives, liberty, and pursuit of happiness!

Get to Work! What to Look for in a Career

All Aquarians have strong ideas and ideals, and you will need to satisfy these before anything else. You'll be happy in a job that is intellectually challenging or that you feel is valuable to humanity as a whole. Money, position, and power do not really interest you, as they remind you of the "good old boy" order of things.

Informal office situations are best for Aquarians who love mixing it up with other people. Lots of protocol or corporate mores will turn you off, as you hate to stand on ceremony. You resent rules and regulations as limiting to human potential (especially yours!). Too structured an environment (with specific offices or cubicles for each worker) will also be counterproductive, as you look for more unconventional surroundings and easier interaction with your co-workers.

Variety and stimulation are necessary for Aquarians, and you should seek these when looking for a position. Each of your days should be somewhat unique. While you can take some mundane tasks for short periods of time, these must be varied, with different things, people, and places. Dealing with others in such diverse positions as sales, customer service, or management can often provide Aquarians with just such an outlet—as handling people can be the most unpredictable task of all! A young Aquarius man doing market-research surveys is a successful telecommunicator because he finds it stimulating to talk to different people and learn about their diverse opinions, attitudes, and lifestyles.

Aquarians like people, and while you always need to have independence on the job, you also like to work as part of a team. Working as part of a group effort or just having others around you will bring out the positive Aquarian tendencies.

An Aquarian editor we know enjoys her position because it presents her with a variety of tasks, most of which involve working with people and ideas. She evaluates proposals, answers queries, and corresponds with writers. Working with the large corporation's contracts, publicity, and advertising departments provides her with diversity as projects progress. Perhaps one of her most enjoyable tasks is editing manuscripts, where she uses her objective judgment independently to evaluate the work.

You do need to take charge of your own duties and to proceed with your work at your own pace and in your own way. The strong Aquarian independent streak must be satisfied, or you will resist authority or control.

Part-time or freelance positions can provide diversity

and variety. Over the long haul, however, unless you have advanced to consultant status, you would prefer long-term or permanent commitments to occasional work or one-shot deals.

What's Your Line? Your Vocational Choices

You Aquarians can fit into most any career situation that piques your curiosity. Independence is stressed and can lead to innovation. Many of you are attracted to work with groups or high-tech occupations.

Aquarius is very often drawn to electronics work. This field offers mental stimulation, variety, and is expanding. An electrical engineer received a master's degree in motion-control engineering so he could work in robotics, specializing in microprocessor-control electronics. He held permanent positions and freelanced, and he invented several electronic-motion controllers that were patented. He is now returning to school for an MBA so he can have even greater independence with his own company and opportunities elsewhere.

In whatever field you choose, you'll want to break new ground. This is true of filmmaker David Lynch, who began his career studying fine art at the American Film Institute in Los Angeles. He was the creator of the cult classic *Eraserhead,* which epitomized not only his unique Aquarian vision but the fixed sign's tenacity as well: The project took five years to complete.

Lynch went on to offer the public such unique films as *The Elephant Man, Dune, Blue Velvet,* and *Wild at Heart.* All of these are remarkable for the Aquarian quality of uniting such disparate elements as horror, black comedy, and the surreal with everyday life. In the television series "Twin Peaks," Lynch continued in his unusual Aquarian mode but was able to reach a mainstream audience with this mystery thriller-soap opera. His success is primarily the result of bringing to life his off-beat ideas.

Air Force pilot and Aquarian Chuck Yeager is another innovator, but one who put his talents to use toward achieving practical goals. He began his career as a mechanic for the Air Corps (many Aquarians are attracted to engines as well as air travel). Later he became a pilot and flew on over sixty missions in Europe in World War II.

After the war, Yeager became a flight instructor and later a test pilot, both Aquarian jobs. And he broke new ground in 1947, becoming the first man to survive flying past the speed of sound.

Retired from active duty in 1975, Yeager reached cult status as the hero of the film *The Right Stuff*. He has capped an extraordinary career with other Aquarian activities: as a lecturer to groups and performer in television commercials.

Aquarian Oprah Winfrey has used her likability, understanding of people, and intelligence to become a top talk-show host. Attracted, like many Aquarians, to the electronic media, she was a television and radio reporter while still young, and she became the first black woman to appear as an anchorwoman in Nashville while only nineteen.

Committed to work in her medium, Winfrey nevertheless went through several positions in her first years, as many Aquarians will do. She was a hit as a talk-show host in Baltimore in 1977 and has been successful ever since, co-starring in the popular film *The Color Purple* and hosting her nationally syndicated show. Through it all, her gregariousness and personable Aquarian manner, love of people, and tenacity have helped her achieve success.

Put a checkmark next to each question that you'd answer with a "yes." If there are several checks for a few career groups, review these first and think about the career suggestions we've listed. If you believe that one of these areas is right for you, investigate your selections further or those closely related to them. Also, take a look at the rest of our suggestions for other possibilities.

___ Do you have mechanical, scientific, or mathematical talents?

___ Do you want to find out more about the reality of our world?

___ Would you like to help other people learn or know more?

___ Does the latest technology excite you?

___ Could you implement goals and ideals in a practical way?

You are a Practical Science Aquarius. There are many space-age fields in which you could satisfy your ideals as well as serve humanity. Your scientific and mathematical bent can be applied in the areas of aviation, radio, television, radar, sonar, or atomic energy as a specialist, technician, or equipment operator.

Specific examples of these jobs include aircraft or diesel mechanic or engine specialist; work with radio and infrared telescopes, rockets, and space machines; laser/electro optics technician, electrician, or electronics manufacturer or supplier; equipment technician or repairer; lighting or telecommunications specialist; television or radio broadcast technician, manufacturer, or dealer; telephone or telephone line installer, repairman, or operator; computer operator, programmer, or service technician.

Specific positions in the medical field that may suit you include X-ray, laser, EKG or EEG technician, radiologist, CAT scanner or medical equipment specialist, nerve specialist, or operator of a medical referral service.

___ Do you have scientific and mathematical talents?

___ Does working with high-tech equipment stimulate you?

___ Can you come up with new ideas and solutions to problems?

___ Do you want to have independent control over your own work but function as part of a larger group or enterprise?

___ Would you welcome the opportunity to break new ground?

You are a Creative Science Aquarius. Your innovative ideas and progressive outlook can put you on the cutting edge of technology. You can succeed in the many design and engineering fields, including those relating to computers, aerospace, aeronautics, electronics, robotics, nuclear power, or metallurgy. The positions of inventor, mathematician, astronomer, physicist, meteorologist, astronaut, space pilot, test pilot, or laser or electro-optics researcher could all be good choices for you, as would being a computer programmer or systems analyst.

___ Are you seeking a stable, secure position?

___ Do you want to have independent control over your own work but as part of a larger group or enterprise?

___ Can you function well in an environment where some rules and regulations are necessary?

___ Does the exchange of ideas with others excite you?

___ Do you like being of service to others?

You are a Business Service Aquarius. You can succeed in many business-affiliated positions that offer variety, stimulation, and a steady paycheck. Some specific positions that would put your ability to deal effectively with others to good use are personnel administrator, project coordinator, group project manager, communications consultant, company training manager, group lecturer, and teacher. Your ability to understand others could help you succeed as an attorney, government official, advertiser, public relations spokesman, employment counselor, or sales representative.

____ Do you have high ideals?

____ Do you want to do something for the good of humanity?

____ Do you feel you have a unique view of life to share with others?

____ Can you function as part of a large team effort?

____ Would you gain satisfaction from working toward future goals?

You are a Social Reform Aquarius. You would be particularly suited to work with one of the many organizations around the world that help others or encourage progressive ideas. Many special interest groups dedicated to improving social consciousness in issues of race, religion, sex, or the environment could use your talents. You may be interested in social work, directly helping the underprivileged, or philanthropic or educational organizations raising money for the needy. You could succeed as a sociologist, human resource specialist, human relations aide, ecologist, counselor, psychiatrist, psychologist, neurologist, therapist, chiropractor, or nurse. Aquarians also make excellent teachers and child-care workers, as you will encourage independence in others and are tolerant yet firm.

___ Do you crave an unusual or unique position?

___ Are creative talents part of your makeup?

___ Do you want to do your work without much outside limitation?

___ Would you like to incorporate your high ideals into a career?

___ Do you need to use your heart as well as your head?

You are a Creative Aquarius, the most creative of the creative, as you need progressive thought to be part of your work. Use your excellent mental capabilities to succeed as a novelist, dramatist, or nonfiction or science fiction writer. Other creative jobs for Aquarians include composer, songwriter, musician (especially keyboard and electronic instruments), music teacher, performance artist, painter, sculptor, special effects artist, television or radio broadcaster, video producer, outré fashion designer, or aerial show performer.

As we approach the dawning of the Age of Aquarius, many Aquarians are attracted to the New Age field. Among the many opportunities here, you would enjoy work as an astrologer, gem specialist, color healer, herbalist, metaphysicist, clairvoyant, or hypnotist. You could also do well as a writer, lecturer, or counselor in any of these fields.

___ Do you resent the limitations and control of others?

___ Do you want to put your original ideas to the test?

___ Can you think up some unique concepts to help others?

___ Are you committed to your specific ideals to the exclusion of much else?

___ Could you work within city, state, and local business regulations?

You are an Entrepreneurial Aquarius and should own your own business. Look over the previous quizzes to find a field that's right for you. Whatever you choose, you're sure to use your progressive instincts to create something truly unique.

Happy Hunting! How to Get That Job

You Aquarians always want to do something that is a little bit off the beaten track. You should begin by assessing what individual contribution you can make to the working world. A good sourcebook for you would be *Off Beat Careers: The Directory of Unusual Work*, by Al Sacharov (10 Speed Press, 1988), which will introduce you to many unconventional professions. Aquarians always prefer the nontraditional or doing things that are special in some way. You may already have several ideas.

Most Aquarius people need to spend some time (years, perhaps) early on in the career just experimenting. Don't worry about settling down to a long-term, full-time position right away. While you may go through a few jobs quickly because of this tendency, the time spent will not be wasted. You'll learn more about yourself and others through this trial period, make contacts, and probably solidify your ultimate goal. Don't turn away from a career track while young because you feel it's a commitment to Corporate America. It doesn't have to be that way for anyone and especially for you. And do you know what? Many Aquarians do function exceptionally well in the business world once they've found their niche. Try it, you might just like it!

In looking for a position, it does help to first narrow down your choices. Aquarians have such diverse talents; you can be interested in and able to handle many different types of jobs. Don't allow yourself to become scattered by following up on a wide array of possibilities. Choose one, two, or at the most three for your search. A common fault is trying to pursue too many things at once or not committing fully to one occupation.

Follow through on your ideas. Something may stimulate you today but be forgotten tomorrow. Go the extra mile to investigate job possibilities with those already in the field. Most professions do have affiliated groups and organizations. Find out what and where these are and go to them for information. They will probably be able to provide you with facts and figures and even possible employers if you join; all can help you decide on a specific job or eventually find one.

You should also spread the word around. Ask all your friends and acquaintances about job opportunities and let everyone know you're looking. Aquarius people are likable and usually have lots of acquaintences. You are good at asking people for recommendations and may just know an important boss's niece without realizing it! Remember the adage that with three phone calls you could contact anyone in the world, and use it to your advantage.

Special interest groups or organizations to which you belong in your community can also be helpful in your job search, even if the group's purpose doesn't directly relate to your field or profession. Many are there to serve their members in whatever way possible, and they will provide more contacts for you to use. Easy introductions to important people are possible when you have a common interest. The larger the organization, the wider your network can become, and you might find a future employer in that friend of a friend of a friend within the group.

An Aquarian man we know let people know he was

dissatisfied with his work as a mechanic. A relative of a friend of his knew someone at AT&T, and he soon found a job there as a phone electrician, which he kept for over ten years. At that point, he had made enough associates in the field to enable him to join an electricians' union. This organization now places him in long-term freelance positions.

You'll benefit from seeing and interviewing with several different organizations, and will probably get a better idea of what you'd really like from what you turn down. Interviewing can be a learning process in itself if you use it properly. You can find out the difference between large and small firms, pay schedules, and employers' expectations, for example.

Aquarius has such a natural ease with others that you'll have very little to worry about in terms of successfully completing a job interview. Your friendly nature immediately makes others feel at ease, and since first impressions last, you'll benefit here.

But make sure you play it by the rulebook for the interview. We know you Aquarian men probably hate to wear suits and ties and you women may prefer slacks to skirts, but most interviewers expect you to *appear* conventional, at least this one time. You may make an impression if you're dressed for a party or lounge, but you'll probably not get that job, even if you're the most qualified.

We're not suggesting you compromise your ideals— you couldn't possibly! Just this once, dress more conservatively than you ordinarily would, and it'll pay off. If you want to show off your uniqueness, wait till *after* you're hired. Long hair should be neatly coiffed, shoes shined, and earrings unobtrusive.

And don't reveal all of your wild and wacky interests right away. You may feel that you don't want to work for someone who won't take you for what you are. But interviewers see very little of the whole person in a half-hour session and will make judgments on anything.

In a competitive job market, your hobby of raising snakes just might put you out of the running. When the employer knows you better, your unusual pastime will be seen as fascinating. Wait until the proper time for these details that don't really have anything to do with your fitness for a job.

If you're called back, try to talk to some of the other employees while you're there. You'll get a better idea of the atmosphere, actual work, and expectations if you can do so.

You are healthily assertive and won't accept positions or pay that are beneath you. Do some homework to find out what's currently being offered to those in your position, and you'll succeed in closing the deal to everyone's satisfaction.

Getting Ahead: How to Do Your Best on the Job

As Aquarius is an air sign ruling the mental functions, you should use your logical, objective mind whenever possible on the job. You have a natural curiosity to understand all that is around you and are always eager to see and get to know new people, places, and ideas.

Perhaps your greatest mental asset is the Aquarian ability to come up with ideas. You enjoy the lure of the innovative and are able to study a problem apart from traditional solutions, business requirements, or other restrictions. In this way you can reach unique solutions with a different perspective and viewpoint from most other employees—one that is fresh and progressive. You will always be able to come up with a positive contribution in any business meeting or discussion.

You are also a rational, thoughtful human being. While you may get sudden inspirations, you should always think over their merits carefully before presenting them. You can wisely use the time for calm deliberation, as your best decisions are made by thinking things over. You will

STAR SUCCESS

learn from experience by trying out your suggestions to see if they actually work. If they don't, you'll learn something more. You're not married to predetermined solutions but, rather, will develop them through speculation, experimentation, and moderation of thought. While you can get excited over some new task, your calm and rational demeanor will aid in its implementation.

You have great powers of concentration; even while engrossed in a project, you will absorb knowledge by thinking, feeling, and sharing with those about you. Writing and speaking come naturally, and you express yourself fluently and succinctly.

Your versatility can help in getting any job done if you look with curiosity on some aspect of each and every task. You are capable of handling most any business situation if you use your mind and discernment to lead you into action.

You Aquarians are extremely idealistic, with your own strict code of behavior and ethics. Yes, these will differ from most, but generally you are loyal, honest, and tolerant of those about you. A humanitarian at heart, you will be quite committed to *your* beliefs and decisions, but you will never push them on others. You also promote goodwill with co-workers because you invite discussion rather than provoke quarrels or show-downs. You will get along extremely well with many diverse clients and customers, as you will work with their personalities, demands, and requirements.

Many of you can stay with one job for a lifetime once you have found your ideal position. When you've made a decision, you will be determined to stick to it and reach your goals.

While you will ordinarily resent restrictions of any kind, most jobs have some. You dislike being tied down to a specific schedule of duties but can manage by varying your routine or the people around you. Many Aquarians really do settle nicely into nine-to-five positions, but these are usually jobs that are more flexible or casual. If you're feeling frustrated by a routine, try a different approach to getting the work done. Sit in a different place if you can, join forces with co-workers when possible, have a meeting or write a memo instead of making a phone call, talk business over lunch, or simply explore new people and places within your firm during breaks. You'll find all of these to be refreshing alternatives, and some can be implemented into the most restrictive environment.

Most jobs will require you to make specific appointments or commitments from time to time. While you may rebel at these, force yourself to get out your calendar and commit your time. You'll find it easy to follow through on such appointments and will probably enjoy the diversion and variety they provide.

But Aquarians occasionally get lost in the world of ideas to the exclusion of practical reality. Don't allow your thoughts to become scattered, as many Aquarians do. Make sure your suggestions are applicable to the tasks or problems at hand and not just eccentric whims. You are naturally future-oriented, but you should stay in the "now" as much as possible. Your duties can provide a logical framework for the organization of your thoughts.

You should also guard against taking too much time for deliberation. If your ideas are practical, they can be readily applied. If you find yourself continually thinking over a prospective course of action, it's probably time to come up with a new plan! Also, remember that certain emergency business situations will call on you to take immediate action *without* predetermined thought. These can be unnerving for you, but once again, if you try to stay in the *now* you will do better in these situations than taking the time to imagine possible future contingencies.

Your keen mind makes you alert but can also indicate a sensitive nervous system. You may become overexcited by too many people, too many thoughts, or too many demands on your time. The stress can put you in a hypermental state from which it's difficult to come down. If you go through such a period, take time out to organize your thoughts, prioritize your tasks, and think things through. Make sure you rest and relax while at home; physical exercise can also help return you to your usual calm and collected state. And a regular routine, as much as you dislike it at times, can be a lifesaver during these difficult periods. Knowing that you'll leave work at 4:30 P.M. no matter what can help you clear your system as well. Don't try to do too much! Mental exhaustion can eventually lead you to a depressed physical and emotional state; use your good sense to avoid continued stress.

While you don't judge the actions of others, you may become too independent yourself. Your superiors probably trust your judgment, but remember to always let someone know where you are and to get your boss's clearance when you think it may be necessary. For you Aquarians, it's better to err on the side of caution. Once again, those company rules usually have to be followed, even if you know you have your superior's implicit permission to pursue a project. He or she may just know something more than you in terms of timing or the overall goals of the firm. Don't resent authority—work with it!

If you find yourself over a period of many years switching from one job to the next of your own volition, you should reevaluate your goals. Yes, you *can* find that ideal position if you look long and hard enough, but are you possibly making changes simply because of an inner restlessness?

If you genuinely feel that your ideals of independence and satisfaction are not being met, it will be time to move on. If you feel frustrated or thwarted in your goals, you will become stressed out, which will affect your health. Once you've ascertained that your decision is not just a whim, take action!

What *are* you seeking? Greater independence, a

chance to innovate, or the ability to pursue your goals more directly? Think these through carefully before your next job search.

Do you find your work rewarding? If not, review our vocations section once again. If you really feel your choice of vocation is right, you might think about working on your own or in a freelance position. But remember that any formal job situation will have certain regulations. And understand, too, that most of us will do best in the career world if we commit to one specific career choice or goal over a long period of time.

You'll be excited by the prospects that a new position or promotion can provide you with. While the routine and structure may take some getting used to, you'll soon be happily at work, hopefully in that ideal position that will last for perhaps the next ten years!

Do

- Use your intelligence and your innovative and progressive ideas.
- Utilize common sense and deliberation.
- Make use of your tenacity.
- Use your friendly nature to get along with others.
- Find a position that offers variety and versatility.

Don't

- Be obstinate or rebellious.
- Go against office rules and regulations.
- Be too unconventional or unpredictable.
- Allow yourself to become overstressed.
- Leave a job just for the sake of doing something different.

PISCES

February 18 to March 21

"We can make people feel better about themselves,
give them hope that anything is possible."
—Sally Jessy Raphael, *Newsday*

Go Fish!

Pisces is symbolized by two fish swimming in opposite directions. Not one, but two, which represents the duality in the Piscean character. They understand and can sympathize with many different points of view. The symbol also evokes the concept of yin and yang, as one point of view dissolves into the other while still remaining its complementary opposite. Pisceans are conscious of the larger whole, and their inner life is most important. Compassionate and often selfless, they can lull others to a relaxed state of consciousness and encourage them to be caring, giving, and open. Their ambitions are not for money, acquisitions, or position but intangible rewards like well-being and doing things for the good of all.

We can get a good idea of what Pisceans are like if we observe the fish in their natural habitat—water. Like fish, Pisceans really do live in a different world, or at least a different state of mind. They prefer the freedom and the sense of weightlessness that a watery environment provides. These people don't allow themselves to be limited by obstacles. If you think of them as existing within a mind and body floating effortlessly in a pool of water, you can understand why Pisceans aren't good at committing themselves to deadlines; they prefer to move at their own pace and when the mood strikes.

Like goldfish in a tank, they can be happy swimming around in a limited space as long as it's pleasant and rewarding. They will begin to droop and drift, however, if there are too many restrictions to freedom. The open seas remain the best habitat for Piscean fish!

Pisces people are good at any task that utilizes their imagination and creative faculties. Right-brained by nature, they need to bring out their visions to everyone else here on Earth. They will often seek out periods or places of solitude in order to recharge their emotional batteries.

Pisceans can make tremendous emotional and creative contributions to the workplace. They are warmhearted and giving people who need to help others and like to do good things. But as any fish can be slippery in or out of the water, Pisceans may exhibit a tendency toward indecisiveness or evasiveness. Still, they get along easily with others and usually like to go with the flow.

Get to Work! What to Look for in a Career

You sensitive Pisceans need a pleasant workplace. A quiet and peaceful atmosphere surrounding you is most beneficial to bringing out your productive capacities. It's also best if your co-workers are likable, helpful, and caring. A flexible schedule or one where you don't need to watch the clock is also desirable for you.

You seek emotional satisfaction and should look for a

field you enjoy and where you feel you can make a positive contribution. Your strong ideals and great understanding can inspire others in many ways. Any service-oriented vocation is good, from the social services to the health field, or even positions in business where you can help others. You have a strong inner life and imagination, and this can help you to succeed in many jobs that require an artistic, creative outlook or thoughtful problem-solving.

You should avoid positions that demand aggressive behavior or competitiveness in order to get ahead. You will be upset by jobs that require a "hard sell" or involve power struggles. Stressful positions, such as those with strict deadlines, also go against your sensibilities.

You Pisceans often succeed in positions that remain behind the scenes or ones where you contribute as part of a group. You may find yourself drawn toward work for large institutions like libraries, universities, museums, or hospitals. City, state, or federal government employment may also be for you, so look for civil service positions or perhaps the post office.

As Pisces is a water sign, you may find yourself drawn to work near large bodies of water where the waves provide the perfect restful, natural background. A young Pisces man we know worked his way through high school and college at a seasonal seaside resort. Because he worked hard and returned every summer, he was given greater responsibility each year. He eventually carved out a real career by the sea, working out of his own beachhouse as a freelance communications consultant—another Pisces career.

What's Your Line? Your Vocational Choices

The choice of vocation for Pisces can be all-important. You'll be successful, productive, and happy in a position that is geared to your often unique talents. On the other hand, because of your great sensitivity, you will flounder and maybe even sink in an unsuitable field.

Sally Jessy Raphael got her first radio job while only fourteen. Many Pisces people find themselves doing a variety of things to reach career success, and Raphael is surely no exception. In over thirty years in the public eye, she's acted and hosted many different radio programs, including rock and roll shows.

Raphael's success as a talk-show host is primarily due to her Piscean compassion, tolerance, and accessibility. She seems like a trusted friend with whom callers can open up easily. She has received more airtime over the last few years than any other woman in broadcasting, thanks to nationwide TV and radio programs.

The magical world of film is something very Piscean, as anything is possible in this medium. Although considered foremost a filmmaker, Spike Lee uses his many other Piscean talents to write, direct, and perform in his pictures. The most popular black filmmaker today, Lee nevertheless has not compromised his relaxed lifestyle.

Although at times controversial, Spike Lee strives to present the black experience in America. In his films *School Daze, Do the Right Thing*, and *Jungle Fever*, he challenges viewers to understand racism between blacks and whites and within the Afro-American community as well. His Piscean humor and understanding of emotionally charged issues have both helped him to succeed.

Piscean talents are many and frequently include music and poetry. Composer and lyricist Stephen Sondheim, one of the most prolific writers in the theater, has used many of his Pisces abilities to build his career.

Sondheim studied lyric writing with family friend Oscar Hammerstein II while still a boy before majoring in music in college. He wrote the lyrics for *West Side Story* and *Gypsy*, then penned the words and musical score for such blockbuster Broadway hits as *A Little Night Music, A Funny Thing Happened on the Way to the Forum, Sweeney Todd*, and *Into the Woods*.

Sondheim's music and subject matter often exemplify Piscean characteristics—original ideas plucked from a variety of sources, a distinct mood presented to the audience, and mixed feelings often conveyed in an emotionally complex dialogue.

Put a checkmark next to each question that you'd answer with a "yes." If there are several checks for a few career groups, review these first and think about the career suggestions we've listed. If you believe that one of these areas is right for you, investigate your selections further or come up with those closely related to them. Also, take a look at the rest of our suggestions for other possibilities.

___ Do you have a talent for expressing yourself?

___ Are you interested in a position in the creative arts?

___ Do you want to use your imagination and intuition?

___ Do you want to have some independence in your work?

___ Would you like change and variety in a position?

You are a Creative Pisces. Your ability to use your talents to imagine new projects or designs can be a great asset in many fields where creativity is necessary. You may try the myriad jobs available as a writer of poetry, prose, plays, screenplays, humor, music, or comic strips. Businesses also require writers for in-house publications or in the advertising and promotion of products. Many Pisceans have talents that can be put to use as an actor, comedian, dancer, choreographer, magician, mime, singer, musician (especially string instruments), filmmaker, or director.

There are lots of creative jobs that *don't* require you to write or perform. Behind-the-scenes jobs in film, theater, radio, and television are often higher paying and easier to get than the ones up front. Designers of sets and costumes, hair, makeup, sound, and special effects can all be Pisceans. You could be a dance, music, or art instructor, cinematographer, or photographer. Many different kinds of artists, painters, and sculptors are also Piscean. Other creative positions include fashion model, fashion designer, flower arranger, cake decorator, food stylist, and color forecaster.

___ Are you drawn to helping people?

___ Do you like to work with others?

___ Would you enjoy working as part of a large institution?

___ Would you like to find out more about altered states of reality?

___ Do you want job security?

You are a Humanitarian Pisces. Your understanding, sympathy, and ability to deal effectively with others can help you succeed in jobs in the medical and public counseling fields.

Work in the civil or social services such as a probation or parole officer, prison official, criminologist, narcotics investigator, penalogist, foster care official, and school or welfare administrator could also be of interest to you and give you personal satisfaction.

The medical field is ideal for many Pisces people. There is always a demand for trained physicians, psychiatrists, nurses, internists, or diagnosticians, and you could utilize your intuition and empathy in these positions. Other specific jobs include podiatrist, anesthesiologist, sanitarium attendant, respiratory therapist, chiropractor, acupuncturist, chemist, pharmacist, toxicologist, medical assistant, or veterinarian.

___ Do you want to use your imagination and intuition?

___ Are you drawn toward helping others?

___ Are you interested in the emotional and spiritual realms?

___ Would you like to serve a real purpose in life?

___ Can you use your sympathy and understanding to inspire others?

You are a Spiritual Pisces and have the ability to give of yourself to others for the benefit of both. You might be attracted to work for charities, political movements, or social welfare. You could help rehabilitate others as a counselor, therapist, natural healer, hypnotist, psychiatrist, or psychologist.

If you feel a real calling, you might want to look into becoming a clergyman, priest, minister, rabbi, spiritual counselor, monk, or nun. Other related positions include philosopher, mystic, psychic, yogi, or esoteric advisor. These jobs all include finding your own way through teaching, lecturing, writing, and counseling others.

___ Would you like to enter the world of business or industry?

___ Do you want to have career independence?

___ Can you go with the flow of business?

___ Are you attracted to jobs that serve others in a practical way?

___ Do you want to have a basic service-oriented job?

You are a Public Service Pisces. There are many positions in business and industry that need good people with Pisces talents to help serve a real need.

You could function well as a communications consultant, petroleum engineer, oceanographer, seaman, diver, public utility worker (particularly with water organizations), toxicologist, or poison or pollution control specialist. Many other areas of industry are also ruled by Pisces, including hatcheries, bait and tackle shops, and seafood restaurants. Or check out distilleries and breweries, as well as work with platinum or tin, the boating industry, and the graphic arts industry. You might like being a wine merchant, bartender, bottled water distributor, or a house or boat painter.

___ Would you like to enter the business world?

___ Do you want to work for a large firm with greater security?

___ Do you have big ideas?

___ Could you function best as part of a team?

___ Can you work practically to achieve business goals?

You are a Corporate Pisces. There are many jobs in the business world in which you could excel in an executive or administrative capacity. Any enterprise connected with the production, refining, or marketing of oil, petroleum products, paints, chemicals, perfumes, or volatile substances is ruled by Pisces.

The professions relating to advertising and mass merchandise are also Piscean. Try magazine publishing, the preparation and marketing of food and drink, or footwear manufacturing. Sales and distribution relating to these fields are also appropriate positions.

___ Do you resent the restrictions of others?

___ Would you like to work only when you choose?

___ Do you have original ideas and talents?

___ Can you roll with the flow of business?

___ Have you found a purpose in life that you'd really like to accomplish?

You are an Entrepreneurial Pisces. You should own your own business, but let a good accountant help you with financial matters. You may also work best in a partnership, especially with a more aggressive partner. Look over the preceding quizzes to help you think of a business that could fill a need and satisfy you as well.

Happy Hunting! How to Get That Job

Since your imagination can be of great help to you at all times, dream up your ideal job. Then go one step further and write out your job description, hours, location, and pay. We all know it's unlikely that you'll find this exact job, but use it to help you zero in on what you want. You may actually end up with two or three ideal career choices to aid you in your job search.

Many different strategies can work for the Pisces job seeker. Employment agencies can help you gain a more objective evaluation of your talents and can also make up for your lack of aggressiveness in finding a position or discussing salary.

In answering newspaper advertisements, you will be more assertive and in touch with exactly what you want when alone. Opt to write letters or fax them with resumes when possible. In placing a situation-wanted ad you can utilize your writing talent to sum up what you'd like in a position, as well as what you have to offer.

Your creativity can be put to good use in designing an

eye-catching resume. You may find that an unusual typeface or the paper's color, texture, and weight all convey a little more of what you're about. While you'll certainly want to include all the essential facts about your education and experience, you can detail your employment history in a style that gives a real impression of exactly what you can do for a prospective employer. This can be very important if you're pursuing a position that requires creativity: Your resume will be the first example of your talent.

Once you have your resume completed, a mass mailing can be very helpful in bringing you to the attention of many employers. Get a list of companies in your field from your local library's career and business section, a trade association in your field, or even a mailing-list service. Try sending resumes or query letters to those large institutions outlined in the previous "Get to Work" section as well; these places often offer a great variety of positions.

You may have to make a few phone calls to get a name to address your query to or find out where the personnel or employment office is located. Include a note with each resume, expressing your interest. If you don't have too many letters going out, these can be personal. If you've got dozens and don't have a computer, you can get a word processor to do a mail merge for you with a standardized letter, usually for a reasonable fee.

It's important for all of you Pisceans to keep looking, keep trying new sources, and to make a real concerted effort in your job search. See, talk, and write to as many people as you can as often as you can. Don't just drift along and hope a job comes to you. Get out there and take action!

Pisceans are great visualizers, so try to use this technique as well. As you relax or are falling asleep, imagine yourself in your ideal job. See yourself as productive, happy, and successful. This will help you keep a positive attitude. (Anything that can help in your job search should be utilized!)

You Pisceans are such likable and self-effacing people that you usually do quite well in interviews. Write down all of your appointments in a diary so you don't forget the specifics of when and where. Punctuality is not a Pisces strength, so make sure you leave in plenty of time to arrive early. The interviewer doesn't have many things to judge you by—showing up on time is usually one of them.

You respond well to questions when asked and can use your ideal job description to help in some cases. Speak up! You will usually err on the side of being too quiet. Your personal reticence may look like indifference to a prospective employer, so if you're really interested in a position, say so in no uncertain terms. Talk about what excites you about the job, as well as those things that you feel you can contribute. Show them why you think you're the best candidate.

Be as direct as possible in conversation. Look the interviewer in the eye. Try to keep up a positive and cheerful facade, even if you're nervous and feel like crawling into a hole. You *can* use your imagination to help you appear more calm.

Don't be afraid to ask questions, especially in a second interview. Practical considerations may not be that important to you, but you'll find that many will make a big difference. Is the nine-to-five schedule rigid or flexible? What about benefits? It can be helpful to write out a list of your concerns before the interview. Don't be afraid to refer to your list before you leave; you'll be seen as efficient and capable, not forgetful!

You Pisceans are usually not concerned with finances, but money is one of the reasons you're working—don't forget it! You may have a tendency to accept less than you deserve. If you're asked what you want to earn, quote a higher price than you think you'll get. Most employers will talk you down a little. Or ask the employer for a bit more than his or her first offer because many "low-ball" it initially. It's easier to talk salary at the time you're hired than to ask for more money later. And given the Pisces tendency to be satisfied with what you've got, you'll probably avoid asking for a raise later on. Do yourself a favor and be as assertive as possible when hired.

Getting Ahead: How to Do Your Best on the Job

Understanding and compassionate, you get along easily with others at the workplace. Your modest, unassuming manner makes you a good listener, and this can make you a favorite with co-workers and supervisors alike. You have an easy manner and are comfortable with others. Your gentle ways make you a nice person to have around, whatever the circumstances.

You are able to adapt yourself to the demands of others or to a variety of business situations. You are not usually upset by changing circumstances. Use this quality to advantage when supervisors need you to shift gears to a new approach or when an unexpected deadline pops up.

You are also able to adapt to a power structure and easily fit into it. Your self-effacing personality will keep you outside of direct confrontations and power struggles. You're just not interested in these things, taking a more objective view toward the ambitions of those about you.

While you don't enjoy a strict schedule or the control of others, if your job demands certain restrictions, you'll accept them rather easily. You don't resent authority and can be sparked into action by the influence of others.

A Pisces executive we know needed the signature of his boss on much of his paperwork before it could be processed. Because the supervisor put things off, the approval came only sporadically. Several predecessors had quit in frustration, but the Pisces adapted by doing other work when he could and ensuring that when his boss got around to it, all the accumulated papers got signed.

You are by nature an intuitive individual. Your mind is usually quick and clear, and you understand meanings without being explicitly told. There is often a wonderful fluency in speech and prose that you should try to utilize in letter and memo writing, demonstrations, and meetings. Strive to include facts and details whenever possible, as you easily convey feelings and the larger picture.

You can also have remarkable mental talents, which may even include a geniuslike ability to process information. Unfortunately, however, many Pisceans never get the knack of arithmetic, spelling, or other mundane chores. Work with whatever limitations you have by stressing what you *can* do! After all, in today's world, adding and spelling can be done by a computer.

Your good sense of humor can make you popular, as well as help lighten heavy business discussions. Make your personal correspondence and speech something looked forward to by others whenever it's appropriate.

As most Pisces people enjoy at least some time alone, you can score points by performing solitary tasks that others may not enjoy. You'll actually find it refreshing to sit quietly for a while. Here you can also move at your own pace without restrictions or the interference of others.

Because you like to give of yourself, you may find co-workers asking for favors. Your instinct is to help out, but don't let this tendency undermine your own work. It's enough to lend a sympathetic ear and give advice— you don't always have to actually *do* the job too. You can exhaust yourself by trying to do too much for other people. Learning how to say "no" is a difficult lesson for Pisceans, yet it can be essential in maintaining a pleasant, regular position.

You are very sensitive and will at times be disturbed by the emotional excesses of those about you. Try to avoid some disturbances by tuning them out. If possible, find a quiet place to get involved with a project. Any work that needs to be done with others of a more chipper nature can also help pick up your spirits at times when you're feeling low.

Your ability to empathize can cause you to be easily influenced. When it comes to decision-making, you may become indecisive or change your mind easily. Learn to trust your intuition in decision-making, and if you doubt yourself, try to find some time alone to clear your mind. You'll find you make the best decisions in times of repose and relaxation.

All Pisceans can benefit from assertiveness training. You can get a lot more accomplished if you'd just take action. Too often a good Pisces worker will let someone else leap ahead because of speed alone. You have wonderful ideas and solutions to problems—share these with others. Don't just think about them, but act! Follow through! Get yourself excited about some aspect of your job. Look forward to it and then actually give yourself the satisfaction of accomplishment. Yes, the anticipation and the memory *are* often better than the actual work. But you can create a mood or feeling about almost anything you wish to undertake. Do these things, and don't just daydream about doing them.

Many Pisceans don't plan far enough into the future. If you have a job that demands advance preparation, it's time to write things down. Get in the habit each day of doing a few of those tasks you'd rather avoid. And don't forget to look at your list! The skeleton of a regular routine, staff meetings, and assigned priorities can also help you get things done on time.

You can have great powers of concentration, but you need to take control of these if you are to succeed. Don't drift off into personal problems, worries, or anxieties. If you train yourself to be able to do this at will, you'll be much more productive. You'll also find an escape from personal problems at the workplace—and who couldn't use that from time to time?

Most difficult of all is concentrating on tasks that don't interest you or that you dislike. We all have some of these in every job. You can be inattentive or absent-minded about things that seem unimportant. Yet many of these things *are* important to supervisors and need to get done. You are great at avoiding things, but work is not the place for this behavior. Make a decision to accomplish a few of these unpleasant tasks on a regular basis. You'll be relieved when they're over with, and you will have the satisfaction of knowing that you really have helped someone else along the line get their job done quicker, too.

You can benefit from working with others in many situations, and you'll probably develop a number of friendships on the job. Simply the presence and emotional support of another may be all that's needed to light a fire under you. Just don't pick someone who only helps you procrastinate even more. A change of scene to more pleasant surroundings and the addition of music can also put you in a working mood.

You'll easily become bored repeating the same tasks over and over. In order to get them accomplished, vary your schedule, the workplace, or cohorts when possible. Break up the day by attending to one thing at a time and then switching gears. Returning to that long, drawn-out and boring work periodically throughout the day will help you get it done while keeping you fresh and stimulated by other chores.

Keep track of the time; you may find yourself whiling away an hour on the phone before you realize that your lunchbreak is over. Try to be punctual and keep track of your overtime hours, too. No one is going to pay you for time that you don't report, and you deserve all that's coming to you. A good watch and calendar can be indispensable to Pisceans. You can even buy a watch with an alarm to remind you when to make a call, begin another task, or go home: all positive, practical uses on the job.

An incompatible job can be disastrous for a Pisces. If you feel you don't really have the right skills to handle your work, if you have difficult co-workers or are emotionally uneasy in your position, you won't do well. And you won't feel well, either. You'll often try to do too much and may not know when enough is enough. If you're overworked or miserable at your job, you could even develop physical symptoms such as headaches, nausea, or fatigue. Listen to your body!

You may abruptly decide to leave when the mood strikes. Make sure this is not just a passing fancy. Discuss your plans with some trusted, objective friend and confirm your feelings when you're more relaxed.

You're not the most practical person in the world, but you know it helps to plan ahead in this situation. The traditional advice is to make sure you have another position lined up before leaving. If this isn't possible, begin an active search right away. And if you're not finding exactly what you want, consider temporary employment. You may locate a position you'll want to keep this way while remaining financially solvent until the perfect job comes to you.

If you've been offered a promotion, take it! Sure, find out whether or not you have the right talents and skills for the position as well as a good feeling about it. But remember that you can be too insecure at times. When in doubt, take the more assertive course and plunge in. Don't think *too* much about what you should do; you'll never be able to see what this new opportunity really is until you try it.

In any promotion, you should also get a raise. Changing jobs is the perfect time to ask for more money, and it should be expected if you're taking on more responsibility. Don't sell yourself short by accepting less than you really deserve.

STAR SUCCESS

Do

- Develop concentration, determination, and willpower.
- Use your imagination and intuition.
- Try to improve your memory and be reliable.
- Develop self-confidence.
- Use adaptability and flexibility.

Don't

- Be too sensitive on the job.
- Feel inadequate or insecure.
- Be passive or take the easy way out.
- Procrastinate.
- Be too trusting.

Part Three

WORKING WITH OTHERS

ARIES
March 20 to April 21

The Aries Co-worker: High Spirited

Aries co-workers are engaging, friendly folk who like people. It's a good bet that if there were a vote for most popular sign, Aries would win. People born under the sign of the ram are so energetic and high spirited that they infuse all activities with excitement and appeal. "Who wouldn't want to be an Aries?" they imply as they get one hundred and one tasks done in a seemingly effortless manner.

You will succeed in your working relationships with these people if you can remember one rule about Ariens: *What you see is what you get.* These people are candid and straightforward. Their tongues are apparently linked directly to the brain; as soon as they have a thought, you'll hear it! Don't look for hidden meaning, covert implications, or subtext in their conversation. It's not there. You may hear someone referring to an Aries, saying, "What do you think he meant by that?" The answer is always crystal clear—just what he said, no more, no less.

Ariens can amuse and stimulate others with their frank

manner but can cause some hurt feelings along the way. They feel so comfortable and at ease with others and are so absolutely unself-conscious about themselves that they'll really just say anything. They don't have a clue about how they come off to others. The more sensitive signs like Cancer, Scorpio, and Pisces will be thrown by what they may consider to be the ridiculously tactless behavior or obnoxious attitude of the Aries co-worker. No matter what sign you are, realize that an Aries is an open book. Yes, Ariens can be too outspoken at times, but you can count on them to be completely honest about their feelings and desires.

Aries people have so much vitality that they are decisive and action-oriented. They like to be on the go and can get a lot accomplished. When delayed or thwarted, they'll easily get excited. If you raise your voice to an Arien, expect to be instantly responded to in kind. These are impulsive, impatient people who easily let off steam. You may even hear one too many unkind words about yourself!

The remedy? Forget about it. Ariens don't hold grudges and are too busy doing what they're doing to remember they were mad at you. And they genuinely like people and accept them as they are. They just have ten times more adrenaline flowing through their veins than most of us, that's all, and generally forgive and forget. Remember, too, that apologies are not their style. Raising the voice is no big deal to them, after all. If pressed, you'll probably hear "You drove me to it!" and the argument will begin anew. Accept as your apology the fact that the Aries on next meeting will be just as charming and friendly toward you as before.

If an Aries really deeply resents you for some reason, he or she won't bother hiding it. You'll get the cold shoulder and brusque words when your paths cross. The way out? You could ask what the problem is (you probably know already), but expect a harangue. A big fight may clear the air, as Ariens genuinely want to be liked. Don't try innuendo or sarcastic remarks with this person, though—it will go right over the ram's head! Stick with the most direct approach possible. Hopefully, sooner or later the conflict will blow over, as most do with this impulsive sign.

Aries people are not the best solvers of complex problems. They need to attack conflict directly and have no finesse when it comes to negotiation or diplomacy. If you've got an argumentative Aries with whom you need to compromise, remember that the Aries bark is often worse than its bite. The name of the game for these people is *expediency,* and they can be flexible if it means solving a problem once and for all.

Ariens have such a wide circle of acquaintances that they generally know at least something about everyone and are always happy to share any and all information. If you need to know who can help you, what to expect in a meeting, or who reports to whom, an Aries can be a lifesaver, especially in larger companies. And it's the rare Aries who doesn't tell all at the drop of a hat.

You'll probably be excited to share an assignment with one of them. Their enthusiasm makes them extremely likable companions, and any Aries will dig in with all the excitement nature allows.

Aries will quickly take the lead and make decisions and expect you to follow through. If you can handle this, you'll make an excellent team. If you can't, you'll have trouble. Capricorn, Cancer, and Libra co-workers especially can have problems with the Aries insensitivity and inability to come to group decisions. You'll also find that Ariens have a hard time planning ahead. They want to get things done *now* and move on to the next project, becoming distracted by the excitement of the *next* new job. Aries co-workers will usually see lengthy discussion and meetings as a big waste of time. If you're stubborn enough about your point of view, you'll win out in the long run—an Aries frustrated by lack of action will eventually compromise just to get something done!

In dividing tasks, remember that Aries people love to deal with people. Errands outside the office, telephone calls, and discussions with many and different co-workers will all stimulate and amuse the ram. Excess paperwork, delay, and discussion over details will always frustrate and squelch their fiery tendencies.

In most business situations you'll find Aries to be companionable, hard-working, and honest. If you don't mind the excitement of a high temperament and can overlook some blunt remarks, you'll have a loyal and amusing friend on the job!

The Aries Boss: You're in the Army Now

We liken the Aries boss to a military leader because many of them are. If they're not in fact they will be in behavior. You'll be expected to obey orders and snap to attention unless otherwise indicated. Are you the sensitive type? Do you gravitate toward a calm and relaxed atmosphere at work? Then this is not the boss for you. Pack up your things and go—your Aries supervisor won't even expect you to give notice!

Ariens are leaders *par excellence*. They are completely at ease when in charge and will expect others to be as quick, active, and optimistic as they are. If you're a laid-back type who needs to take lots of time and are working directly for an Aries boss, you won't last long.

Ariens will almost bark out instructions. Whatever is happening *now* is usually top priority. If you can easily drop what you're doing and instantly obey commands, you'll do fine. If you're thrown when a long-term project is interrupted several times a day, you'd better learn to like the stimulation.

Aries supervisors like to feel they're in command; they

want to be looked up to and recognized as the one in charge. They are easy people to get along with and are usually personally likable, but they can be quite demanding of employees. Ordinarily they'll go through their work day as if there were deadlines looming imminently. Strangely enough, however, in real crises they keep their cool and get no more excited than usual. There will be a greater intensity to their actions and orders at these times, but a challenge is Aries heaven. Don't argue in an emergency, just do what you're told! Ariens can explode over delays or problems and will blame *you*. Their short-sightedness will often not allow them to admit themselves as the cause of any problems.

A secretary we know found herself filling in as an Arien's assistant one day. As luck would have it, the Aries suddenly had an unexpected meeting in his office with a client. He expected the temp to do everything his usual assistant would do to prepare—at once! She was shouted at and replaced. The secretary was upset for weeks by the incident and was shocked to hear the Aries president tell her soon afterward, "You're doing a great job!" This scenario illustrates many Aries characteristics: They have to act immediately and can be intolerant of others' shortcomings and unsympathetic in times of stress. And yet they really don't hold grudges. Temper tantrums are usually just passing incidents. If an Aries supervisor likes you and feels you're productive, a shout-down does not influence his or her overall estimation. Don't you make too big a deal over an incident like this if your boss doesn't!

In general, these people can be easy to work for, as they are independent and expect others to be. If your supervisor sees you're getting the job done in an efficient and timely manner, you'll probably be given more responsibility and less supervision. These people like to have others worry about follow-through, and if you are reliable you'll score points here, too. Most Ariens will like to take suggestions and original ideas from anyone. Yes, they're in charge, but they're not up on a high horse as some bosses can be.

Aries superiors are not clock-watchers, and if there's not a lot of work at the moment, you won't be criticized for talking, lounging, or having a good time. Ariens view networking as something both enjoyable and necessary for advancement. Just remember that when work comes in you'll be expected to hop to it with no questions asked. Your Aries boss will expect you to work overtime when necessary and will not even hear arguments. Your boss is probably very ambitious, and work is the most important thing, followed by efficiency in getting it done.

You may find that your boss cannot anticipate deadlines; he or she may be so tied up in this week's problems that next week's due date seems minor in comparison. Go your own way and do what you can to prepare.

Don't be afraid of being assertive with this boss. Ariens are very straightforward and relate to you best when you're that way as well. If you want a raise or time off, don't expect this supervisor to pick up on hints. Asking for what you want is a good way to find out what your supervisor really thinks of you. After your query, you will probably be met with a comment like "Why do you think you deserve it?" Be honest in your reply; the Aries will make a quick decision and that'll be that. Don't be surprised, however, at a curt response, like "You have some nerve coming in here considering your laziness!" A nice direct "What can I do to improve?" will fit the bill nicely at this moment.

While Ariens can make snap judgments of people, they realize that things change and they're not afraid to move into the future. Your show of renewed enthusiasm and a willingness to please will go far in setting you aright in the boss's eyes. Take seriously whatever your supervisor has criticized. Don't try to read between the lines but follow suggestions to the letter.

"'Ten-shun!" Good. If you can meet the demands of

working for this boss, you'll be all that you can be in no time. All right, "at ease."

Gift Ideas for Aries

You'll have fun choosing a gift for an Aries. Just keep in mind the idea of suitability for an active lifestyle. Aries people like things that can help them do tasks in a quicker and easier manner. They also enjoy diversions. Avoid all gifts that require elaborate preparation to enjoy. While Aries people like putting things together, they don't enjoy long-term projects.

Sports-related equipment is a good choice; many Ariens pursue several different sports as hobbies and would be interested in learning new ones if they're fun and easy. Bodybuilding or exercise equipment, target or skeet shooting gear, a trampoline, tennis rackets, a dart board, badminton set, horse shoes, table tennis equipment, pool equipment, or bowling equipment are all good choices. Beachballs, basketballs, frisbees, a baseball bat or mitt, roller skates, surfboard, or skateboard would all be enjoyed by these fun-loving people. A stopwatch or mileage meter would be appreciated as well.

Aries love their cars, so auto apparatus can make good gifts for them. Car, motorcycle, or bicycle tools and accessories such as a flashlight, sun visor, seat cushion, tire inflator, maps, or tapes are all good choices. Even miniature cars, trains, and trucks will be enjoyed by adult Ariens!

Aries people like to do things themselves, so a work bench, tool kit, knife, or scissors would all be useful. Woodcutting and cloissoné sets might also be appropriate.

If you'd like to buy a book for an Aries, make sure it's exciting! Subjects that are good include sports, racing, military, aeronautics, or biographies of explorers or self-made personalities. To fit the Arien's short attention span, subscriptions to such magazines as *Popular Mechanics* or books of short stories would be read and enjoyed.

For the home, choose gifts that help the Aries be more independent or do things faster. A Walkman, answering machine, VCR, coffee maker, microwave, or automatic lighting equipment will be used often. Other home ideas include an iron, toaster oven, waffle maker, food processor, minichopper, hand vacuum, curling iron, or blow dryer.

The casual Aries style makes it easy to choose clothing. Exercise clothes, sweatsuits, beach paraphernalia, a sweatband, or sports cap are usually needed by active Ariens. Any comfortable sweaters, shirts, blouses, and shorts that allow for freedom of movement will be enjoyed. Aries colors are red and other bright hues.

Jewelry for Ariens should not get in their way either, even for formal occasions. Choose bright and flashy stones and metals. Aries rules all red stones, including red jasper and garnet, as well as diamonds and fire quartz. Aries women and men enjoy metal bracelets, necklaces, and earrings.

Flowers for Aries are the red rose, tulip, poppy, and honeysuckle. Scents include those with a rose base or jasmine.

Aries people often enjoy sporting events, so tickets to a game can make a nice gift. They would also like race car events, variety shows, and rock concerts.

TAURUS

April 20 to May 22

The Taurus Co-worker: Consistency Personified

Taureans seek a peaceful existence and are usually kind, warm, and gentle. You can tell a lot about them by the way they speak—quietly and calmly, often with beautiful voices.

They like serene environments and tend toward good-natured reserve. Taureans will mind their own business and attend to the work at hand. While they enjoy friendships with co-workers, they need to get to know others over a long period of time before they can really trust them.

Your co-worker likes things to stay the same and can be an absolutely immovable, permanent fixture behind a desk. The Taurus will show up at the same time every morning, with the same breakfast items and the same newspaper. Part of the reason these people maintain such placid dispositions is that their inner security is well grounded.

Like the bull, Taureans go about everything they do in the same unhurried, unruffled manner. They crave material security, and most will eventually own property or have extra money in the bank for a rainy day. They'll dress in soft fabrics, in pastel or earth-toned colors. Some may even wear the same suit constantly or keep it for many years.

The good thing about working with Taureans is that you'll always know what to expect. They will be found in the same places, will react predictably, and tend toward accepting the status quo rather than attempting to change things as an Aquarian or Sagittarian might. They are extremely straightforward and genuine—what you see is what you get. Literally. When these people say they'll do something, they can be counted on to do it, although they will usually take their time. If you confide in them, they'll never tell. Once they like someone or something, it's final. Taurus people like to maintain permanence in their relationships, and it's in their nature to be loving and giving.

There is a great quiet strength in these earthy people, but while they'll let a lot roll right off their backs, they can be pushed too far. Taureans won't be hurried and won't allow themselves to be pressured into quick decisions. This is the most stubborn and obstinate of all signs once a decision or conclusion has been reached. Some co-workers may continually impose on their generosity, thinking that it will continue forever.

A Taurus co-worker can be taken advantage of for quite some time but will finally and resolutely fight back. It won't matter if it's an associate or the boss who's at fault—when the Taurus has had enough, everyone will know it. He or she will explode into such a rage that many associates will be shocked. But it takes a lot to provoke such violent emotions. If it's enough to rock the typical Taurean placidity, it's enough to cause a loss of all control. Be forewarned: If you sense resistance, don't push this person too far.

As you get to know your Taurus co-worker, you'll really get a sense of the reliability and loyalty inherent in this sign. You'll find your associate to be protective, supportive, and giving. If there is a deadline, your Taurus friend will pitch in. If there's a crisis, you can rely on the bull to keep a cool head and help as much as possible.

If you want to get to know your co-worker better, suggest going out to lunch or an early dinner after work. These people love food and drink and consider them the chief luxuries of earthly existence (they are the type who will invite the boss over for dinner and cook up a gourmet meal). Over a rich dinner, your Taurean associate will become more relaxed and may even become a bit more expansive and talkative. Just be aware that many of this sign are often dieting as a result of being too indulgent.

In working with Taureans, remember that they can be extremely opinionated. Once they latch on to an idea, it can be nearly impossible to dissuade them from it. Yet they remain practical business people. If the facts and figures are on your side and profits are at stake, you will be able to change a Taurean's mind. Just be prepared for a long, detailed session, complete with extensive cross-examination. This type of discussion can make even the most patient co-workers lose their cool, so be prepared for the long haul when dealing with a stubborn Taurus. Even after you feel you've made all your points clearly and convincingly, you'll still find that your associate will have to chew things over alone before making a decision. The earthy Capricorn and Virgo people will have an easier time handling the plodding Taurus, while Leos and Scorpios will have the patience and determination to see the struggle through to the end.

Avoid losing your own temper, which many of you may be pushed to do, a Taurean's sometimes incomprehensible stubbornness can be provoking. If your co-worker senses blind opposition or anger, he or she will dig in and become even more committed than before. It's a curious thing, but the more others oppose Taureans, the more determined they become to prove themselves right. This can result in stand-offs, antagonism, and nonproductivity, none of which are recommended for the workplace.

Be reasonable, practical, and patient with Taureans when working out problems. They respond to kindness as well. If you've gained their friendship, you may even be able to appeal to the soft Taurean emotions. They have been known to bend when people they like plead their case emotionally.

Taurus rhythms are a bit slower than the rest of ours, and you should be aware of this when sharing information with a co-worker of this sign. They are not mentally quick or sharp and often not even curious about things that don't seem to have a direct effect on their lives. Yet once they have taken the time to study and digest facts, they will never forget them. And once they've learned something from experience, they don't ever forget the lesson.

Bulls are almost childlike in the way in which they view the world. They can be somewhat naive compared with more worldly or complex personalities. They tend to accept what they see and what they're told and can be falsely led into a trusting relationship. Because of this characteristic, they may sometimes suddenly see a person in a different and negative light.

If you have unwillingly upset or hurt a Taurus co-worker, just apologize and explain. The more stubborn and inflexible Taurean may not accept your apology and will hold a grudge for a long time. You can expect sulking silence and avoidance if this is the case. No Taurus will be so foolish as to jeopardize his or her career by refusing to work with you when necessary. Yet the warmth will be gone, you will get single-syllable responses to your questions, and it will take a long time to regain your previous relationship. These people will never be aggressive, mean, or overtly antagonistic, but they can make you pretty uncomfortable nevertheless.

For the most part, however, Taureans are sweet and

reliable co-workers. If you can consistently show them concern and friendship on the job, you'll be sure to have a loyal, trusted associate for a long time to come.

The Taurus Boss: Rock Solid

Taurus supervisors are not particularly gifted, except in one area—they have an innate and complete understanding of the value of things. This can mean that they have good artistic taste, financial vision, or great practicality. Maybe all three. But recognizing value is of great importance in the business world. Many Taurean bosses also earn quite a bit of money. This sign seems to attract wealth, and with cash and stable investments, a Taurus will build a business based on a solid foundation.

Taureans are realistic, they know what's practical, what's possible, and their market. Their common sense and no-nonsense approach leads them to build careers on the tried and true—hard work, determined effort, and that ever-reliable sense of value. As a result, their positions are usually of long standing. A Taurus businessperson who reaches a position of power will keep it, period.

Like most people of this sign, Taurus supervisors are pleasant, peaceful individuals, with even dispositions. They are so down to earth and real that positions of power, responsibility, and superiority don't faze them in the least. Like Taurean Billy Joel has said in the *Celebrity Register*, "I don't think I'm so special. I just do what I do." This attitude makes them friendly and considerate supervisors. If anything, they are nurturing toward employees and will give their time and emotional support to help those they like feel comfortable and do the job properly.

Taurean bosses work hard and are often self-made people. They feel that anyone who is dedicated over a long enough period of time will succeed in the end. They always take their time, even over the most simple matters. You'll have to wait, if necessary, for your boss at times. Get used to it.

Your supervisor, like most Taureans, has probably succeeded to a large degree because of patience and determination. These two traits taken together imply stubbornness. While any Taurus on the street is a tough customer, those who have reached positions of power are even more so. When Taureans find something that works, they stick with it, permanently. Many who have achieved success have only reinforced this tendency.

Your boss will not be easy to oppose, convince, or side-track. This sign has been likened to a steamroller and also the Rock of Gibraltar. When you get resistance to suggestions, it's best to try and forget the whole thing. You'll save yourself a lot of aggravation, frustration, time, and trouble if you learn early on that your boss is a strong-willed person.

Most bulls are tradition-bound and are thus at least somewhat conservative. The hierarchy of the workplace is important to them. Taureans accept as a given that you should listen to superiors in order to get ahead. If you do so, you'll be more likely to move up, too. These people don't want bright, aggressive employees who offer suggestions; they prefer those who can be relied on to listen to instructions and get the job done. If you are independent and innovative, as many Aquarians or Aries people are, you may have problems working for a Taurus.

These people are so easygoing, however, that if you cover the basics of the job, they'll overlook a lot of problems. First, get to work on time and don't leave early. Put an honest effort into what you do and take pride in your work, whatever it may be. Try not to overestimate how much work you can accomplish in a given period. Your boss just wants to know that you do your job well, not fast. You should strive for thoroughness and accuracy, rather than speed.

Taurus people hate being betrayed or lied to. They will

think the most of you if you are up front about all circumstances. If you're caught in a lie, your Taurean boss will never be able to completely trust you again and will forever wonder just what is the truth and what is not. Be as candid with your supervisor as possible. Remember promises and commitments and make sure you keep them.

Your boss won't make a hasty judgment of your abilities but will evaluate you over a long period of time. You'll be given plenty of opportunity to prove yourself. Because Taureans are so practical, your supervisor won't get upset or angry over small mistakes due to human error or unfamiliarity with the job. This can be very refreshing in a world where employees are often expected to be constantly correct—or else.

Your boss will take time to explain things to you carefully and thoroughly. Taureans' instructions are usually to the point. If you don't catch on to an idea or procedure, just speak up and ask questions. Your boss will take whatever time is necessary to make sure that you understand exactly what is needed.

Taurus people need to have a peaceful atmosphere, and you should strive for an even-tempered emotional outlook while on the job. Highs and lows or wild fits of temper or enthusiasm can upset your boss's equilibrium. Avoid these when you can. If you like using a radio or cassette player, and if the music is soothing, it can have a positive effect on your boss.

Taurus trust is earned over time, and you can't count on keeping a reputation that you don't live up to day after day. You must continue to have a good attitude and routinely do your work in a responsible manner if you want to keep your boss's regard. And if you can be there when emergencies strike, you'll be appreciated even more.

Taureans know the value of their workers. They'll pay employees what they feel they're worth. If you're important to the company, you should expect to earn the going rate, if not more. If you come in early, stay late, and complete your work with accuracy and in a timely manner, you will probably receive more from your Taurus boss. These people will be generous when they feel that you are.

But don't expect your supervisor to immediately give you the raise you ask for. He or she will have to think about it first. If you're not a valued employee, you just won't get an increase, no matter how you push. Sometimes Taureans can have prejudices, too, and even if you feel you're working your butt off, if your boss doesn't believe it for some reason, you won't get the increase.

The same will hold true for vacation time, although your Taurus supervisor will give you time off without pay if the firm's not busy. It's just a practical matter: If there's no work to do, it makes sense not to pay someone to hang around.

It's very easy to get along with a Taurus boss on a superficial level and more difficult in a close working relationship. But if you are willing to listen and do what you're told even when you disagree, you'll have no problem working for this boss. And you'll have as your reward a stable, secure position that you can enjoy for a long time to come.

Gift Ideas for Taurus

Taureans love possessions, especially things that last. They appreciate high quality and good value in gifts. No matter how small or inexpensive, try to make it the best of its type. Taureans also enjoy practical gifts that help them through their day-to-day lives. They appreciate things that are simply beautiful or those that appeal to their sensual nature, too.

Taureans would enjoy books that cater to their interests in cooking, baking, nature, gardening, flowers, plants, and trees. Coffee-table-type books or those on painting, sculpture, interior or exterior design, or decoration can also make good choices. Biographies of successful businesspeople and romances are possibilities as well, as are subscriptions to magazines relating to these subjects.

A gift certificate or evening out to a fine restaurant is an excellent gift, or treat Taurus to a wine or food tasting or cooking show. Tickets to a dinner theater, musical theater, classical concert, symphony, ballet, art exhibit, or museum would all appeal to the Taurean appreciation of the finer things. Or they may also enjoy seeing nature shows, farm exhibits, going horseback riding, hiking, attending a boxing match, or taking a tour of the stock market or other financial center. Taurus would also appreciate a gift certificate for a massage or sauna.

Taureans prefer clothing of comfort, simplicity, and value. They have a strong sense of touch and are attracted to soft, natural fabrics like silks, velvets, lambswool, and angora. Pastel and earth tones appeal to them, as do the colors blue and rose pink. Choose plain practical sportswear with no excess trim.

Taurus is associated with the violet, columbine, foxglove and daisy, and Taureans will enjoy exotic and lingering scents. There are many gemstones which they would be drawn to, including pink coral, rose quartz, green jasper, lapis lazuli, and emerald.

Personal items that make good gifts for Taureans include a necklace or choker, brooch, cameo, or tie tack. Cushiony pillows, fluffy blankets, down quilts, silk sheets, satin dress hangers, music boxes, crystals, prints, sculptures, figurines, or knickknacks would all be appreciated. Other possibilities are decorative dolls, scented candles, soaps, and oils.

Or help Taureans in the kitchen, with cooking and baking equipment, gourmet gadgets, utensils and pans, a cake icer or decorating set, bread mixer, ice-cream maker, fondue set, coffee grinder, espresso or cappuccino maker, ceramic mug, mug warmer, waffle iron, crock pot, wok, or any other equipment. Perhaps buy a wooden salad bowl and spoons, a rattan fruit basket, butcherblock cutting board, snack tables, a picnic basket, linen tablecloth and napkins, placemats, coasters, a spice rack, canister set, trivet, china, platters, or glasses for a domestic Taurus.

Most Taureans would love gifts of food. Assorted candies, chocolates, cookies, jellies, meats, and cheeses are sure to please the Taurean palate. Or prepare your own homemade cakes or pies, purchase gourmet pastas, a bottle of good wine or liquor, whole-roasted coffee beans, or flavored teas.

Many Taurus people enjoy gardening. If your co-worker does, consider garden tools and equipment, such as hedge clippers, knee pads, a sun hat, gardening gloves, flower seeds, bulbs, saplings, small bushes, potted plants, an outdoor umbrella, patio chairs or table, hammock, barbecue grill, or bird feeder.

Taureans also enjoy comfortable furniture, such as an overstuffed chair or recliner and home or office accessories like a portable television, thick area rug, fireplace logs, stereo or Walkman, and cassettes of show tunes or mood music.

Many have creative hobbies, too. Painting equipment, art supplies, ceramics kits, a sculpting set, and afghan or patchwork quilting equipment can all be appropriate. Or buy Monopoly for your favorite Taurus would-be tycoon!

GEMINI
May 21 to June 22

The Gemini Co-worker: Variety Is the Spice

Your Gemini co-workers are affable people who love to talk, share ideas, and mix it up with others. Their friendly manner, mercurial temperament, and easy-going disposition make them a pleasure to talk to and have around.

No matter what their age, Geminis appear youthful. They have a vivacity, restlessness and insatiable curiosity typical of the young. They give the impression of being here, there, and everywhere. They don't like to be tied down to routine and can be seen exploring the workplace or keeping abreast of the latest news.

If the Gemini body isn't in motion, the mind and mouth usually are. Typically social butterflies, Geminis need to have people about them to be happy, and in turn enlighten, entertain, and fascinate co-workers. Geminis are at once familiar, casual, and bright. They speak with ease and fluency, can provide a near-constant stream of information, and have a light way of communicating. Many Geminis also have an infectious sense of humor as well. They enjoy clever wordplay, jokes, and witty repartee. They'll never come on too strong, but their amusing observations can be sharp and to the point.

Geminis make popular co-workers because of their ease and likability. They are rarely at a loss in any business or social situation because they have the gift of gab. They often become everybody's favorite lunch companion. Undemanding, unpretentious, and equally comfortable with the boss or the cleaning crew, you'll soon find your Gemini co-worker to be a welcome change of pace from the day-to-day grind.

Geminis live in the moment and are always alive in the present split-second. They can therefore be changeable and unpredictable. The Gemini symbol of the twins implies two personalities in one, and this is generally the case. They can be restless, moody, or even somewhat schizo at times. Their constantly moving, busy minds can forget their promises. It's easy for a Gemini to say, "I don't remember saying I'd *definitely* finish the report today." If you must work closely with a Gemini, get used to the roller coaster.

They are generally not ambitious, preferring instead to remain free from the constraints of overtime, heavy commitments, and responsibilities. Geminis usually do remain somewhat cool and detached. You can get to know a Gemini very easily, but to *really* get inside the Gemini heart, mind, and soul is very difficult, something very few co-workers will succeed in doing.

These people can do just about anything—their talents are multitudinous and they know a little about almost everything. From fixing a desk lamp to knowing how to handle a difficult personality, they are up to any challenge, as long as it can be resolved quickly.

Geminis will also know an awful lot about their business associates. This communicator knows the personalities, eccentricities, talents, and histories of one hundred and one co-workers. You'll be entertained as you gather the information. Need to ask the super of the building for a favor but don't know how to approach this key person? Ask a Gemini. You'll find that your co-worker will be on a first-name basis with an enormous number of people, many of whom will owe a favor to your mercurial friend.

Geminis are often kind and generous. Because they like to keep busy, they often volunteer to help. If they can do it *now,* they probably will. If the promise is for tomorrow, chances are it could be forgotten. A Gemini promise has a fifty-fifty chance of being broken. Some of this sign are more reliable and grounded than others; you'll just have to get to know a particular Gemini co-worker well to find out for yourself. And don't hesitate to remind the twins—they'd love to hear from you!

Geminis are so quick-witted and personable, they're the perfect people to take along to meetings. They can easily entertain clients, customers, and associates, and they speak intelligently on a wide range of topics. Generally diplomatic and often quite persuasive, Geminis can often get the most stubborn persons to change their minds simply by rephrasing a proposal.

When working in partnership with the twins, you'll find easy cooperation. Geminis don't usually make a big deal about anything, are adaptable to circumstance, and will agree to go along with the majority. They will always provide a rational take on the subject or problem at hand and can come up with any number of solutions to a particular problem, able to discuss the pros and cons of each.

Because Geminis are easily bored, they may prove to be unreliable on long-term independent projects. Always check up on their progress! If you wind up working with a particularly slippery or unresponsive Gemini, it can help to actually sit down and do the work together.

The final flaw in the twins' character is that they can talk too much. You may find your co-worker prefers to chatter aimlessly rather than get the work done. Yet Geminis are not usually forceful, and gentle nudgings can quiet them down. Or try to split up the responsibilities to make a task more interesting to the Gemini temperament. Most of them will love phone work, talking to others, seeking new information, skimming documents, or writing. And they must have variety, above all else.

Unhappy or disinterested Gemini co-workers can tread water without getting anything accomplished. They may concentrate on criticism and socializing at the workplace. And the negative side of Gemini charm can turn some into con men or calculating manipulators. Even the nicest Geminis can sometimes be flighty, impatient, and argumentative.

Yet these people are for the most part so likable, you'll easily forgive them their faults. Like a breath of fresh air, a Gemini can make you feel alive again. This sign knows that life shouldn't be taken too seriously and especially not *work!* Accept the twins as they are, don't be upset if they forget to say "hi" one morning when they're in a mood, and don't restrain their effervescent spirits too much. You'll find you'll have a stimulating friend, an entertaining cohort, and an endless supply of information in your Gemini co-worker. Have fun!

The Gemini Boss: Dynamic Duo

Geminis who become bosses have gotten there not because they are such good supervisors, but because they're good at what they do and understand exactly what all their employees are up to. Your supervisor will probably restlessly ramble about the workplace, chatting with one, arguing with another, but ultimately finding out what's being done. The Gemini curiosity will be very evident in those with power. There will be many questions to routinely answer, so always be on your toes. The what, where, when, how, and why of your current project will be probed by your boss to ascertain just what's going on.

STAR SUCCESS

Don't let the Gemini inquisitive streak fool you into thinking your supervisor is a control freak. Far from it. Gemini executives are very easy to work with because they adapt the system to what their employees can deliver, give ample opportunity for you to give more, and let you work without restriction or pressure. These smart folks know better than to try to change you but may give you enough rope to hang yourself if you're not careful!

Gemini supervisors won't play favorites, although they may have employees whose conversation they prefer. They're objective intellectuals at heart and base their decisions on nothing but the facts. If you ever break into the personnel files, you'd find all of their employee reviews to be equally cool, accurate, and unbiased. You'll be evaluated on your fitness for the job, your ability, work habits, and performance. Geminis like variety, and your sex, race, religion, or ethnic background will generally be ignored in terms of evaluation but will be appreciated on a personal level because of the added diversity they give the workplace. Neither autocrats nor powerbrokers, Geminis respect everyone equally as individuals and believe in the democratic theory—the majority makes the decision.

Long hours picking up the pieces or finalizing projects are not for this supervisor, who prefers to have trusted managers run the shop. This is someone who will not be tied down. You'll probably find your Gemini boss leaving with the gang when the clock strikes five, or maybe earlier; these people have active social lives and probably several hobbies for good measure.

Your Gemini boss will no doubt have a brilliant, analytical capacity, which is usually evident from their brisk manner and fluent speech. Your workplace will probably be a flurry of activity which may send you reeling, especially if you are a more sedate sign like Taurus, Cancer, or Scorpio. Your supervisor, on the other hand, can clearly see how all the cogs fit together to provide a functioning whole.

This executive will be a restless soul, not able or willing to sit behind a desk for long hours. He or she is better suited to evaluate propositions, attend meetings and conferences, or come up with new ideas, rather than study the payroll ledger. Gemini supervisors can get the information they need at a glance and will skim the *Wall Street Journal* in a matter of minutes for the key facts, figures, and trends they're interested in. Gemini will also welcome inquiries.

While most Geminis have a variety of interests in life, including career, the rare "all for work" Gemini can be difficult to keep up with. If you have this type of boss, you'll find that your supervisor produces an incredible amount of work in a short period of time. Do your best to keep up but don't be afraid to suggest the hiring of additional permanent or temporary employees if the workload gets to be too much.

Geminis can change their minds, moods, and ideas very quickly. Gemini Walt Whitman said, "I am vast. I contain multitudes." A secretary was exasperated with her Gemini boss's reworking of proposals. He'd change a sentence in one version and then change it back in the next. Thankfully in these technological times computers are more quickly responsive to the Gemini change of opinion.

These people like variety and change. You may find that your Gemini boss routinely moves the furniture around in the executive suite, but you'll probably be more disconcerted when your department's location or schedule is next on the hit list. Changes are no big deal to a Gemini, and you should get used to them. Your work schedule may be changed as a matter of course; equipment, systems, and procedures will often be in a state of flux. They'll be keeping up with current developments in the firm and will probably provide for greater organization and efficiency. But if you've become attached to regular ways of doing things, you'll just have to get used to making changes.

You'll also have to get used to your boss's unpredictable behavior. Be aware of his or her particular eccentricities and avoid close contact when the Gemini pendulum swings the wrong way!

Because the twins don't often stand still, it may be difficult to find them when you need to. And when you've found your boss physically, it can be even more difficult to get his or her undivided attention. While you can pop in on most of these easy-going people without an appointment, getting a Gemini to pay attention to your problems for ten minutes could be a near impossibility if your boss is a busy type.

Be prepared to get the most out of your boss by clearly outlining in your mind the problem at hand. Don't risk boredom by reciting the whole history and details—get right to the important facts. Try to be clear, concise, and quick. Assume that your boss's mind is way ahead of you. Be entertaining when you can to keep the Gemini attention. You should then receive a fast and direct answer. If you actually have an interesting mental problem to solve, your boss may become so involved that he or she will actually do it for you in about half the time it would've taken!

When asking for time off or a raise, remember that your supervisor is rational and objective. Geminis can't really be talked into things that don't make sense and won't be emotionally swayed. But they're not tight with money either and are more generous than not. Try to catch your boss in a good mood, make some scintillating conversation, or tell a few jokes if you're good at it (Geminis love humor). But don't take too long with the preliminaries or your supervisor may skip out the door before you've gotten to the point!

There really should be some hard facts you can point out to support your query. Don't be put off by double talk—if your boss wants to avoid the subject, there are one thousand and one ways to do this. You may be agreeing it's not a good idea before you realize it! Keep your wits about you and keep to the subject at hand; if you've been doing your job you'll probably be successful.

For all their inconsistencies, Gemini bosses are easy to work for because they allow you to have the freedom to do what you do best. Add to that an entertaining, charming personality and a light-hearted attitude, and you'll probably agree to stay with this supervisor for some time.

Gift Ideas for Gemini

Geminis enjoy gifts that appeal to their intelligence and communicative nature. Anything that's fun, novel, entertaining, and light will attract the Gemini. If you can find a gift that makes a good conversation piece as well, it'll be all a Gemini ever wanted! Geminis usually prefer things on the small side.

For the home or office, consider a bookcase or book shelves, book light, magazine rack, word processor or accessories, fax or answering machine, calculator, long phone cord, alarm clock, compact tape recorder, portable radio or cassette player, electric pencil sharpener, rolodex, letter opener, date book, calendar, Filo fax, box of greeting cards, or audio cassettes.

Geminis love to read but like short and light subjects. Buy them a dictionary, thesaurus, book of short stories, trivia, jokes, crossword puzzles, cartoons, or brain teasers. A magazine subscription is also a good idea. Maps and travel guides make good choices for these people, who like to see many different places.

Geminis have extensive social lives and tickets for an evening out would be appreciated. They'd enjoy concerts, theater, musicals, comedies, lectures, museums, and car racing. Some other fun events for Gemini include tickets to a scavenger hunt or audience participation theater.

Games and hobbies often pique the Gemini curiosity.

STAR SUCCESS

They'd be pleased to receive Scrabble, Trivial Pursuit, picture puzzles, and handicraft sets like crocheting, knitting, hooking, woodworking, or painting. Or buy a miniature train set, toy racing cars, model airplane, boat kit, or computer games for your Gemini friend.

Geminis lead active lives and often have an interest in sports, usually those involving other people. You can purchase a tennis racket, badminton set, pool table, golf equipment, table tennis set, horseshoe game, or croquet set for a Gemini. Or try roller skates, a ham radio, walkie-talkie, radar detector, or CB radio for the car.

They prefer casual, colorful, sporty, or trendy clothes in lemon yellow, slate blue, green, and violet. A pair of running shoes also makes a great Gemini gift.

Gemstones ruled by Gemini include agate, green topaz, watermelon tourmaline, and yellow citrine. When choosing jewelry, remember that Geminis prefer small and delicate objects. A ring, bracelet, cufflinks, cigarette lighter, and watch with alarm all make good gifts for this sign.

Flowers that Geminis would enjoy are lily of the valley, yellow jasmine, camellia, lavender, and bittersweets. Or purchase a mixed bouquet. Scents for Geminis should be light, airy, or abstract.

These people love to travel and are always on the go. Consider a travel case, overnight duffel or tote bag, driving gloves, sunglasses, briefcase, manicure set, travel clock, travel iron, or portable games.

CANCER

June 21 to July 23

The Cancer Co-worker: Family Affair

It's important to remember that your Cancerian co-workers are reserved and often shy individuals who need to be treated with care. These people are very sensitive emotionally, at times overly so, and you'll avoid a lot of hurt feelings and misunderstandings if you remember this. Cancers can appear stand-offish or even cold, but this is only because they are not easily able to get to know or feel comfortable with other people.

Loud, boisterous types will put Cancer the crab off, as will those who are presumptuous or come on too strong with cheeky remarks or ribald jokes. When Cancerians feel put off, they'll withdraw into their emotional shells. They can also be extremely self-conscious; if you want to make friends with them, don't poke fun or draw attention to their shortcomings. Their reserve is most often obvious in groups—in meetings they will often "clam up" if not used to the people or situation.

Cancer workers need harmonious surroundings and will do all they can to encourage a nice atmosphere. However, their own moodiness may produce just the opposite at the workplace. These people can be up one minute and depressed the next. It's usually impossible to predict their emotional swings. If you can avoid being influenced by this behavior, so much the better. You can encourage them toward evenness with your own consistent up-beat attitude.

Cancerians can be sweet, sentimental, and even motherly at work, whatever their sex! They like to create family circles and when they're comfortable will usually be a joy to have around. These are the people that bake cookies for the crowd or bring M&Ms for the receptionist's desk. They'll be protective of those they're attached to and can be loyal and endearing to associates they care for. Often insecure, all Cancerians can benefit from the nurturing attention of those about them.

Your Cancer associates are collectors—of facts, memories, and things, as well as people. When the supply room is out of pens, paper, or what-have-you, ask a Cancer. You'll find this co-worker will have all the necessary supplies to avoid getting caught short. You may also be politely reminded to return that pencil you borrowed!

This collect-a-mania can pose problems for those near Cancers at work. So much stuff! Their files, desks, or lockers will be loaded with things that others will view as junk. They don't like to throw anything out and may overflow onto surrounding areas with files, piles, boxes, and bags of who knows what? Well, whatever it is, it's extremely important to the Cancer individual, who will be quite upset at any aggressive attempts on your part to do away with it.

If you have a special project to do with a Cancerian, try to be sympathetic and helpful above all. Sugar-coat any direct criticism, as Cancerians are extremely sensitive to critiques and anything that will make them feel ridiculed. Your Cancer friend may also be a little bit on the low side of energy levels. Yet if you've developed a rapport (this usually takes some time), the crustacean will prove to be a considerate, cooperative worker who'll do a good share of the job. Cancer people think that everyone else is as sensitive as they are, you see, so they'll go out of their way to show support. And while they may be somewhat slow at accomplishing things, they are steady and will get much more done when working at their own pace.

Deadlines may frighten these people, so try not to put direct pressure on them. Reassurance works much better. "Don't worry, we have plenty of time" will soothe jangled Cancerian nerves, but you may have to step up *your* output at the same time! Just remember that Cancerians are not at their best when under pressure and can become confused, unhappy, and anxiety-ridden in such situations.

They ordinarily dislike having to work late or being taken off a regular schedule. If you're open, it can help to give the Cancerian the option of when to schedule meetings, conference calls, errands, or appointments away from the workplace.

Unhappy Cancerians make miserable co-workers. They can brood, drag, and idle away time gazing out a window or into space. They need to keep in touch with their families and may spend endless time on the phone if they or important relatives are feeling low. Remind them *gently* that you need those reports and offer some advice on their problems. Cancers are always much more cooperative with those they feel warmly toward, and they'll feel warmly toward you if you give them emotional support and personal attention.

If you're working with a Cancer who has a negative attitude, or if you're not doing *your* share of the workload, be prepared for a slow and tortuous response. Cancerians will complain ad infinitum when in discomfort or upset. They can nag and harp at you until you do what they feel you should. It is a little childish, but it usually has the looked-for result. You'll eventually say, "I'll do it, I'll do it, just shut up already!" Forceful and direct Aries, Leo, Scorpio, and Sagittarius people should especially avoid losing their temper with Cancer co-workers. They'll resent you for a long time to come, and you'll have further problems dealing with them.

Cancerians have many positive qualities that you can seek out to help in your job. They have excellent memories and can recall people, names, faces, and facts. Those "collection" tendencies generally ensure that they'll have a full Rolodex as well. And among all those piles that you thought were junk, the Cancer will probably be able to dig out just the thing that you threw away last month and now need desperately.

As Cancers live in an emotional world, they often have accurate impressions of others. You may think Mr. X is jovial and hardworking, but your co-worker can tell you right away he's a blowhard and slipshod, something you wouldn't find out for several months.

So be nice. Be diplomatic. Be *sensitive*. Once you develop a friendship with your Cancer associate, you'll find a person who is warm, generous, supportive, and loyal.

The Cancer Boss: All My Children

"You're ruining my life!" the Cancer boss angrily shouted before he slammed down the phone. Would you believe the conversation was with a messenger service? This incident illustrates Cancer tendencies at their worst. There's the supersensitivity, anxiety, and blowing a little thing out of proportion. And there's also the habit of taking everything too personally.

Most Cancer bosses don't rant and rave all the time, but they *are* feeling people and can let their feelings get the better of them. Don't provoke a Cancer boss who's in a mood because it'll only end badly. You'll get to know pretty quickly when one of these moods is on. If an upset

Cancer isn't throwing a temper tantrum, he or she will probably be brooding or sulking in a remote silence. Leave them be.

Somehow Cancerians in positions of power seem to let it all go more than employees of this sign would. Whatever the case may be, do your best not to be the target of one of these rages. Don't press issues that seem to aggravate your boss, or you'll be the one to ignite the fuse. Try at all times to keep up a pleasant demeanor and supportive and helpful manner.

The positive side of these emotional beings is that they're wonderfully sympathetic and caring and can have insight into their employees' thoughts and feelings. Cancers are usually warm individuals who don't like to take advantage of others. While they may often appear childlike, they will act the parent role the rest of the time. If you do your job and have a good attitude, you'll be taken care of. The Cancer boss can be downright motherly, making sure everyone is feeling right, eating right, and taking care of personal business. In larger companies, Cancerian supervisors will look out for those under their charge, assuring employees a reasonable workload, promised days off, and full benefits owed.

Positive Cancer bosses usually cover up their softhearted manner with a businesslike, mainstream appearance. They are ambitious and want career and financial security above all else, and they usually have a good idea of the firm's market, ability to move ahead, and future outlook. Cancerians don't take bold risks but make progress in smaller steps over time. They'll retrench and go "lean and mean" before they lose any money. Make sure you're not the one who gets laid off. Cancerians absolutely hate to be the cause of others losing their jobs, but if a decision has to be made and you're not pulling your weight . . . well, you're the fat to be trimmed.

Be aware that your supervisor will remember everything you say or do, as well as your attitude. Try to become someone your boss likes to have around. If the boss is pressed for time and needs you to help, offer assistance. If someone must work late, volunteer. The Cancer will remember you as the one who helped the team out when the chips were down, and this could be to your benefit come review time.

If you're looking for an excuse *not* to work late or to take a day off, Cancerians do sympathize with personal obligations. There is usually no need to make up an outrageous lie for a Cancer boss. If you have to get home because of family obligations, your supervisor will understand.

Cancerian bosses are at times uncertain and insecure but will usually not ask for help in decision-making. Be supportive, and if you feel you have better solutions, offer them with tact. These supervisors aren't "full of themselves," as many can be; they're looking to make the most money in the most efficient way possible. Make sure your suggestions don't criticize. Grace and diplomacy are generally needed in working with a Cancerian to come to a joint decision.

Cancers like to oversee the work and will take charge in a quiet way. They don't order others about; that isn't their style. They may be exacting, though, so make sure the work is up to par. If you're not doing your bit, even a Cancerian supervisor will resort to nagging and carping. They may also complain to you about others, and you may at times feel torn in your loyalties. A good solution is to be sympathetic to your boss's *feelings* while not actually coming down specifically on the co-worker. Cancerians can at times appreciate mediation as well. Be careful how far you go when intervening in problems of this type, however. If it doesn't work out well, your boss will have a tendency to blame *you*. A heartfelt "I don't think I should get involved" may be appropriate in some sticky situations, and the Cancerian will understand.

In general, Cancer is unprogressive and likes to cling to the old ways of doing things. If you can prove that your innovations will result in financial growth, you've taken the surest step in getting your supervisor to move ahead.

Cancerian bosses are notorious penny-pinchers, so you may get less of a raise than you expected, or you may have to ask for one. If over a year goes by with no offer, it's time to ask. Appeal to the Cancer's sympathy, emotions, and feelings. Hopefully, your boss already likes you personally. If not, you may be out of luck. Yet if you can point out how much more efficiently you're doing your job than a year ago, how much more responsibility you've taken on lately, or how much business you've brought in, you're more likely to get that raise. Ask for a specific amount, too, as a Cancer will probably offer less than you should get!

Get to know your Cancer boss and become a supportive member of the team. The atmosphere can get a little dicey at times, but in the long run you'll have an individual who cares about *you*. And you'll probably also have a safe, secure job for many years to come.

Gift Ideas for Cancer

Cancerians are warm individuals who will be touched by your gifts. If they're really struck by your thoughtfulness, their eyes may fill up with emotion, and they won't know what to say.

If you'd like to buy a book for a Cancerian, make it moving or family-oriented. Those old tearjerkers are perfect for these people, as are collector's manuals, history books, cookbooks, and those on decorating, home furnishing, or landscaping. Time-Life household-project books would be ideal for many a Cancer, as are romances or melodramas.

Most Cancers have strong ties to the home, which is their haven away from work. Decorative objects with useful purposes like ashtrays, vases, crystalware, candlesticks, linens, blankets, and quilts would be enjoyed by Cancerians. They'd also love a diary, camera, camcorder, picture frames, or photo albums for snapshots of their loved ones.

Home appliances are also good ideas, especially if they combine with the Cancer's love of food. Try crepe, waffle, or pancake irons, juicers, blenders, yogurt or ice-cream makers, and food processors. Bakeware is also a good choice.

Yes, Cancer loves to eat and would appreciate foods, especially those that are sweet or doughy. Buy baskets or boxes of cakes, cookies, chocolates, or petits fours for them. Rich foods like fine cheeses, lobster, caviar, lox, or gourmet pastas can also make nice gifts for a Cancer. (Make sure your friend is not on a diet, though!)

Tickets for a cozy dinner for two or the theater, such as a romantic comedy, musical, melodrama, or historic plays would be appropriate. Or tickets for attending a museum, aquarium, or movie would be appreciated, too.

Jewelry should be delicate, small, and tasteful. Cancerians would especially like silver, moonstone, pearl, milky opal, or crystal.

Think light and soft for cologne as well as flowers. Cancer rules all lilies and white flowers, as well as wildflowers. Potted plants or seeds can be good, too, as Cancers like to nurture gardens.

Gifts of clothing for Cancerians should be soft, comfortable, and snuggable. These could include robes, sweaters, slippers, scarves, and gloves in white, pale green, and light gray colors.

Many Cancerians are collector-hobbyists, so you can add to their collections of coins, stamps, autographs, or books. Hummel figurines are excellent for many because of their emphasis on simple domestic life. Some

Cancerians may enjoy Norman Rockwell-type prints or plates.

They love to spend time with the family, so games geared to this are also a good idea. Trivial Pursuit, Monopoly, or any of them, really, are excellent choices, as are videotapes, which the whole family can enjoy.

LEO

July 22 to August 24

The Leo Co-worker: Life of the Party

Your Leo co-workers have firm handshakes and will always be the first to introduce themselves to new associates. Warm, outgoing, and gregarious, they are usually very "put together," especially in business situations. These people often judge others and their positions from their appearance; subtle power struggles are beyond their understanding. They always need to be the center of attention in some way, to prove to others and themselves that they are important and in control. They also have a dramatic flair, able to make even the most insignificant trip to the deli for a sandwich sound like an epic adventure when retold.

The Leonine trait of always being personally involved in everything they do causes this behavior. It's also the reason for their often magnanimous natures: Leos want to do good, whatever they perceive it to be. They'll try to take pride in any task they're asked to accomplish.

Leos are just what they appear to be. Open and straightforward, they won't plot, scheme, or hold grudges against others at the workplace. They generally do mean well, want to be well-liked, and are real softies at heart. If you apologize for whatever mistakes you've made, Leos can't help but forgive and forget—even if they still believe *you* were wrong!

Leos like to have a good time and can indulge in gossip and office romances more than the average co-worker. The excitement and drama inherent in these activities is what attracts them. Even the hardest-working Leo will often enjoy lunch, dinner, and after-work drinks with associates. You'll find them lively and fun on these occasions, as they really know how to relax and have a good time.

You'll soon notice that Leos like to talk about themselves. In some cases, this is the *only* topic of conversation! You may have to interrupt forcefully to present your side of the story. Although business discussions can be somewhat one-sided, if you're firm and stick to what *you've* got to say, you'll end up in a lively exchange.

People of this sign like to stick to their guns. They will rise to the challenge of tough competition, so your dialogue could eventually get out of hand, especially if you're another of the stubborn signs like Taurus, Scorpio, or Aquarius. Leos will maintain their opinions as a point of honor and really do believe they're right. They often have a hard time understanding others' points of view, too. While you can always agree to disagree, shake hands, and go your separate ways, most business situations are not so easily handled. You can try to convince the Lion, but the tougher the competition, the more Leo will resist the opposing view. Although aggravated by continued opposition, Leos on a certain level actually *enjoy* this kind of sporting showdown and will be in no hurry to resolve the issue.

Probably the most successful way around stubborn Leos is to prevail on their good nature. Compromise is difficult for these people, but if you can allow the lion to save face by utilizing some key Leo points in the final decision, this will go a long way toward a compromise.

Whereas signs like Aries, Sagittarius, and Aquarius have their own points of honor and will not like to stoop to manipulations of flattery and admiration, they are the only sure-fire ways to the lion's heart. Suffice it to say that if you do appreciate and admire your Leo co-worker, don't hesitate to say so! These people love and need recognition, acceptance, and support. If you like them, they'll like you—it's that simple. Leos can often be caught hanging around with undesirables for this very reason.

In meetings Leo co-workers will want to take center stage, and you'll again have to force yourself to get in your points. Don't insult these naive co-workers with preplanned group opposition or trickery to dupe them. You may have your way for the moment, but your associate will later want to win back the lead more than ever and can become much more competitive than before.

Any Leo will appreciate up-front dealings. Try to get around direct opposition from this person by emphasizing such phrases as "your work is always so thorough" or "you usually know what's right" before coming to the big "but maybe we should do it my way." Leos usually do try hard to resolve conflicts and don't like to let go of a problem till it's solved. If you genuinely try to work things out in a friendly manner, you're more likely to be successful with them.

Leo co-workers also like to tell others what to do, and if they're not your superiors, this can be hard to take sometimes. They just can't see why you wouldn't always want to do things their way! Try to make light of this whenever possible, and explain your own point of view as clearly as you can. While you could eventually find the lion's nudgings irritating or even obnoxious, remember that this co-worker is only trying to help you.

Leos will dive enthusiastically into special projects, and if you're assigned to work with one, it could be both stimulating and enjoyable for you. They need to prove themselves and take action, and you'll find the job will usually get done in a very conscientious manner. But if your Leo friend hates the project, the job, or resents *you*, that stubbornness will once again creep in. Your coworker might spend much of your meeting time chatting about wind surfing, last week's date, or the attributes of the latest celebrity cologne. Try appealing to the lion's innate pride in these cases. Negative Leos could call you "no fun" or a "bad sport," but if they realize *they* will look bad if the job isn't done well, you'll have more cooperative co-workers.

Leos are typically generous, and if you need assistance on any task, they'll be happy to help. You've flattered them by acknowledging they know enough to help out, you see. Even the most overworked of Leos will usually lend a hand; it makes them feel good to aid others, especially people they like. Remember to thank them profusely for all they've done, and you'll quickly have a loyal friend on the job.

They may talk too much and may at times be lazy, but Leos are certainly a lot of fun to have around. Your workplace would probably be a lot duller without them!

The Leo Boss: Hail to the Chief!

So you've got a Leo boss: You'll probably work harder, play harder, and at times resent this person more than anyone you've ever known. Leos in charge can be demanding and uncooperative. This sign really knows what power is all about and won't easily let you forget it!

Symbolized by the lion, king of the jungle, the dignity and self-confidence of the Leo personality find their greatest expression in leadership. Leo bosses can be generous with both their time and the company's funds. They don't understand pettiness and will back up their smallest argument with broad ideals and principles.

But they are detail-oriented, too, and will want to know about *everything* that goes on under their supervision. They have the ability to run a business efficiently but can at times produce a stifling atmosphere by wanting too much control. If you do your job well and have a good attitude, you'll probably have no problems. You'll find your boss supportive, protective, and loyal. A good Leo supervisor can delegate responsibility and create a well-oiled machine by utilizing the strengths of all employees. He or she will infuse others with enthusiasm and will receive genuine admiration and respect.

People born under this sign like to remind everyone that they are in charge. This can be done by issuing commands or by dressing elegantly and formally. They love the perks of a gorgeous office with a stereo system, bar, and big upholstered couches and chairs. The desk must be bigger and better than anyone else's, with a chair to match and, if possible, an imposing scenic view. They'll take great pride and enjoyment in driving the company car, or may even have a chauffeur. If they want to be called "Mr." or "Ms.," make sure you do so: Even if you've developed a real friendliness with them, many Leos feel these honorifics demonstrate your respect for their authority.

If Leo supervisors don't feel they're getting proper respect from employees, they will do everything possible to put them in their place. Highly conscious of the power structure, they will be assertive about reminding everyone that they are a part of it. Rule number one in working for a Leo boss is: Remember who's in charge. Show deference and appreciation. If you disagree, arrange for a private meeting and be tactful but open in your conversation. Your Leo boss will appreciate that you had enough respect and honesty to discuss the matter in a civilized way.

Think of your Leo boss as a father figure, regardless of age or sex. Leo likes to give advice. If you're having a problem and want to solve it, the Leo is your perfect foil. Your supervisor will be supportive, protective, and encouraging to those who show proper respect.

Ambitious and driven, Leo superiors will work you hard and demand excellence. Yes, they will ask you to do things that they wouldn't do themselves, but they will never ask you to do something they don't believe in. Even the most difficult worker will be given a second and third chance if a Leo really believes they're trying to give the job their all.

Leos can have bad tempers and will not be shy about expressing their disgust if they feel an employee has behaved in an underhanded or unfair manner. If you're the victim of a Leo's outrage, *apologize*. Agree. This works wonders. Your Leo boss will find it more chivalrous if you admit your mistakes and promise to do better than if you try to make excuses.

Leos who have negative attitudes and hold positions of power can become domineering and arrogant, demanding that everything go their way. They may be overly impressed with social status and appearance and treat those low on the totem pole severely. They can play favorites and may be swayed by yes-men and flatterers, while being oblivious to the faults of those they like. Some Leo bosses can also rest while everyone else does all the work. But let's face it, where else can you get such obedience if not from those whose salary you pay?

If you're doing your share in good faith, you'll probably get that raise or bonus. Don't be ashamed about asking for one either, as this person appreciates your candor. You'll have to prove yourself, though, so make sure you have a list of the accomplishments to back up your claim.

If the company's large, there will probably be a regular time for reviews. Don't try to usurp this policy. But if your boss forgets, a polite reminder should be all it takes, as Leos feel obligated to fulfill promises. Don't expect it all to be easy-going. While you may be taking home more money next week, you'll also have to work for it. The Leo boss will pull no punches about your problems or performance. Do your best to correct anything the boss points out. If you disagree, *explain* why; you'll probably still need to change in the end, but you will feel better for at least airing your views.

A Leo businessperson may sacrifice showing affection in order to run an efficient shop. If you remember that your Leo boss would really rather be a king or queen and can behave in that manner, you'll probably develop a long and enjoyable business relationship!

Gift Ideas for Leo

Leos love the excitement of getting presents. As they are talkative and open, many people at the workplace will be aware of their personal tastes, needs, and wants. Remember to make the gift special in some way—not necessarily expensive, but showy. And the more personal, the better the Leo will like it. *Any* gifts are appreciated by this warm, fiery sign, but Leos like celebrations and events, and it can be important to make an impression with your choice.

Most Leos are too busy leading their active lives to read a great deal, but coffee-table or photography books are potentially suitable. Books about theater, sports, and entertainment companies or stars will also be enjoyed. Romance, melodrama, gaming, and parenting books are all good choices for Leos, too.

Leo natives enjoy a night out on the town, so tickets for an evening's entertainment are a nice idea. They'll likely enjoy attending the theater a concert, Ice Capades, comedy club, fireworks show, sporting event, casino, or even the circus.

If you'd like to buy clothing for a Leo, think sophisticated. For women, silks, satins, and beaded blouses and sweaters will be greatly admired. The old stand-by tie for men can be made more appropriate for Leos by choosing brighter colors with coordinated pocket handkerchiefs. Leo men and women enjoy things that set them apart from the crowd, like a silk evening scarf or personalized sports gear. Leo colors are warm yellow, orange, and red.

Bouquets are loved by many Leos, and gladioli, marigold, zinnia, tiger lily, and yellow tea rose can be special favorites. They prefer jasmine and rose scents.

Jewelry is generally appropriate for both Leo men and women, as they tend to like large and ornate decorations. If the office needs to buy a special gift for a Leo man, a diamond ring or cufflinks would be ideal. Gold or gold-toned jewelry is most appropriate, and Leo rules the gemstones amber, topaz, golden opal, yellow jade, and gold quartz. Leo women like big earrings and pendants and will appreciate whimsical brooches. Style is more important to them than quality.

Many Leos enjoy recreation, and gifts relating to their favorite activities can be good choices. Sunglasses or a monogrammed sports bag or jogging suit will be used often. For more expensive gifts, a tennis racket, golf bag, golf clubs, or bowling ball should be considered. For the Leo who loves to see it all, field glasses, binoculars, or a telescope are also good choices.

Leo people like to enjoy themselves, and fun gifts like games or even toys will be enjoyed. Try an ornate deck of cards, gambling chips, dice, or other games of chance. Computer games like Leisure Suit Larry or Wheel of Fortune can be entertaining, as can almost any gag gift.

Other good gifts for Leos include anything monogrammed or personalized, especially glassware, stationery, or grooming sets. Decorative jewelry boxes, gold-plated picture frames, good cologne in fresh scents, grooming tools and accessories like manicure sets, a blow dryer, hair-curling set, or high-quality brushes and combs to tame the leonine mane will all be gladly accepted by your Leo co-worker. Additional possibilities include gift certificates for a make-over, massage, or photo session.

VIRGO

August 23 to September 24

The Virgo Co-worker: Workaholic

Your Virgo co-workers may brush and floss their teeth regularly in the washroom after lunch and can stay home at the first hint of a cold. But their prudent sense of health and hygiene extends to their work, one of the few things that are of equal importance to Virgos. They make pleasant, likable companions at the workplace and can be helpful and supportive co-workers.

Virgos usually just *work*. They are very responsible about the duties entrusted to them and will put in a lot of time and effort to get things done to perfection. They are usually quiet and reserved, as they put more emphasis on the work than on socializing. You'll rarely see them engaging in idle chitchat, and they can be brusque if you want to talk when they've got work to do!

Modest and unassuming (some may even exhibit shyness), they are approachable and easy to talk to. They'll gravitate to individuals rather than groups and will usually go out of their way *not* to attract attention.

When you get to know them, you'll find your Virgo co-workers witty conversationalists. They have excellent minds and are quite discriminating. They see people, things, and situations for what they really are. Trappings, clever facades, and put-ons will never fool a bright Virgo who knows who's who and what's what.

Virgos seek high quality in whatever they do. They won't move themselves from the tasks at hand for just *anyone,* and if they ask for your advice or suggestions, they must really respect you. Virgos seek out intelligent, interesting individuals with whom they can enjoy stimulating discussion.

These co-workers have excellent perception and notice even the smallest details. Nothing will escape their keen scrutiny and shrewd analysis. They have a wry sense of humor, but more often their criticisms and summations of people and situations are so frank that they'll inspire laughter without intending to. Virgo Senator Daniel Inouye's muttering during the Watergate hearings "what a liar" after John Ehrlichmann's testimony is a fine example. Simple, concise, and personally felt, Virgos have a knack for understating the obvious.

Virgos will routinely offer suggestions and criticism. This is one of their few real compulsions; they're so keenly aware of trying to improve that they want to get everyone to do their best. Although the delivery may not always be pleasant, Virgo criticism is generally meant to be constructive. Try and overlook the fact that the advice was unsolicited. If you're of a more sensitive disposition, like Cancer, Pisces, or Scorpio, take solace in the knowledge that Virgos mean well and realize that the comments are far from personal. They'll criticize everyone, including the boss!

There's real value in Virgo observations, and if you can take some of their advice, you'll often find it fruitful. If you're hopelessly lost in a messy desk, disorganized routine, or red tape, ask a Virgo to help sort things out. This associate will be happy to do so, and you'll soon realize how easy it is to maintain orderly habits. Virgos understand how little things can add up to big results.

They believe in the sagacity of the old adage "For want of a nail the shoe was lost, for want of a shoe the horse was lost, for want of a horse the rider was lost."

Some Virgos can be walking drugstores, so intent are they on maintaining their health. Besides the toothbrush and toothpaste, they probably have a first-aid kit, Tylenol (never aspirin—too hard on the stomach), antacid tablets, vitamins, breath mints, chewing gum, and a laxative in their locker or desk drawer. Now you know who to go to if you need any of these items. They may also have sewing kits, safety pins, and a change of underwear and stockings on hand as well.

Perhaps their greatest strength is in knowing how to help those in need. Virgos handle emergencies with the same calm composure they do anything else. In times of crisis, they'll save the day with their dedication, know-how, and service. Depend on them to come through when you need them.

But don't rely on Virgos too much, and don't take advantage of their kindness. Most Virgos know how to "just say no" when put in an intolerable situation. While they'll help you out often, there will come a point when your co-worker will realize you're not doing enough work yourself. Virgos have no sympathy for associates who don't exert themselves, and they will hasten the demise of lazy co-workers by forcing them to accept the results of their own irresponsible behavior.

Overall, these people are wonderful to work with. They are adaptable, will do their best, and will follow and work with those who take the lead. They will always do their share, if not more than their share. If you're working on a project together, they'll be organized and systematic about getting the job done right.

In working closely with a Virgo, prepare yourself for some practical advice and criticism. Virgos will be vocal but will never be pushy, so although they may feel disgruntled with what they perceive as sloppiness or incomplete work, they won't usually provoke a big conflict.

Virgo people strive for perfection, and some can get carried away. If you're stuck working with a finicky Virgo who insists on redoing a report seventeen times to get the typing perfect, it's time to put your foot down! Overemphasis on perfection can become inefficiency, and you just might point this out, gently. Or give your co-worker a practical talk about how difficult it is to attain perfection in the business world (but make sure it's a practical talk, as Virgos have no use for philosophy).

Virgos make better co-workers than many others, except in those situations where they may show you up! Follow their example, if you can: They are the real workers of the zodiac. If you befriend one, you will have the extra bonus of getting diet and exercise advice and free Alka-Seltzer when you need it!

The Virgo Boss: Nitpicker

Virgo bosses are capable managers who concentrate on the details in order to attain results. Bit by bit, in a systematic way, they will see to it that everyone is working effectively and efficiently to produce a sound product or service. But these people can be quite difficult to work for, primarily because they are so exacting in their work and will demand it of you, too.

Yet Virgo bosses are easy if you follow a few simple steps and do *exactly* what's expected of you. You'll get explicit instructions on what is to be done and how to go about it. Follow these to the letter. If you are unclear as to how to go about something, a Virgo boss will never mind taking the time to explain in more detail so that you fully understand. Make sure you do before beginning any project.

Virgo bosses are straightforward and approachable.

Their goal is to get the job done, and their personalities will never get in the way of their objectives. They can give you a good background on the basics of the business world; if you are lucky enough to have a Virgo boss as your first employer, you will be well prepared for success in the future.

From the orderliness and cleanliness of your supervisor's office, you can learn a lot about the inner person. Virgos are practical and industrious to a fault, setting fine examples for their employees because they work harder and accomplish more than they'll ever expect you to.

Virgo standards and expectations are high, but once again, the specifics are most important, and there are particular guidelines that you can follow to please your boss. Show him or her respect and deference, but don't overdo it. Virgo knows the genuine thing and will never be taken in by flattery or fake compliments.

First of all, listen to the advice and criticisms of your Virgo boss. Try to understand exactly what you should improve and how you're expected to do it. No Virgo will ever hesitate to expand on advice and instructions. Leave your ego at home—your boss, usually upfront and honest, is only helping you to be your best. If you can learn to take criticism constructively, you'll be on your way to becoming a better employee.

Come to work on time and keep yourself busy. Strive for accuracy in all you do. Avoid sweeping generalities and broad opinions, unless you can back them up with facts. Virgos love facts! Listen to what's going on around you, pay attention to deadlines, and make your work presentable. Virgos hate dirty hair and fingernails. Dress conservatively but, most important, neatly. Comb your hair and brush your teeth at lunchtime. If you look squeaky clean you will at least be a prospective candidate for promotion.

Above all, take control of your work habits. Think things through and don't rush yourself. Double-check all that you do for even a minute error. Don't allow yourself to become careless in what you do or say. Bone up on your grammar and maybe invest in a word-a-day book. Better yet, invest in a word-a-day calendar, put it on your desk, and use it to make your self-expression more articulate. Your boss will be impressed by your attempt at self-improvement and may even join you in your studies.

Try to express yourself succinctly whenever possible. When writing letters or reports for your boss's approval, cut, cut, cut! Trim all the fat from your paragraphs and keep only the meat. Virgos don't appreciate flowery language, artsy expressions, or self-aggrandizement. They like clever, exact language.

Develop a good attitude toward your work and cultivate patience and a sense of humor. Virgos demand only that you do your best. Take the time and care to do it right the first time and learn to pay attention to those details that your boss always seems to be a stickler about.

Try to be as orderly and organized as your boss is. We know—it won't be easy! Your supervisor can have that one particular paper you're seeking in hand in a minute, though faced with banks of filing cabinets. Could you do the same? Learn the organization of records available to you well enough so that they work *for* you. Your supervisor will be impressed when you, too, can have that specific document in hand in the blink of an eye.

Virgos know the worth of a good employee, and if you are willing to work for results, you'll do well with this boss. You must prove yourself through dedication and commitment to excellence. Virgos will always be fair in pay, benefits, and vacation time. Check your own records thoroughly before questioning a mistake your supervisor may have made. It is helpful to keep your own records of holidays, vacations, overtime pay, and other compensation. A Virgo boss will always want to see documentation to support your claims.

Be careful when spending company funds, no matter how insignificant the purchase. Make sure you get good value for your money. Always get a receipt! Virgos are sticklers for recordkeeping as well.

Virgo bosses will pay employees exactly what they're worth. Your supervisor knows exactly what your market value is and will pay you just that. Don't expect to get a raise if you haven't improved your output.

Be prepared if you feel it's necessary to request a raise or time off. Your boss knows just what you do well and what your weak points are. Expect a detailed discussion about what you have and haven't done to fulfill expectations. Bring hard evidence of your accomplishments to your meeting. Don't be afraid to refer to a list or memo of all that you've done and explain your assets point by point.

Don't be surprised if your boss takes out a list as well. Be prepared for criticism. If your supervisor is slow to give in to your request, suggest a compromise. Guarantee that you'll improve according to the supervisor's directions in a month or so, and schedule a second performance review at that time. If you try honestly to prove that you can and will do what you claim, your boss will willingly reimburse you for superior service.

Virgos are not sentimental and won't be influenced by sob stories. If you are in a real jam that you couldn't avoid, however, they'll do all they can to help, including advancing you money and giving you time off.

There are a lot of little things that your Virgo employer will concentrate on. But if you pay attention to them, the big things will take care of themselves. You won't get excess praise or kudos from your Virgo supervisor for doing what's expected of you. What you can expect is a good working relationship, respect, and the rewards of knowing you've done your best. What more can you realistically ask for?

Gift Ideas for Virgo

Virgos enjoy gifts of value and usefulness. Don't worry if your budget is small—they enjoy small things and prefer quality to quantity. Choosing a gift that is practical for the home or office is ideal.

Organizational gifts are wonderful, and Virgos will love them (check first to see that your Virgo friend doesn't already have the item). An umbrella stand, bookcase, bookends, file cabinet, computer diskettes, file folders, drawer organizers, blotter, pen and pencil sets, pencil sharpener, bulletin board, magnets to hold notes, Rolodex, note pads, paper clips, stapler, hole punch, datebook, calendar, and letter holder will all be appreciated and useful for home or workplace. For more expensive gifts, the Virgo might enjoy a fax machine, closet organizer, or typewriter.

Virgos always like tools and equipment that help them do things more efficiently. For the home, a bathroom scale, massager or shower massager, facial sauna, heating pad, Water Pik, iron, or steamer are all good choices. Cleaning equipment like a Dustbuster, minivac, or feather duster are useful, as are kitchen utensils, a water purifier, a timer, juicer, electric chopper, blender, vegetable steamer, and yogurt maker.

Many Virgos exercise, so hand or foot weights, a bicycle, or home exercise equipment and accessories are appropriate. The Virgoan interest in gardening may prompt you to purchase hand gardening tools, gloves, or knee pads.

Virgos dress conservatively and like accessories. You might purchase gloves, galoshes, a hat and scarf set, shawl, cotton or wool sweater or vest, briefcase, keyholder, or wallet. Virgo colors are navy blue and earth tones.

Personal and decorative items should also be useful.

Things like a clock or watch, barometer, sewing basket, cheese tray, fruit bowl, trivet, garlic press, nutcracker, food scale, cutting board, bread basket, spice rack, and canisters will all appeal to the practical Virgo nature.

Many Virgos enjoy cultivating plants, so hanging or potted plants, fresh flower arrangements, small shrubs or saplings, planters, terrariums, and herbs or vegetable seeds are all good choices for the Virgo home or workplace. They'd prefer bouquets of hyacinths, asters, forget-me-nots, bachelor's buttons, or blue violets.

Virgos would also enjoy afghans, patchwork quilts, towels, a linen tablecloth, napkins, placemats, coasters, and fireplace logs. Cotton, flannel, or linen sheet sets might also be appropriate.

Virgos generally bathe quite often, so you can buy soaps, bath beads, body lotion, natural shampoos, and manicure sets for them. If your Virgo friend wears cologne or perfume, choose clean, fresh scents as gifts.

Books and videos on cooking, health, diet, exercise, gardening, pets, and household tips, as well as a dictionary or thesaurus would be good choices for Virgos. Tickets to a flower or animal show, health lecture, business seminar, or a spa or gym membership are appropriate. Consider treating the Virgo to a dinner out at a vegetarian or health-food restaurant.

Virgos would appreciate food gifts, but be sure to make them healthy ones, like natural foods, nuts, dried or fresh fruits, spices, and cheeses.

Most Virgo people would prefer delicate, unostentatious jewelry. The stones yellow jasper, carnelian, blue star sapphire, and moss agate are ruled by this sign.

Many Virgo people are active hobbyists. Zero in on your co-worker's specific interest, or choose jigsaw puzzles, crossword puzzles, word games like Scrabble, handicraft or needlework kits, card games, or Mah-Jongg.

LIBRA
September 22 to October 24

The Libra Co-worker: You and Me Together

Libra co-workers are gracious and considerate. They're everyone's ideal of what a refined, cooperative individual should be. Highly aware of the needs of others, they strive for harmony and peace at the workplace.

You'll probably recognize Libra co-workers at a glance. Elegant and sophisticated, they dress in lovely colors, avoiding the flashy, trendy, and plain in favor of pleasing combinations and tastefully appropriate clothes. The corporate version of Libra can make even the standard business suit look like something special!

They need to have people around, and they know just the right thing to say at awkward moments. So the waiter just spilled a whole bowl of pasta and tomato sauce in the big client's lap? Don't worry. If a Libra co-worker is with you, the event will be smoothed over with such finesse that the client will probably remember it as an interlude from *A Midsummer Night's Dream* rather than the most embarrassingly painful moment of a glittering career.

Librans make very pleasant companions at the workplace. Even their small talk has a likability that goes far beyond content. Librans concentrate on the "how" and always make it with decorum. They can talk a lot, but they are also good listeners, instinctively understanding the give and take necessary to a good relationship.

They are outgoing and know how to work at relationships on the job. They need to be liked by all, and their ambition will cause them to network, negotiate, compromise, and smile all day. The number-one Libra credo is: "You must get along with others in order to do business with them." Succeeding corollaries are: "If they enjoy doing business with you, they'll do it again," and "If they like to talk to you, they'll talk to you."

Librans are the "have a nice day" people. And even if you think that saying that phrase regularly is stupid or insipid, there's certainly nothing rude or difficult about it. The speaker is at least making some effort to be nice. And yes, it *can* cheer you up and make you smile, too. Which cashier would *you* rather turn to, the one that said, "Have a nice day" or the one that chided, "You sure don't know how to choose avocados, buddy"?

Librans are cautious not to ruffle anyone's feathers. If you're busy and can't talk, just say so. They'll back off politely and won't take it personally. Understanding and considerate, they have the ability to adjust to others' needs. They'll never be pushy about any business dealings.

Do you understand them yet? Think the "pleasure principle": They want things nice and trouble-free. Librans try to avoid unpleasant, uncomfortable, or distasteful situations. More mature people born under this sign will attempt to make a difficult situation less so by putting up a good front, taking an optimistic attitude, and playing fair. They need to live in a supportive and stress-free atmosphere.

Librans can help disparate factions come together because they believe in the benefits of negotiation and are objective in their views. This makes them wonderful to work with on projects. They'll always do their share and will be cordial to everyone involved. When teaming up with a Libra co-worker, expect to have your talents utilized and your flaws covered.

Librans connect, look good, sound good, and make others feel good. They are civilized and won't be forceful or make scenes. Should this be necessary in order to get the job done, don't expect a Libra to do it! If you're working with a Libran, you'll probably be elected to handle it.

Likewise, more down-to-earth and frankly spoken co-workers will turn Librans off. They are sensitive and easily upset. Approach them on their own terms if you want results.

Try to curb your temper when around Libra co-workers. Flying off the handle with them is a big no-no. They can retreat, and it may be difficult to work well with them again. Anger just doesn't work with these people. While Librans may at times appear to be yea-sayers, they will politely extract themselves from any situation they find too sticky.

Librans can also be indecisive as a result of their need to see every point of view. If you're decisive, you'll probably work well together. But expect a devil's advocate if you ask your co-worker's opinion. Libra loves discussion and balancing different views. You may need to cut this short because of deadlines.

Remember that Librans want to maintain peace at all costs. They will compromise easily but can go to great lengths to guarantee behavior and decisions that they feel will be for the good of all. And Librans can make practically *anything* sound as if it's for the good of all! If you disagree with them, speak up.

In reading Librans, it's especially important to look beyond the facade of cooperation for what's really there. They don't often let down their guard at work and will try to maintain a good relationship with the most difficult co-workers. Don't worry if they're genuine or not, just let the relationship work for you!

Some Librans are such pleasure seekers, they don't like to work at all. They'll concentrate on their love life, spending money, and surrounding themselves with beautiful people and things, especially if they don't enjoy their work. If you need to get some work out of one of these reluctant types, use reasoning, the concept of fairness, and a polite but firm attitude to get results.

Librans in general, though, do much more good than harm. And just like the "have a nice day" cashier, they can often be benign when at their worst. At their best, they're cooperative individuals who can be diligent, ambitious workers, completing projects for the benefit of all concerned. And they're also the perfect people to chat with in idle moments!

The Libra Boss: The Diplomat

Firm but always fair, a Libra boss will understand and accept you as an individual with opinions, talents, and values of your own. Your boss will treat you as a partner in the business, able to combine your talents with those of your co-workers to capably get the job done.

Your supervisor will be friendly and open, encouraging feedback and conversation. You'll probably feel free to share your thoughts with this communicative superior. The Libra boss will solicit opinions from everyone at the workplace in order to come to democratic decisions and policy choices. Yet you'll always feel that your supervisor acts in a businesslike manner; these people don't talk to lay the law down or engage in manipulations but simply to exchange ideas.

Communicating is something they do extremely well. If you see your boss in action on the phone or in meetings, you'll realize that he or she is a master of business negotiations. Libra supervisors will be some of the most polite, well-mannered, and well-meaning of executives.

You won't be shouted at, abused, or scolded by this boss. If and when you make a mistake, you can expect kindness and clarification. Librans will talk *with* you, not *at* you! This in itself is a big relief and change from the autocratic type of supervisor.

You'll find that Libra bosses feel that in business, the relationship is the important thing. They wait, they weigh, they compromise, and they negotiate, but above all they deal fairly and usually get what they want in the end.

Librans gravitate toward people who represent their ideal: those well-spoken and emotionally in control. If you want to be truly accepted by your Libra boss, you'll have to be classy.

Don't raise your voice, don't be forceful, and couch what you say in a friendly manner. Bone up on those old traditional niceties that go beyond "please" and "thank you." Learn what you *should* say and how and when you should say it. Learn the proper use of utensils, especially if you must go to breakfast or lunch meetings. Believe it or not, there are all kinds of social rules about these things that most of us in the nineties were never taught but that Librans instinctively seem to know. These may seem insignificant to you but can make all the difference to your Libra boss.

If you are from Brooklyn, Tennessee, or another area with a strong regional dialect, you may want to take elocution lessons to standardize your speech. Everyone can benefit from learning the proper use of the speaking voice in a well-modulated, soft-spoken, and clear tone.

Cultivate an attractive appearance as well. Pay attention to your hair and don't wear excessive jewelry. Even if your employer has no dress code, look neat, clean, and fashionable in whatever you wear.

Once you've gone through this beautifying transformation, your boss can begin to consider you promotable. In the Libra view you'll now have the ability to make a pleasing impression as a representative of the firm, since you speak effectively and can be trusted to carry on business with decorum and tact.

Your boss can see both sides of the coin at once, and if you think about trying to do this, you'll realize why he or she can take such a long time to come to a decision. You may at times just have to wait . . . and wait . . . and wait. Don't push your boss, and if you must, be polite. Libras can change their minds, so learn to take this in stride as well. Don't add more information down the line; if you do, you'll just wait longer. Yet if you want to take responsibility for the decision, perhaps your boss will let you make the choice.

Librans can also avoid unpleasant dirty work, and you may be just the person who gets to do it—that's what these people have employees for! Yet if you get fed up with a constant stream of shouting clients or reluctant suppliers, don't hesitate to discuss it with your boss and have a solution ready. The technique of airing your views combined with suggesting new procedures can be most effective in dealing with a Libra supervisor.

If you've got a self-indulgent Libra boss, all hell can break loose as long as things look good, and many complaints can go unnoticed as long as the Libra doesn't have to hear them. You probably won't want to stay in the position if things have deteriorated to this point. But there are ways to get a Libra supervisor to straighten things up: Force him or her to understand the unpleasantness that's going on all around you. If your boss has any pride left, things will improve. Perhaps you may also have to be decisive and implement appropriate action.

As Librans are always fair, you can expect to receive your due in salary and time off. If you must ask, do so in the most refined way possible. Look your best, speak nicely, and pay attention to the established procedures.

Don't expect your boss to give you an answer right away. Your supervisor will probably want to review your work record, attendance, and performance. Calls will be made to other associates regarding your progress, attitude, and ability. Finally, a review will have to be made of your co-workers' salaries to make sure that everyone's being equally compensated. It's a long process, so don't push for a quick answer.

You'll have a wonderful atmosphere while working for a Libran, and your co-workers, if chosen by the Libra boss, will be cooperative and kind, too. All of us can quickly get used to being a little more civilized and liking it!

Gift Ideas for Libra

Librans have fine taste and appreciate gifts of beauty and value. They enjoy delicate and exquisite objects as well as those that enhance their own enjoyment of beauty.

You might want to first visit a traditional giftshop, one which sells knickknacks and figurines. As long as something looks good, it will be appreciated by Librans. You can buy pastels, watercolors, prints, picture frames, decanters, vases, china, crystal, silver, perfume atomizers or bottles, a demitasse set, candle holders, music boxes, mirrors, or an ornate telephone. They also enjoy compact beauty, so you need not spend a fortune to buy something of quality.

Silk or dried flowers, bonsai trees, and live flowers such as pink roses, daisies, dahlias, and hydrangea will all appeal to the Libran's aesthetic nature. Perfume or cologne in delicate scents, potpourri, fragrant or decorator candles, body oils, soaps, and bath oils will appeal to the luxurious leanings of Libra.

Librans will enjoy cassettes or CDs of classical, soft, or mellow music. They'd like coffee-table books of photographs, art, decorating, and fashion. Any beautiful book on a subject they enjoy will be appreciated.

Clothing is a good choice for Librans of both sexes. Your choice should be in pale pastel shades or muted vibrant hues, somewhat conservative or classic, but never plain. They'd especially like designer clothes, elegant fashions in rich fabrics like silk, satin, and velvet, and accessories of fine leather. Women may enjoy lacy lingerie, a bedjacket, or night clothes.

Personal items like delicate jewelry of sapphire, rose coral, pink jade, tourmaline, or peridot are wonderful; or jewelry boxes, grooming kits, a jewelry cleaner, well-crafted desk accessories, wind chimes, stationery, silk sheets, damask or linen tablecloth/napkin sets, artist's materials, or a paint set can be appreciated by Libras.

Good food and exotic teas, gourmet delicacies, fine wine, champagne, and imported candy or cakes can all be good choices. Most Librans would love being taken to an elegant restaurant.

You can probably give the most pleasure to a Libran by a gift of pleasure! Tickets to a classical concert, the ballet, and art exhibits or lectures will touch the Libra heart. Many are artistically talented themselves and would enjoy a gift catering to a specific hobby such as jewelry making, flower arranging, or painting. Or buy a magazine subscription about one of the subjects your Libra enjoys.

SCORPIO
October 23 to November 23

The Scorpio Co-worker: Behind Closed Doors

Your often quiet and polite Scorpio co-workers certainly don't *seem* to be walking time bombs, but this is one way of thinking about them. They're full of a tremendous amount of energy, and if it's properly directed, it may never explode on the job. But if you observe one long enough you'll possibly see the fuse ignite and—*ka-boom!* Whether the eruption is big or small depends on the circumstances.

Most often, however, Scorpios are completely in control of their strong emotions and hide them well, at times behind an almost stuffy formality. They'd never want it to get out that they're not totally professional. So they play it cool instead of hot and probably have most working associates fooled into thinking they're detached or disinterested in the people and events around them. Remember that Scorpios are not shy or insecure, just reserved. Try to let them keep whatever distance they need.

All of this may give you the impression that Scorpio workers are self-absorbed, and they are emotionally.

They're also quite sensitive and can be overly conscious of co-workers on a very deep, almost psychic level. They'll have pretty definite opinions about most of them, and it will take a long time or dramatic events to ever change them. They can perceive and utilize subtle relationships and power struggles on the job, which can go unnoticed by many of us. You either love or hate Scorpios: They generally don't produce indifference.

The Scorpio co-worker will observe and calculate before taking action. You'll see your associate seemingly casually place all papers out of sight before leaving the desk and most likely there will not be pictures of family members or significant others. You may get the impression that he or she leads a double life, being so mysterious. Your co-worker may change the subject when asked a direct question or, inexplicably, not answer it. Instead, your co-worker is watching you and wondering why you wanted to know that anyway.

Most people don't get to know Scorpios at work really well, but if they like you, or if you've known them a long time, they can be the most powerful friends you have on the job. They will be ferociously loyal and back you up even when you are wrong. If they open up to you, you'll wonder how they ever hid such strong and intense feelings before. Be patient and kind with this often misunderstood sign, and you're sure to make a positive impression. Some days your co-worker may brood, and it's best to be sympathetic and not pry at these times. If you can distract the Scorpio with some interesting work you share, so much the better.

When you get to know your Scorpio co-worker well, you'll realize you've found a resource. If you need to find out who can help you get something done or details on another associate's character or personal problems, ask a Scorpio. For someone so tight-lipped you're sure to wonder where this worker came across such classified information. Scorpio just takes a back seat, listens, and learns, often becoming so unobtrusive that others don't even notice.

Your co-worker is a good friend to cultivate for many reasons, including the ability to make life miserable for you if you're disliked. A Scorpio isn't someone you can force to do anything, especially when it concerns personal likes and dislikes. If you're not genuine and are merely trying to *cultivate* a friendship, you won't be trusted at all. If you have invited your co-worker's enmity for some reason, watch out—you'll get it back tenfold. These people will politely accept your apology but will inwardly seethe. It may take months, it may take years, but when there's an opportunity to return what's felt to be your due, it'll be done without a qualm.

Don't expect an upfront explanation if you can tell by those not-so-subtle signals that you've upset your co-worker. Scorpios are notorious for not sharing their feelings when they've been hurt and will even lie to avoid a showdown. Then they'll take that back seat again, observe some more, and shift their opinion of you based on your current behavior. But Scorpios don't like to let go of real relationships, and if you've become friendly and trusted, your friendship should remain intact. If your associate unexpectedly yells at you about some minor personal slight, you've really got a friend in this co-worker. *Any* expression of personal feeling is not shared lightly, so try to be as sympathetic as possible.

If Scorpios like their work and are on the right career track, they'll plunge into it fervently. Although they're painstaking, they can get more done than anyone when motivated. They have the ability to get to the heart of any matter, can find their errors with complete research, and may show up everyone.

These people can often be difficult to work with closely, as they're not really team players and like to take charge. Some simply have abrasive personalities. Scorpio views can be dogmatic, and they may be inflexible about what you should be doing or what they'll contribute. "Not my job!" is clearly a Scorpio phrase, and they'll stick to it when applicable. They often like to follow established procedures and can be sticklers about rules. Scorpios don't like being pushed but will feel free to push you to do your share. If you dare to mention this fact, don't expect any cooperation. Your Scorpio associate will sit on the work as long as possible just to take control, figuring you'll change your attitude and treat him or her more kindly next time.

A lot of Scorpios just work for security and cash; their personal lives and relationships are much more important. Even so, highly developed types will still display the positive Scorpio capacity for hard work and the ability to handle difficult tasks and situations without blowing their cool.

If you're stuck working with a Scorpio who hates the job, he or she can be sullen and difficult. Scorpios will often keep positions they don't like just because the paycheck and benefits are good. They may resent the boss or the power structure and will prove that they really don't care what anybody thinks, ignoring work or getting others to do it while spending a good part of the day on personal calls. Scorpios keenly understand co-workers and are aware of what they can get away with. Your disgruntled associate may even make life miserable for everyone for months before getting fired and collecting unemployment.

If you can ascertain what's really important to your Scorpio co-worker, you'll find it a lot easier working with this sometimes obsessive individual. Is it doing exactly what the boss says, doing the job a certain way, or collecting *all* the background material before committing to a decision? Don't listen to what's said, but observe what's *done*, and this will soon be clear. When you have a project to share, you'll know what to expect and where the Scorpio won't bend. If you really want to understand this co-worker, realize how different he or she probably is from you, and you'll go a long way toward developing a positive and mutually rewarding working relationship.

The Scorpio Boss: Anything Is Possible

Scorpio bosses can be angels or devils and on a day-to-day basis probably are a little of both. How they behave toward you is likely to reflect their personal feelings and current state of mind. Scorpios are some of the most emotional individuals you're ever likely to encounter, and if you think they are icy and aloof, you only see their superficial appearance.

To understand this boss, realize that Scorpios are complex and passionate. If you haven't worked closely with your supervisor for ten years, you probably think that this is hardly the case. Look a little closer. Weren't you surprised last week when you heard a loud guffaw from behind the closed door? Ever catch your supervisor on a very personal call? You were probably surprised at how vulnerable he or she suddenly seemed.

Yet vulnerable is hardly the word you would apply to this superior on the job. Always businesslike, the more they're aggravated, the more exaggeratedly businesslike they can become. They work *hard,* sometimes alone all day long without a break, and often into the night, if necessary. Try not to interrupt with petty matters during one of these phases. If you disturb a Scorpio unduly, you'll get a sarcastic comment and no information.

What do these people get by on? Sheer strength of will and desire. If you need to do preliminary work in order that the boss can continue, you'll do it; it's as simple as that. It's not easy to say "no" to a Scorpio. Your supervisor may at times bark out orders but will more often tell you politely and succinctly what's required. If you put it off or forget, anticipate a long and regular series of Scorpio reminders. By the time you're subjected to a few of these, you'll realize it's a lot easier to quickly make the boss's top priority yours and be done with it.

Scorpios can be quite demanding, but they won't ever ask you to do anything they wouldn't. The only problem is, they'll do just about anything. If they want to be hamburger, they'll put themselves through a meat grinder.

There are different types, of course. Even executive Scorpios can be more interested in their personal lives than work and may be in secure positions that they've held for the past fifteen or thirty years. At quitting time this particular boss is out the door as quickly as most employees. Yet the greater number of Scorpios in positions of authority are seeking more control and the financial security that accompanies promotion.

Don't question requests or offer any arguments. Excuses for not completing a job on time will be met with silence, public embarrassment before co-workers, or possibly verbal abuse. But if you're a hard worker with energy and enthusiasm, you'll love working for a Scorpio. Your boss will always take all that you can give and increase your responsibilities if you're competent.

Reliability is a key. The Scorpio boss is always on the job when needed. Personal problems, including illness, never get in the way of work. Scorpios have an almost superhuman ability of mind over matter. If you can exhibit the same behavior and attitude, you'll get much respect and admiration.

While a Scorpio superior will be direct about how you should behave professionally, how you are expected to behave *personally* is far more difficult to figure out. Train yourself to pick up on what the Scorpio behavior and implication *mean* rather than what's specifically *said*. Reading between the lines can be a tricky business, especially for more direct signs like Aries, Leo, or Sagittarius, and you'll at times find yourself confused or hurt by your boss's mixed signals. If you're sensitive, intuitive, and open, however, you'll fare much better with this occasionally moody character.

Don't raise your voice to your Scorpio boss and don't get into an argument unless you really feel personally close. Both can spell disaster. If this supervisor wants to get rid of you, your life will be made so miserable that you'll probably soon quit in disgust. Or you may one day get a call from personnel regarding your layoff. Scorpio rarely deals directly when angry, and you may not even suspect that your boss had anything to do with your dismissal. Think again. If in response to your query last week your supervisor said there was no problem but continued to behave as if there was one, you've just been shut out. Scorpios never forget slights, no matter how small, but never forget kindnesses either, which can be your greatest asset.

If you haven't been given the raise or time off you feel you deserve, this boss can prove to be a really tough nut to crack. Scorpios are masters of avoidance. Make your requests clear and concise and be stubborn. Are you consistent in temperament, easygoing, and adaptable to the demands of your job? Do you work hard? Do you try to work with your Scorpio boss to help attain goals? If you can confidently answer "yes" to these questions, you should be rewarded accordingly. Yet if your boss has taken a dislike to you for some unknown reason, don't expect to get a raise. And don't ever go over your supervisor's head unless you want to be hit between the eyes with Scorpio venom.

As time goes on, you'll begin to see the inner workings of the Scorpio executive: passion, determination, and commitment. You'll find there's a lot more to this person than meets the eye. You may just click with your supervisor, find a warm and loyal friend, or develop a close and important associate. Scorpio can be judgmental and trusting of instincts, which tend toward caution: It will usually take a long time for your boss to let the Scorpio guard down.

Take any confidences, no matter how seemingly insignificant, as important rewards for your loyalty. And don't break one of them unless you want to sever your relationship forever. Your boss will always respect *your* privacy. And you know what? When some personal emergency comes up that keeps you from work, the Scorpio will really be the first one to understand.

No matter what, don't become romantically involved with this supervisor, unless you're really serious. If you decide you want to see the boss personally, quit your job immediately and seek another. Business and romance just do not mix with Scorpios, especially Scorpio supervisors. You'd be reckless to even attempt a casual fling and will likely suffer greatly from your mistake.

When treated with respect and a healthy dose of compassion, a Scorpio boss can be someone who's really a joy to work for. Give it your all, and you'll develop a good working relationship over time.

Gift Ideas for Scorpio

Scorpios can be the most difficult co-workers for whom to buy a gift; if you don't know them well you may not know their personal interests. Gifts should appeal to their emotional tendencies and allow the recipient to feel indulged in some way. Unusual or metaphysical things that pique the Scorpio curiosity would make suitable gifts.

Many Scorpios are readers, and there are lots of categories, both fiction and nonfiction, which appeal to the penetrating Scorpio intellect. Try detective, espionage, murder mysteries, horror, psychic, occult, astrology, psychology, or philosophy books. Other interests include satire, sexuality, home improvement, finance, the stock market, real estate, and taxes. Financial magazines are especially suitable for Scorpios. Some Scorpios may have an interest in the martial arts, t'ai chi, hunting, firearms, or battle histories. Books on these subjects, too, are good choices, as are biographies in any Scorpio subject of interest and exposés on government secrets.

Scorpios may enjoy tickets to operas, dramas, heavy metal or rock concerts, mystery plays, lectures on the occult, boat races or expositions, boxing or wrestling matches, demolition derbys, or fireworks displays. Nature walks, natural history museums, and antique shows will also appeal to the Scorpio.

When these people have hobbies, they are probably all-encompassing. You may purchase gifts to cater to these interests, which can include photography, bodybuilding, diving, snorkeling, boating, deep-sea fishing, hunting, boxing, wrestling, or surfing.

Scorpios love to indulge themselves, and rich or exotic foods will appeal to their palates. Wine, fancy liqueurs, fine cheeses, coffee, meats, chocolates, marmalades, caviar, lobster, and smoked salmon should all be enjoyed by your Scorpio friend.

In choosing personal gifts, you may consider stocks or bonds, fine leather goods, perfume or cologne (particularly musky or oriental scents), body oils, lingerie, an astrology chart, crystal ball, or healing gems and stones. Most Scorpios have significant domestic lives, so cutlery, household tools, car-repair tools, or car accessories can also be appropriate.

Scorpio flowers are heather, red rose, geranium, gardenia, chrysanthemum, and brambleberry. These people are drawn to heavy metal jewelry and stones such as bloodstone, black amethyst, ruby, red coral, and black pearl.

If you'd enjoy buying clothing for a Scorpio co-worker, black is usually your best bet. They prefer soft, comfortable, or sensual clothing, including silks, velour, and velvet. Other colors enjoyed by this sign are wine, maroon, deep red, and tapestry patterns.

For fun gifts, try games of chance, tarot cards, Monopoly, whodunit games, and puzzles. A microscope, chemistry set, telescope, or binoculars could also appeal to Scorpios with an investigative bent.

SAGITTARIUS
November 22 to December 22

The Sagittarius Co-worker: Free Spirit

Your Sagittarian co-workers will arrive at work with newspapers under their arms and a lot to say about the latest events. They will likely be at least a few minutes late in arriving (they're probably not even aware of it) and will tell you all about what's happened to them since they last saw you. You'll love to hear their amusing anecdotes and amorous adventures, and you'll wonder where they found the time to do so much since 5:30 P.M. yesterday when all *you* did was have a cold dinner and watch television. But Sagittarians, after all, have a zest for life. If your particular co-worker also has zeal for the job, you've found someone great to work with. If not, you'll be working with a person who's entertaining at best, but distracting and obnoxious at worst.

Symbolized by the archer, Sagittarians need to share their ideas and are stimulated by what others have to say. They'll love to hang out at the coffee cart with the gang. Often funny and insightful in their criticism of superiors, they can be quite outspoken, especially if they feel they've been treated unfairly. They've probably already discussed the situation with the boss, to no avail. Idealistic, Sagittarians will be bitter about office politics, hating to admit that the brightest and hardest working aren't always awarded their due. Yet they won't let this get in the way of the job and will refuse to admit that they could fall victim to manipulations or unseemly gossip. They're right—they probably won't.

Sagittarians have their own principles at work—a combination of doing the right thing and having a lark. They have a strong sense of themselves and won't be influenced by others. Taken to an extreme, it can result in a devil-may-care attitude. Sagittarius can also be self-righteous at times. But if you believed you did all your work faithfully and truthfully, wouldn't you feel the same way? So whatever goofing off they may do, they'll always feel justified.

Lunch with Sagittarians will always be an adventure; they can introduce you to the wildest exotic restaurant in town or some of their foreign friends. Their lives are open books, and before you even feel you know a Sagittarius well, your co-worker will be telling you all about his or her personal life, feelings, and goals. You'll be so comfortable with the Sagittarian character, you might open right up, too. Think twice before you tell Sagittarius anything you'd rather be kept secret, though, because tomorrow everyone will know who you think is attractive or how you secretly want to seduce the boss's spouse. Sagittarians don't talk to be obnoxious or spiteful—they just take glee in spreading the word. They may even repeat back what others have said about *you*. Remember, don't respond to this unless you want *your* comments repeated. But your Sagittarian associate will honestly be upset if you mention how horrified you are at this indiscretion; it's far easier for you to exercise a little prudence.

If Sagittarian workers like their jobs, they'll enthusiastically tackle any project, no matter how large or problematic. You'll find them eager to discuss their work, size up problems within the firm, and share contacts or shortcuts. Sagittarians like to help, and you will find in them an endless source of information on people, places, and things. They'll even happily commit to sharing some of your workload if you're overburdened.

These people are easy to work with because they're so adaptable; they understand that others have different points of view. If they agree with you on principle, details never ruffle their feathers. Sagittarians may digress from the topic at hand, but you can easily get them back on track. In the face of a deadline, they will enthusiastically give their all and, if available, will be happy to stand in for you and earn overtime.

Unfortunately, they don't always follow through with all they've committed to. Remember the project Sagittarius promised to help you with? You'd better, because your co-worker is likely to forget. It's a good idea to check with your friend well before the work is due, or you just may end up doing it yourself. Your co-worker can realize too late that there's an important meeting looming but will try to keep a promise. If the Sagittarian really has other commitments, expect a sheepish apology about this forgetfulness. In the end, you'll be told frankly what will or won't be done.

If you're working closely with one, good-natured reminders to finish what's started are in order, too. If your associate is not genuinely interested in the project, it'll be difficult to get anything of consequence done. Perhaps you can try to engage the Sagittarian in some way, making the work sound exciting, or you can divide your responsibilities differently. Anything to do with people, ideas, or moving about will appeal to the archer. Anything tedious, repetitive, or quiet will not interest Sagittarius in the least.

If Sagittarians in fact hate the job or don't believe in the company or a boss's values, you'll have a difficult time dealing with them at all. You may have a hard time even *locating* your co-worker! Off procrastinating by the water cooler with a member of the opposite sex, in a rest room discussing the existence of God, or taking an extended lunch or coffee break, Sagittarius will avoid the tasks at hand. Even if your associate is where you expect, he or she may be involved with guests or on a personal call.

This unhappy co-worker will probably be cranky in response to your sixth reminder for those figures that are needed in order to get on with *your* job. And after the boss calls the archer in to ask what the problem is, your co-worker's response will be an involved argument about why the firm doesn't get more productivity from its staff, or how the managers are irresponsible in allocating assignments. Sagittarius will probably be candid, too, in sharing *your* shortcomings with the boss, and expound on how difficult *you* are to work with. But if Sagittarians are that unhappy, they usually don't stick around too long, anyway.

In general, though, Sagittarius is more a charmer than anything else, and if you're friendly, any differences between you will be quickly forgotten. Take the archer out for a drink after work, talk about your congressman, and you'll be on your usual genial footing again.

The Sagittarius Boss: Truth, Justice . . . Adventure!

If you've got a Sagittarius boss, you're in luck. This boss is a lot of fun. You won't be bored working for a Sagittarian. The daily grind just isn't a grind when working with someone as spontaneous, idealistic, and jovial as the archer.

These people are generous to a fault, so if they take you to lunch, it's their treat (if it's not, you'll be told up-front). And you're sure to learn a lot about the world, including their theories of life and details on international politics and current events. They may even recommend the latest hot paperbacks or magazines.

The most noticeable quality about your employer will be a sense of freedom. This boss doesn't come on heavily with discipline or restraints and won't be looking over your shoulder as you do your work, either. You'll be trusted to behave in a responsible manner, and it's important that you live up to this faith in you. If you do, you'll be given more freedom and commensurate pay.

Sagittarians are so frank they can't hold back what they really think and would feel dishonest to do so. As a result, you'll have to learn to take such comments as "You look lousy today" with a grain of salt. If you've made a mistake or have been giving less than a full effort, Sagittarius will tell you. As the sign can also be excitable, this boss will not be above giving you a good dressing-down. Take this in stride—it's just a passing fancy, really. Once your supervisor has let off steam and you eagerly correct your error, any problems will be forgotten.

Be sure to take criticisms in a positive frame of mind. Don't expect your boss to apologize, either—it's not the Sagittarian style. Just remember that it's in your boss's nature to forgive and forget and not hold a grudge. Don't you hold one, either. If you disagree with what's shouted at you, say so tactfully. Sagittarians appreciate honesty and don't mind a good argument, but they can be more sensitive than they think other people should be. Don't critique the *philosophy* behind the chiding, and you'll be all right.

The positive aspects of having freedom on the job are obvious: You can socialize, make personal calls, or take an extra half-hour for a lunch break when it's slow or if you've got personal errands to run. Remember, though, that you had better be there when your boss needs you.

Sagittarian bosses will always take *their* freedom first, and will likely move about a lot. Meetings will take them all over and the necessary networking will do the same. You could thus be a prime candidate for the Sagittarian last-minute call: "I forgot those figures" . . . "Could you bring over my briefcase?" Or "Finish up that special report by the time I get back!" Frantic calls from out of town or even out of the country are also typical. And your boss may at times be difficult to reach when you're in need. Therefore, keep lists of all your questions handy for when your boss unexpectedly calls in.

These people are also not the greatest at planning ahead. They will suddenly realize that a deadline is looming and have to work all night to meet it. Which means *you* will have to work all night, too. Projects that have been neglected will need to be taken care of "yesterday." If you are organized, you might jot down anything your boss mentions in passing (especially deadlines) and periodically try to update yourself. But even this technique can fail, so the best advice is to be loose and try to go with the flow whenever possible.

Your attention to detail will be very important, as your boss only has an eye for the big picture. Sloppy work can easily get past a Sagittarian supervisor, but will come back to haunt you when a client or your boss's own supervisor complains. And you will certainly find yourself at times picking up the pieces when the Sagittarius has rushed off or jumped in too quickly.

You will sometimes feel that the boss has all the fun while you're stuck with the real work. This is true. But you're probably better suited to your responsibilities, and your supervisor is clearly good at being a glad hand. In any case, Sagittarius is still in charge, and maybe someday you might be, too.

Your Sagittarian boss will probably make promises to you regarding work. The possibility of raises, an interesting project, or extra days off are all things that can be guaranteed to you in a warm moment of generosity. However, in the busy Sagittarius day and with such quickly moving minds, these things can be forgotten. *Speak up.* Don't be shy with this boss; you'll get nowhere. Sagittarians will remember what's been promised when reminded, and if you can get them to act quickly, they'll do all they can for you. But you may have to remind them several times before getting any action.

To get along best with a Sagittarian supervisor, try to be flexible. They need someone whom they can trust and who can take action *now*. If you can roll with the punches, you may even find yourself creating a much more interesting position for yourself.

In developing a personal relationship, it helps to show that you're intelligent: Your boss will think highly of you if you can discuss books, politics, or current affairs. Brush up on the subjects the Sagittarian is interested in, read the books the boss recommends, and talk about them. Your supervisor will be pleased and your reputation will soar, even if you just listen to what the archer has to say and ask intelligent questions.

Cultivate a good sense of humor. Your boss loves jokes, so remember those told to you or write them down. And leave your moods and personal problems at home. Sagittarians are cheerful and like to surround themselves with others of the same kind. A winning smile and warm hello for this executive will go a long way in helping keep you in good graces. And doesn't it feel better when you do so? If you can make up for the Sagittarian's shortcomings, you'll find the rewards of working for this boss to be much more than money and position.

Gift Ideas for Sagittarius

Gifts for Sagittarians should cater to their sense of adventure, or their need to pursue their ideals.

It's a rare Sagittarius who doesn't read; almost any book will expand their horizons. Particular interests include wildlife, pets, animal training, sports, camping, foreign cultures, politics, travel, exploration, philosophy, and religion. An atlas, exotic cookbook, or books on the law or higher education would be enjoyed. Also, consider a subscription to *Natural Geographic* or *Sports Illustrated*.

These people love travel and are usually on the go. Suitcases, duffel bags, a travel iron, tie case, jewelry bag, makeup or shaving kit, a voltage converter, disposable camera, and foreign-language tapes or dictionaries are all good choices for Sagittarius sojourners.

Many Sagittarians have sporting interests as well, and athletic gear and accessories such as a football, volleyball, basketball, baseball bat or mitt, hockey stick, ice skates, riding equipment, hiking boots, backpack, bicycle, a dart board, trampoline, wind surfer, or fencing equipment are just some of the equipment they might enjoy.

Tickets to the racetrack, or football, baseball, basketball, hockey, soccer, or polo games would all be enjoyed, as would attending a rodeo, horse show, carnival, or circus, or dining at a foreign restaurant.

Some personal gifts for Sagittarians include barbecue equipment, camping gear, a hammock, outdoor furniture, picnic basket, or live trees, or plants. The Sagittarian could enjoy a compass, binoculars, distance meter, or sports video. Gifts for other Sagittarian interests are a book light, kite, globe, maps, animal poster or calendar, a toy pinball or slot machine, or a leash, collar, toys, food, and accessories for their pets. You may even buy a new pet for a Sagittarian, but inquire as to suitability first.

Sagittarians enjoy games in which they can use their minds, like chess. They'd prefer comfortable, loose clothing, such as a sweatshirt or jacket, T-shirt, sweatsocks, and sneakers. Their colors are rich hues like royal purple, mauve, dark blue, and lavender.

Sagittarians love gold or gold-tone jewelry. Gems that they'd enjoy include blue tourmaline, purple quartz, amethyst, and azurite. Flowers for this sign are deep red carnations, poinsettia, narcissus, or begonia. Scents should be fresh, reminding them of the outdoors.

CAPRICORN
December 21 to January 21

The Capricorn Co-worker: Unassuming Ambition

Your Capricorn co-workers are serious, reserved individuals; perhaps that quiet bookkeeper in the corner is one. They are all business while at work and pretty much keep to themselves. Capricorns seem so unassuming, it's hard to believe they're ambitious, but they certainly are in their own way. Would you believe that young bookkeeper is already planning on being president of the company some day? Well, it's more than likely true. And the Capricorn will probably get there through a combination of hard work, respect for authority, and patience.

Responsible, self-disciplined, and cautious, Capricorns get ahead because they learn the rules of the game early on. Then they wait, and while they're waiting they make themselves the most indispensable people around. When it's promotion time, the Capricorn individual may not be the first one management considers but will be the last, and the only person everyone can agree deserves the position.

You may be astounded when a quiet Capricorn gets

promoted before you. After all, you complimented the boss and networked yourself sick. But the Capricorn worked hard, with an honest commitment to serve, coming in early and staying late. He or she was always relied on in any emergency situation.

Capricorns are quite nice to have around. They do their work and won't butt into anyone else's business. Even the young ones will appear much older because of their mature outlook and sense of responsibility. They are realists, though, and some Capricorns become downright pessimists. While people of this sign have a sense of humor, don't expect to see them rolling in the aisles. Capricorns have a dry wit, which is usually ironic or even cynical. Delivery can be so dead-pan that you'll wonder, "Was that supposed to be a joke?" Laugh anyway. It helps to try and lighten these people up.

Capricorns are really shy and insecure. They may cover it up with a brusque, businesslike manner, but deep down all of them are afraid of being homeless and penniless. Their career drive is just a great need for security, and they'll take the safest, surest means toward being successful.

Get them to go out to lunch with you (they'll only agree if they're not too busy) or, better yet, bring your own brown bag to match the Capricorn's and share a corner. But wait till you know them pretty well before making such a move. Capricorns take a long time to feel comfortable with others, and they may clam up if you come on too strong.

It can be difficult to really get to know these people, as they often don't like to let up on their work. You may get the impression that they only talk when they need something, and this is partially true. Capricorns are purposeful no-frills types who like to use the minimum amount of energy to get a job done. But they also feel foolish just saying anything, and Capricorns never like to feel foolish. If they want to chat, they'll come up with a reason to do so.

When you *do* get to be friendly with Capricorns, you'll find them invaluable for help and advice on how to beat the system. These people know how to use the rules; they accept them as givens instead of rebelling or knuckling under. Then they turn them around and make them work for *them*. A catch-22 is the ultimate Capricorn challenge. If you're not sure which procedure to take or how the boss wants a report handed in, ask a Capricorn. You'll find out everything you always wanted to know about corporate structure but were afraid to ask. Once you win a Capricorn's confidence, however, you may wish you hadn't, because they can be notorious complainers. Yet you can learn something about business even from their daily criticisms.

You might feel their business and career advice is sometimes a little too conservative, but it's always sound. You may think that your co-worker's "save a pencil" idea is silly, but you'll also have to note that the department saved not an insignificant amount of money as a result.

Capricorns are easy to work with because they will share an equal if not greater portion of the work load. They like to work and don't understand about working for a reward—the work *is* the reward. They can take over and organize a project, planning who'll do what and scheduling when each task should be completed. If you can, let them; they're good at it and they love it because it gives them a feeling of control.

Capricorns will also try to take control by warning you about the importance of working hard and finishing on time. If you are an independent type like Aries, Sagittarius, or Aquarius, this can be a bitter pill to swallow. Try to get it down the gullet, though. Sure, Capricorns can be deadline-crazy, but they usually don't miss any. The rest of us can learn a thing or two about work and career from these people. You may be put off by their no-nonsense approach, but when there's a job to do, Capricorns can think of nothing else. They won't chitchat. They may strike you as cold and uncaring, but try to see them as businesslike. When the job's done early, your co-worker just might relax and have a soda with you (Dutch, of course!).

You can depend on Capricorns to be there when needed. They have cool heads in emergencies, and their take-charge attitudes emerge during these times to help everyone else feel more secure. Their instinctive understanding of systems and structures can also help to get a job done in the shortest amount of time.

So don't look down at those quiet Capricorns, working steadily and diligently in the corner. Make friends with them and take their good advice. If you don't they'll be chuckling all the way to the bank and the executive suite. You might as well tag along!

The Capricorn Boss: The Real Thing

Capricorn bosses are here to stay, partly because they want to and partly because they are so good at what they do. They need and want responsibility and will always do what's expected of them, regardless of how they personally feel. These people keep their jackets and stockings on even in the hottest weather. They won't let on that they're just as uncomfortable as you; that would give away the fact that they're not in control! Like stoics, they'll accept whatever the universe presents to them with the same accepting attitude, changing the things that can be changed while working around those that can't.

These supervisors have especially serious manners: They have work to do and know *you* have work to do. Capricorns in positions of power will take on the trappings that show everyone who's boss—conservative attire and a polished speaking voice. But this alone is not enough. They inspire confidence and respect because they know how to handle employees, clients, and crises with firmness and impartiality. Capricorns don't ordinarily raise their voices because they know they don't have to. Their rule is unobtrusive but omnipresent.

Capricorns have a great talent for knowing how to use employees to best advantage and understand how everyone's efforts can be put together to achieve results. They will insist that you follow instructions to the letter, come in on time, and do what's expected of you, including working late when necessary. If you don't do these things, you won't be as valuable as you can be.

If you've been with the firm for many years and have worked your way up to a closer association with your Capricorn boss, you'll find an often gentle, paternalistic type who won't take liberties with others and conducts all business affairs on the up and up (it's too risky to take chances by breaking the rules!). Your supervisor will be willing to help out and offer advice on your business dilemmas. Do exactly what's suggested—Capricorns speak from experience. Most of them have worked their way up to their positions and will know all about doing your job because they probably have *done* your job. And they may have even waited tables and shipped packages somewhere along the line as well. You'd be surprised at the often superhuman ability these people have of putting their noses to the grindstone.

Capricorns just naturally tend to be social climbers and will be attracted to positions of power. They don't coldly calculate to marry into important families, but they often do because they're attracted to everything that wealth and prestige offer.

There's a simple way to get a Capricorn boss to like you—work hard! Your supervisor will admire results. Try to emulate your boss in every way possible. You'll see it's not that easy!

Capricorns resent employees who waste time socializing on the job. Lunch is the time for that. They will especially disapprove if you hang on the phone for long personal calls. Don't come in late and don't sneak out, extend breaks, or leave early. They'll find out. Remember, they're control freaks, and they make it a point to know what's going on.

Dress in a conservative manner. It won't matter if you wear the same clothes every day, as long as they're clean and pressed. Don't put on airs, talk about things you don't know about, or (the worst of all possible sins!) offer advice when you're not speaking from experience. A Capricorn will see these last few traits of behavior as dishonest, and there's nothing Capricorns hate more than dishonesty.

If this sounds like an elementary course in how to succeed in business, it is. Capricorn superiors expect all the traditional spoken and unspoken rules to be followed. How could they promote a person to a position of authority who acts like a jerk and burps after lunch? No way. So swallow your wild impulse to do the lambada at the conference. Say "excuse me" before interrupting, knock on the boss's door quietly, and wait your turn. These things will work wonders.

If all of this seems tough to you, say good-bye to your Capricorn boss forever. You'll never get ahead unless you can master the primer of good business practices. If you are a maverick or an independent exec, you are much better off working for someone who can better appreciate your creative enthusiasm.

What's more, Capricorn bosses won't be subject to flattery, either. They'll politely thank you for the compliment and will inwardly be a little pleased. But this has nothing to do with the fact that you didn't complete your assignment on time last week and will not soften their annoyance at that fact.

Capricorns may tend toward depression. Be aware that their dark moods can last, so be extra cautious to disturb your boss only when it's important. Or try to inspire an upbeat attitude by reporting on a new client, money saved, or other positive office news.

Some Capricorn bosses can become power hungry,

wanting only to get to the top at all costs. Such people may become cold, arrogant, and even cruel to underlings, content only when telling others what to do. There's no fun way to deal with such a person, but if you must, make sure the work is done well and distance yourself whenever possible from this self-absorbed supervisor.

Capricorns are known to be penny-pinchers, and Mr. Scrooge is the perfect example of a cheap Capricorn boss. Some can be money hungry, but the vast majority of Capricorn wage-givers are fair, if modest, in their pay schedules. They are not overly generous but will pay a commensurate salary. If you do your job, you should expect regular wage increases. Capricorns know that in order to keep good people they must continue to make the job worthwhile. You can also expect regular increases in responsibility if you are handling things well.

If you feel you've been overlooked or should be paid more, follow all necessary protocol when approaching your boss. Schedule a meeting well in advance. Be prepared with hard facts to back up your claim, such as working late, greater responsibility, or a heavier work load. Remember that you must *prove* you're accomplishing tasks successfully.

Your Capricorn boss will evaluate your work quite closely, so you may be in for some criticism. And you absolutely won't get a raise if you don't deserve one. If you do deserve one, you'll get *something*. Be prepared to be offered less than you expect. Or start out by asking for more than you'd like in order to compromise on what you really feel is your due.

Don't ever try to convince a Capricorn boss to give you a raise because you need it. Such phrases as "my mortgage payments are so high now" or "the new baby costs more than we planned" will invite censure, not sympathy, from your practical-minded supervisor. Capricorns will think you foolhardy for getting in over your head and will probably think less of you as a result, besides being able to offer several other practical solutions to solving your money problems. In times of unexpected disaster or difficulty (such as the illness of a parent or spouse), a kind Capricorn boss may give you an advance (to be paid back) to help tide you over. Most of them feel that everyone should have money set aside for a rainy day but also understand the realities of unforeseen emergencies better than any other sign. After all, it's what drives them so hard.

Yes, Capricorn bosses can be tough and demanding, but if you're a good worker, you should have a secure future. You won't see the undeserving promoted ahead of you, and you can expect regular increases in position and pay when they're earned. What more could you want? Remember, this is business! Your boss will never forget.

Gift Ideas for Capricorn

Capricorn people like practical gifts, ones that can help manage everyday life, time, or business. These people will not appreciate gifts that they cannot use, such as gag gifts. They like things that others may not consider gifts. Their favorites will be simple and compact things that will last a long time, such as a pencil sharpener, key ring, or fountain pen.

Gifts for the office are naturals for Capricorn co-workers. Filing cabinets, desk and mail organizers, a Rolodex, business-card case, letter opener, desk lamp, briefcase, or sturdy desk chair are all good choices. Capricorns are ever conscious of time, so you might buy an hour glass, desk clock, calendar, appointment book, watch (wrist, pocket, or locket), or Filo-fax.

Capricorns always try to improve themselves and are usually upwardly mobile. They'd enjoy self-help and how-to books, biographies of successful people, and historical and political works. They'd also appreciate subscriptions to business magazines.

While these people don't go out often, they can enjoy

an evening out. They'd prefer tickets to a business seminar or political lecture. Classic plays and movies, chamber music, and operetta will all appeal to their conservative tastes.

Think conservative for personal items, too. Jewelry must be small in size and of high quality to be appreciated. Capricorn gemstones are black onyx, jet, smoky quartz, imperial jade, and Russian malachite. As Capricorn is an earth sign, these people especially enjoy plants and flowers. Pansies, climbing plants, holly, and amaranth all make good choices. Earthy, musky scents will also be preferred.

Wearable items should be of fine materials in subtle shades. Appropriate clothing for Capricorns include business wear, designer labels, tailored blouses, scarves, ties, handbags, wallets, briefcases, and other leather goods. Capricorns like earth tones like charcoal, black, gray, beige, brown, dark green, and white.

Occasionally, they may enjoy some fun and games. Try games like Career, Life, or Monopoly, which cater to business interests. Many Capricorns can have hobbies, such as ceramics, printing, or woodworking.

Capricorn's favorite interests are old things: They love any item that has stood the test of time. Antique prints and coins, cassettes of movie classics, or old radio shows, manual calculators, little wooden cigar boxes, or even modern reproductions of such things would all appeal to them. A fountain pen and ink makes an ideal gift, as it combines many Capricorn tastes—it's useful, beautiful, durable, inexpensive to operate, simple in design, reminiscent of a by-gone era, and doesn't create waste. See if your gift can satisfy all of these criteria!

AQUARIUS
January 20 to February 19

The Aquarius Co-worker: Computer Head

It's not really nice to compare people to machines, especially such friendly, considerate, and often kind persons as Aquarians, but the comparison is apt. Those Aquarians are so *attracted* to hardware, software, and logging on and off that you'll almost think they've found a long-lost relative! They revel in the pure logic, the variety of functions, the "future-ness" that computers possess. And yes, many Aquarians want to be just like 'em when they grow up!

Aquarius people are so *rational*, you see. They like to make decisions based on objective, intelligent thought, and they always try to avoid predetermined judgments. They take their relationships the same way—Aquarians are extremely user-friendly. They are some of the most easy people to get along with at the workplace, as they strive for calm, friendly interaction, without a lot of strings attached.

Aquarians like to mix it up with other people but at the same time are real individualists. You can see them all over—perhaps wearing orange and green ties, spiked hair, and retro eyeglasses. No matter how conventional they may at times appear, you'll probably notice that extra earring or wild streak of red hair. Whatever it is, there will be *something* that sets these people apart, and they like it that way. While Aquarians have a need to be well liked and will treat all co-workers with the same respect and quiet understanding that they demand for themselves, they are die-hard individualists (just like that PC over there that can do anything you want on its own). Remember that old seventies' line "You do your thing and I do my thing"? It was probably dreamed up by an Aquarian. If you leave these people enough space to "do their thing," you'll find them very able working partners.

Aquarians have a great intellectual curiosity. They like the variety and the unexpectedness that the world of human interaction presents them with and are thus excellent conversationalists and wonderful listeners. They are real easy to talk to and be with. These people can truly be "just friends" with both sexes, probably because they are basically that way in most relationships. You'll often see that their chosen compatriots are somewhat eccentric as well. They don't try to change people, seeing each one of us as interesting, unique characters in our own right. They won't get overly emotional or involved with people at the workplace, and it's a rare Aquarian co-worker who will ever show signs of pettiness, jealousy, or vindictiveness on the job.

If you've got a problem to solve or want an objective view, ask an Aquarian. The calm, sane, rational feedback can help you see a business problem in a whole new light. Even tricky personality problems with others will not appear quite so sticky once an Aquarian has analyzed the situation with you. Aquarians always have unique perspectives on *any* situation and can help you see things differently.

They are fond of discussion and like to help. Don't worry, there's no obligation to an Aquarius, although you'll probably *want* to help these people out when they're in need. You'll know—they're not shy about asking.

As much as Aquarians love to be part of a group, they do also need time to work independently. Their best ideas and decisions come after they've mulled over the meeting's proposed suggestions. And while they like to go out with the gang for lunch, you'll also notice that at times they go their own way to the exclusion of the regular routine. Be prepared for the unexpected with an Aquarian co-worker.

These people need to do what they want, when they want, and where they want. Heavy work restrictions can cause rebelliousness and absent-mindedness. If they're unhappy with a stifling atmosphere, they can become restless, unreliable, and depressed. Make your Aquarian friend feel better by sharing lunch in an off-beat restaurant or enjoying a stimulating discussion.

Aquarians don't like to pin themselves down. If you need to set up an appointment with one, be prepared for the worst! They can avoid setting an exact time and date or get back to you after some thinking and schedule-juggling. Aquarians can adapt to the needs of others, but others must also adapt to the Aquarius needs (it's only fair!). Be persistent if need be. Once these people make commitments, they generally stick with them.

But expect the unexpected. You may have thought your Aquarius co-worker all set to take one course of action, only to find that he or she has done the opposite!

Sometimes people of this sign will settle into a regular routine, though only as long as there's enough variety within that routine. When Aquarians are not interested, their attention can wander, and they might just blow off the whole thing. Remember that they don't hold authorities or responsibilities as sacred, and this can make them difficult to deal with. You cannot reason with an Aquarian by saying "The boss needs this by five." Your co-worker believes that imposed structures and restrictions (like a regular schedule and having to answer to a supervisor) are just that—imposed. The concepts of both "boss" and "five" are meaningless to Aquarians who have their own code of ethics. These involve being loyal and fair, but "To thine own self be true" is the top Aquarius priority. If they must sacrifice the boss's approval to be true to themselves, so be it. Sound a little complex? It is. And you'll just have to get to know *your* Aquarius co-worker better to determine exactly what his or her own specific code of ethics is really all about.

Usually, though, appeals to their rationality can help. "You did promise me you'd help" will work wonders, as Aquarians like to keep their word and rarely break promises. If, however, your associate has found that the promise was coerced by you through fraudulent means, it will be regarded as invalid.

All Aquarians need to deliberate long and hard before taking action. They may appear helpless in emergencies because they don't have time to think things through the way they need to, and their systems can even "crash" due to excess stress or anxiety. Turn to someone else when you need quick, decisive action.

Another result of their thinking process is extreme obstinacy. Once they feel they've seen and analyzed every facet of a situation and have come to a logical conclusion, there can be no shaking them. Try telling a computer it's wrong! Yet there are ways around a stubborn Aquarius co-worker: Appeal to everyone's right to their own opinion, present new evidence, or agree to disagree. Most Aquarians will be open to each of these alternatives.

And who can hate a computer for long? It helps you solve problems and can be relied upon for good judgment. Your Aquarian co-worker has these positive attributes, plus the rare ability to understand and tolerate most of humanity's foibles. Sounds like a great combination for the workplace!

The Aquarius Boss: You Do Your Thing . . .

Aquarians usually become bosses mainly because they are so good at what they do. Many even have geniuslike abilities in their chosen field and thus are promoted to positions of higher responsibility. They will fulfill these roles well because of their easygoing and calm nature, as well as their excellent decision-making capabilities. The best of them can even remain detached and distant enough from the emotional chaos around them to function as a sort of wise counselor. But Aquarians are really not cut out to be supervisors in the truest sense of the word.

If you're not the typical employee, you'll probably be able to deal with your boss's often eccentric behavior. If you need a role model, manager, leader, or organizer, you will not get it from an Aquarius, no matter how hard you try. These people dislike giving orders and are such individualists that they really don't understand exactly how to get someone to do something for them. They resent the structures of the conservative business world (like suits, meetings, and kow-towing to superiors) and will often be found in more eclectic fields where they can make decisions and act on them without too much red tape.

Your boss will be a person who will treat you as a trusted friend and associate if you are capable, honest, and have a good attitude. There are never any power plays, ruthless tactics, or double-dealings with Aquarians. What you see *is* what you get—a thoughtful, intelligent, rational person who tries to do the right thing by others. An Aquarius won't prejudge employees or evaluate you based on your job status. This boss will be curious about you as a person but will not try to influence you or change you at all. Aquarians like others who are individualistic, too, and love the excitement and variety of humanity. You can count on quiet understanding from this supervisor no matter what your lifestyle, sex, race, religion, or dress code. If you do your job, you're okay. Expect to share a sandwich at lunch, a cup of coffee, or a friendly chat with your Aquarian supervisor.

There will not be a lot of rules or restrictions to learn or abide by. Aquarians function best in an environment of freedom and will grant independence to all employees. There's not a lot of control exercised by this boss, and those of you who want to get ahead because of your own capabilities and merits like Aries, Libra, and Sagittarius, will flourish with Aquarians. Those of you who need and want a structured environment should probably look elsewhere.

An air sign, Aquarius uses the mind well. Your boss will be able to absorb facts, ideas, situations, and personalities and come to unbiased conclusions. But this supervisor also needs time to think things through. Don't be put on edge waiting for a decision—learn to understand the process.

Aquarians try to maintain friendly relations with all, especially in business situations. Expect lots of interesting associates surrounding these people, who will rarely show distress.

The only real quirk in the Aquarian nature is its essential quirkiness! Your supervisor may step over the threshold every day at 8:30 A.M. and then one day not show up until noon. Aquarians dislike getting into ruts and may change things just for the sake of change. They are also not very good about informing the staff as to their whereabouts. Your list of regular numbers at which to reach your supervisor will continually be out of date. Don't even try to anticipate what your boss will do next. If you can adapt you'll do fine, and you will never be bored.

The Aquarian unconventionality can be incompatible with many formal business situations. Your boss may ignore or rebel against the company rules and regulations. You should be prepared to be the businesslike member of the team, to know company procedures, policy, and routine. You may be able to help your supervisor function more effectively within the imposed limits and can also serve as a liaison between this eccentric genius and the more normal people on the staff.

Your boss is very idealistic and can become angry and impatient with people who misbehave. Don't you be one of them. Although not suspicious or guarded, Aquarians see, hear, observe, and understand a lot about what goes on without having to be told. Don't try to lie or persuade your boss that you really *didn't* promise to stay late today. You'll be caught in an act of insincerity, and your boss's analysis of your character is an ever-developing study. You will not be kept on staff out of loyalty, pity, or compassion if your attitude and work habits are found to be lacking. Give your all, be up front, and explain shortcomings. If you adhere to the Aquarian's basic code, you will develop a real rapport with your boss.

Aquarius can ask opinions from others, and you should be honest if approached. Don't try to outthink your boss by coming up with the answer you think he or she wants to hear. Your supervisor likes to seek a range of opinion and realizes that everyone has a unique perspective. You won't be held to be wrong if the final decision does not reflect your input. Remember that Aquarians *always* grant others the right to their own outlook.

Listen when your boss gives suggestions. Aquarians especially know and understand how to deal effectively with others. You will rarely be forced into a certain course of action, but there is wisdom in many Aquarian recommendations and evaluations. Learn to use them!

Don't be shy around this boss, for Aquarians are open. If it's time for a raise, promotion, or time off, just ask. Your supervisor may not give you an answer right away but will think over your request objectively. Appeal to the Aquarian's intellect and be prepared to make your case in a straightforward and logical manner. Your boss wants to do the right thing. You may have to bring the subject up more than once due to occasional absentmindedness, but just don't rush! This sign needs time to deliberate.

In evaluations, your boss will candidly express concerns and suggestions for improving your work. Be gracious, don't get excited, and above all, share your views. If you have been trying to do your best, you'll most likely be rewarded.

One final note—never tell this boss what to do! Aquarians resent this more than anything else and will take this approach as your presumption to judge *them*. Try to go with the flow. If you can accept the unusual as part of your boss's temperament, you'll do well—and even have fun in the process!

Gift Ideas for Aquarius

Aquarians love the unusual, original, and unique: Keep this in mind when buying a gift for people born under this sign. They'll also enjoy gifts that challenge or appeal to the mind and intellect. Aquarians like to be on the cutting edge of technology; they therefore enjoy futuristic, state-of-the-art, or high-tech gifts.

Gadgets are always great for Aquarians, and the more unusual the better. Small calculators, battery-operated clocks, and mini electronic datebooks are a few of the office items that would please them. There's a wide range of electronic equipment, such as automatic switches for lights or auto-timers, cordless phones, earphones, CDs, videotapes, and accessories that will satisfy the progressive urge. A telescope, camcorder, microwave, cassette player, camera, electric keyboard, ham radio, and computer accessories are all good suggestions for Aquarius if they're the latest thing.

Books for Aquarians could cover the topics of electronics, but you can also try such subjects as science fiction, aviation, space travel, astronomy, or inventions. Biographies of astronauts, inventors, daredevil pilots, or daring individuals will all be appreciated. Many Aquarians enjoy New Age subjects including astrology and unexplained phenomena. Books on tape or a set of lessons on the above subjects are also good choices, as are subscriptions to magazines that cater to Aquarian interests or the latest news.

Aquarians would enjoy piano recitals, rock concerts, performance art, astronomy exhibits, modern-art museums, and laser-light shows; tickets to any of these events would be appreciated.

Fun gifts and games for the Aquarian co-worker need to stimulate the imagination and curiosity. Computer games are always good choices, as most Aquarians either own or have access to a PC and are fascinated by programs. Mini, handheld video games, futuristic toys such as remote control planes and cars, or puzzles, and thinking games like Trivial Pursuit or chess will provide endless hours of fun for Aquarians. They might also like a mounted personalized astrological chart, a Slinky, or one of the unusual metal mobiles or sculptures that pulse or move while the Aquarian deliberates.

For jewelry, Aquarius rules the opal, turquoise, peridot, and blue amethyst. Aquarians also enjoy crystals and New Age settings for stones, unique accessories, astrological charms, pendants, pins, and psychedelic earrings. Flowers for Aquarians include the white lilac, orchid, daffodil, primrose, and carnation. Try modern scents for cologne.

If buying personal articles or clothes, choose day-glo colors, unusual combinations, or wild prints. Colors ruled by Aquarius are bright blue, light azure, and silvery white. This sign also rules the ankles, so ankle bracelets or even socks would be appropriate, as would colorful ties and scarves.

Look for something unique! Cater to a known enthusiasm of your Aquarius friend or come up with something off-beat like tattoo decals, ear cuffs, or membership in a special-interest group.

PISCES

February 18 to March 21

The Pisces Co-worker: Old Softie

Pisceans are wonderful people to work with on a personal level; their kind natures make them ideal friends who will always find time to listen to your problems. They are idealists who want to see everyone be happy and love one another, and they are wise enough not to try to change others. Tolerance is a key word for Pisceans and while they always give of themselves emotionally, they rarely make demands on others.

Generally Pisceans have good a sense of humor, and some are genuine jokers. When in a positive mood they know how to have a good time and how to make others happy. Genial and sociable, they'll go along with suggestions and love going out with the gang. Pisceans often surround themselves with many friends and acquaintances on the job. While they can at times be quiet and retiring, they often need to be with others.

Your Pisces co-workers live in a world of emotions. The day-to-day practicalities of a job might well be things that they don't relate to easily. Tender and caring, they're caught up in their own inner world. If the job can use these personal strengths, that's great. If, on the other hand, the job demands strict adherence to routine and deadlines and has a competitive atmosphere, Pisceans will feel out of place. They can even appear to be misfits in certain business situations, as they can't really relate to acquisitiveness, power struggles, and moving up the way most people can.

Pisces co-workers need time alone to relax and recharge. If they are unhappy with the job, they'll retreat into an office, a secluded corner, or even their own heads. They can be moody and are very empathetic individuals. A sad story can bring a lump to their throats, and sharp words or unconcern from others can depress them.

It's hard to work with a Pisces who's feeling low. The best way is to show your care and concern and offer your help in any way possible. This co-worker will often turn down assistance in a self-effacing way, but you may just get him or her a cup of coffee or a snack to show you care. Or do any little thing for Pisceans that you know they'll appreciate. A positive boost like this could be just the thing to lift the Pisces spirits.

These people may not admit they're upset and will sometimes avoid talking about what it is that's bothering them. Gentle nudging toward some work or project that they enjoy may be in order. If the Piscean concentration is shifted to something concrete, it can also help their temperament.

Pisces people are so loving and giving, they'll find it hard to say "no." If you need help on a deadline, they'll be happy to oblige when asked. Make sure that the task is something they're experienced with and can handle. You may find, after your work is completed, that your Pisces friend is way behind and has to work late to finish up. Offer your assistance to even up the scales, but you'll find that Pisces rarely complains, asks for aid, or lets you know what obligations they have.

Because of these traits, some Pisceans can allow themselves to be taken advantage of by more aggressive types. Undeveloped Pisces people may even put up with and suffer emotional abuse from co-workers or supervisors. You can help by pointing out the obvious and offering your advice. An insecure Pisces may not want to rock the boat and could need someone else to speak up first. If nothing else works, your sympathy and emotional support will always be appreciated.

Pisceans often view the world through rose-colored glasses, and they like to think that everyone is as well intentioned and good-natured as they are. They see things in terms of moods, feelings, and images. The business world will unfortunately often demand seeing things in the clearcut terms of facts and figures, and your Pisces associates can be at a disadvantage here.

Pisceans may be misunderstood because of their communication of impressions rather than facts. They can also be difficult to pin down because they don't relate to specifics well and prefer generalities. Because of their acute sensitivity, they may not always tell it like it is. Pisceans will tell you what you want to hear, what won't hurt you, or what they feel will have the most positive affect on you. With this emphasis, there can be a straying from hard reality, as Gemini, Libra, Capricorn, Virgo, or Taurus would understand it. Back up key communiqués from Pisceans with input from other objective co-workers to get a broader, more accurate picture.

Don't be surprised, either, if various associates report conflicting information from a Pisces co-worker. They were probably given the same impressions and came to different conclusions on their own.

Pisceans are the last people to understand punching a time clock; in their inner lives time is not of significance. They'll work at their own rate and may need outside mobilization to govern pace. They can forget or evade deadlines, promises, or commitments on the job. Getting a Pisces to project a completion date is difficult. Getting the Pisces to actually *do* this, if the task is not something enjoyable, can be impossible.

If you have an assignment to share with a Pisces, you're much better off. These people usually like to work with others and can use your input positively. But Pisceans are not ambitious in the usual sense of the word. They strive for peaceful associations and personal satisfaction. If you can encourage an atmosphere that is conducive to these objectives, your cooperative effort will be much more productive.

Get Pisces people to give imaginative input. They have many ideas and opinions and like the give and take of an open discussion. They are great contributors in brainstorming sessions because their ideas exist for their own sake and are not censored because of practicality or other limitations. All Pisceans have unique viewpoints, which are often quite different from those of the rest of the populace.

In dividing tasks, remember that Pisceans gravitate toward creative work and love to interact with others if they don't have to be aggressive. The soft sell is the Piscean way of doing things; they will avoid manipulating, coercing, or forcing others to do anything.

Your help in reminding the Pisces co-worker of deadlines will insure that your joint project is delivered on time. But you may have to take the lead in this case. Weekly or even daily status-report meetings can have a good effect by updating and enthusing the Piscean on a regular basis. However, don't be *too* forceful with deadlines, or the Pisces will rebel and escape you.

Show concern when you can. If you take a personal interest in your Pisces co-worker, you'll also gain the great trust, dedication, and understanding of a person whose still waters run very deep and who gives all when the chips are down.

The Pisces Boss: The Un-Boss

The Pisces supervisor is a real *mensch*—goodhearted, likable, and a human being first and foremost. He or she will be genuinely helpful and attentive to your needs. A Pisces boss will always take time out to listen to what you've got to say; the only problem is, nothing may ever be done about it. These people often learn to live with less than ideal conditions and could counsel you to do the same. "That's just the way things are" is a Pisces sentiment. And if you want to keep your current position, you'll need to learn to live with some of the inconsistencies and irregularities of the Piscean boss.

This boss can be your friend, and a good one at that—someone to share problems with, who'll sit outside and have lunch on the lawn. Pisceans can be generous with both time and money, even if they have little of both. They are talented, sensitive types—really not "boss" material in the truest sense of the word.

Because all Pisceans like a pleasant atmosphere, they'll encourage a friendly, dormitorylike society in their unit. They don't like to tell others what to do, having an inability, really, to cross over the line of someone else's personal freedom.

This is fine if you know just what to do and don't need to be taught skills or have close supervision. The Pisces boss will be happy to answer your questions, but often the answers you get won't be applicable. You may gain insight and understanding, but you still won't know which peg needs to go into which hole. The best term we can come up with to define working for a Pisces is "experiential." You'll have to find things out for yourself. You'll need to rely on your *own* instincts, talents, and interactive skills. A Piscean can't give you something you don't have. You'll be given all the rope you need to do whatever you think you have to, but some of us will end up hanging ourselves.

Your supervisor acts primarily on emotion and instinct. Pisceans loathe to offer criticism. They may tell you what you want to hear, just to make you feel better, and they certainly have a hard time firing or chastising anyone. They'll shy away from inflicting pain and can at times be overly indulgent of their employees. Even those they don't like will be sympathized with, maybe even *more*. The Pisces reasons, "Employee X has such a hard time here because I can't relate to her. I'd better treat her nicer." Odd logic to you, maybe, but perfectly reasonable to a Pisces. Bosses of this sign can overlook bad work, inadequacy, and more if they feel you're trying, or if they have an emotional rapport with you.

Pisces people are idealistic and will be the first to make sacrifices for the welfare of the whole. Your boss is probably a highly talented individual, yet he or she could still use assertiveness training. Pisceans don't need praise and support to survive, but it helps if they feel needed and wanted. Make sure your Pisces boss knows you care. Tell him or her positive things when you can. Give compliments freely when they're due. Building up your supervisor's image can go a long way toward improving your unit's productivity and everyone's attitude.

Pisceans are often "idea" people that need to have a stable structure surrounding them in order to function best in a business situation. If you are organized, efficient, and reliable, you could be the perfect foil for your Pisces boss, who'll eagerly see you have what he or she can use. A good office manager, administrator, or assistant can bring out the best in a Pisces superior by being the conduit to the "real world" of business. Keeping track of deadlines and appointments with gentle reminders may be all that's needed for the Pisces to be in top form.

A Pisces supervisor can give off mixed signals to employees about decisions and priorities. Expect this

STAR SUCCESS

and use your own judgment in dealing with it. Your boss can switch gears or moods at the drop of a hat. If you can't exist in what many would call this "unbusinesslike" world, you'd better look elsewhere; your Pisces boss is not going to change any time soon.

The Pisces boss can be moody and will withdraw when hurt or upset. It's best not to intrude at these times. If you must, be gentle and kind and keep your own spirits up—they could have a beneficial effect on the boss.

Pisces people are notorious for being evasive, just like the fish that slips away as soon as you've got your hands on it! Asked a question point-blank, they'll usually answer with related issues and not facts. They see the world in a much different way from most of us. If you can tune in to their wavelength, and learn to get the gist of what's being said, you'll do well. Literal-minded or detail-oriented people like Aries, Taurus, and Virgo may be tearing their hair out over what they see as Piscean inattention to important facts. But remembering that your Pisces boss may be looking out from inside the fishbowl can help.

If you need time off or a raise, it's easy to make an emotional appeal to a Pisces supervisor and get what you want. Try to avoid taking advantage of the good Piscean nature, though. Reminders are also in order here, too. Tell your boss that you're leaving again the day before you leave—it may have been forgotten. And you might have to arrange for that extra money with the accounting department yourself (insulted as you may feel). As well intentioned as Pisceans are, they often don't get around to things and may forget altogether after a while.

Don't expect your Pisces supervisor to solve all the department's problems. A Pisces will avoid open conflict and will not mediate disputes, even when in a position of power. Once again, expect to go it alone.

Positive Pisceans can be joys to work for, though, and can create a little bit of that idealized world they'd so like to live in. It can be fun in the fishbowl for you, too!

Gift Ideas for Pisces

Pisceans are so touched at the *thought* behind any gift that it almost doesn't matter *what* you give them. They'll treasure items, however, that draw on their imagination, emotions, or dreams. Remember, too, when making your choice that Pisces people have an ethereal sense of beauty.

Many Pisceans like reading books in times of solitude, and sagas, romances, crime, or mystery stories will engross them. They will enjoy collections of poems, photography, humor, or magic books and those relating to mystic experiences. True to form for the fish, they can also be attracted to stories about sea travel, marine life, or boating.

The artistic side of the Pisces character enjoys an evening out. Tickets to the ballet, musicals, aquarium, or a wine-tasting event will be enjoyed. Many cities near lakes or the sea feature boating tours or restaurants aboard ship, which would be ideal for the Piscean taste.

Most Pisces love music and the movies. Give them tickets to a special film screening, videos or video equipment, audiotapes, CDs, a portable cassette player, or a miniature TV. Again, comedies, romances, mysteries, music, and dance will especially appeal to them, as will soft mood music for those who drive a car.

Many Pisces people enjoy entertaining, and wines, liquors, and glasses are appropriate for Pisces people. Decanters, mugs, shakers, steins, and ice tongs or an ice bucket are practical, but they can be beautiful as well.

In the nautical area, fishing gear, boating equipment, water skis, or a surfboard can be good choices for Pisces sporting types.

There are lots of fun gifts that Pisces people are sure to enjoy. A camera, film-developing equipment, art supplies, water pistol, beach bag and towel, slippers or thongs, an aquarium, foot massager, or positive subliminal tapes are all unique gifts that cater to some of Pisces' special interests. Their mystical bent might like a pendant, pin, or key chain with the Pisces astrological sign or figure; or try healing crystals, incense, or even a crystal ball. The Piscean sense of beauty and love of luxury would make perfume or cologne, body oils, or bath beads all great gifts.

For clothing, try slippers, a beach robe, or any silky, satiny, or flowing item. Pisces colors are aqua, teal, sea-green, coral, and white. Gems ruled by Pisces include the coral, amethyst, aquamarine, and emerald, especially set in silvery metals like platinum or sterling.

Gifts of flowers for the Pisceans should include lilies, lotus flowers, violets, and especially white orchids. If these are not available, delicate and pastel-colored flowers should be chosen for a multicolored bouquet.

Appendix

For Further Study

Not everyone will completely relate to all of the information in their Sun sign chapter. Some people will find themselves drawn more to a vocation not ruled by their sign, and they may even find that a different sign is more indicative of their character. If you fall into this category, don't be upset. It doesn't mean that this book—or any astrology book—cannot be helpful to you.

While the Sun is the strongest element, it's only the first in the study of astrology. (It's a common misconception that "being" a particular sign is all there is to astrology.) A complete birth chart also includes at least the other eight planets and the Moon. Emphasis in another sector of the chart can cause the Sun's influence to be less dominant. Or you may have several planets in a sign different than your Sun sign's, causing that sign's traits to be predominant.

To understand more, you will want to see your complete horoscope based on your time, date, and place of birth. This is easily obtained from any number of sources. Local metaphysical bookstores or astrological

APPENDIX

magazines are good places to start. Computer-generated charts are inexpensive and can offer a wealth of information to the beginner. Personal consultations with professional astrologers are more expensive, but here you can have specific questions answered.

Once you have your own natal chart and know a little more about astrology, you can use this book on another level. The sign on your sixth house cusp represents your work, detailing your experiences as an employee, the type of work situation you'd most enjoy, and the way in which you work effectively. Read more about yourself in the co-worker section under the sign on your sixth house. Keep in mind that this section will only describe how you function as a *worker and employee* and does not indicate your entire career experience.

The Mid-Heaven or tenth house cusp is at the top of the chart and can point you to areas of career growth and development. You could read about how you'd be as a boss or entrepreneur by looking at the boss section under the sign that's on your tenth house. You can also read the entire section relating to your career for this sign. Depending on how strongly placed the Sun is in your chart, you may find yourself drawn to the career as represented by the Mid-Heaven.

Most horoscope charts these days are generated by a computer. If you're unfamiliar with reading a computer chart, don't worry: Take your time and don't allow yourself to become anxious. There are different abbreviations and symbols used to represent the signs and planets, and a key is generally included to translate these. The twelve houses are usually quite clear, so it shouldn't be difficult for you to isolate the signs on the sixth and tenth houses.

Although you might not think so, astrology can be very complex. For example, there may also be planets in your sixth or tenth house, and these will give further information on your career. There are aspects between planets in

APPENDIX

your chart as well, which will further influence your work experiences.

If you'd like a computer-generated chart, contact:

Renée Randolph
P.O. Box 396
Seaford, NY 11783

Send your date, time, and place of birth, along with a check or money order for $5.00 for your birth chart, $15.00 for a basic interpretation or forecast, and $25.00 for a compatibility delineation (include information for both parties). Or write for further information.

For your own personal career interpretation of your chart, write to:

Karen Christino
P.O. Box 396
Seaford, NY 11783

This is a completely individualized report of at least ten pages, and you may ask questions which you'd like to have answered. Or write for more information.

Suggested Reading List

General Astrology Books

The Astrologer's Handbook, by Frances Sakoian and Louis S. Acker (Perennial Library, Harper & Row, 1989).

The New A to Z Horoscope Maker and Delineator, by Llewellyn George (Llewellyn Publications, 1990).

Secrets from a Stargazer's Notebook, by Debbi Kempton-Smith (Bantam Books, 1982).

How to Judge a Nativity, by Alan Leo (Fowler, 1969).

Heaven Knows What, by Grant Lewi (Llewellyn Publications, 1978).

From Pioneer to Poet, by Isabelle M. Pagan (Theosophical Publishing, 1969).

APPENDIX

Career Astrology Books

Vocational Astrology, Personality and Potential, by Sue Ann (American Federation of Astrologers): The signs, planets, and house placements are all used to discuss career potential.

Planets in Work: A Complete Guide to Vocational Astrology, by Jamie Binder (ACS Publications, Inc., 1988): This book uses the many astrological factors to take you step by step through the analysis of vocational potential in a horoscope.

Astrological Life Cycles: A Planetary Guide to Personal & Career Opportunities, by John Townley (Inner Traditions, 1987): The author uses your birth information to create a different way of looking at astrological forecasting. Career cycles are discussed, as are some scientific studies of astrology.

Cosmic Influences on Human Behavior, by Dr. Michel Gauquelin (Aurora Press, 1985): This renowned investigator presents scientific research to back up the influences of astrology on career.

Vocational Selection and Counseling (2 vols.), by Doris Chase Doane (American Federation of Astrologers): These are two advanced astrology books intended for astrological career counselors. Volume I helps isolate individual vocational abilities, and Volume II shows how to synthesize them.

Pattern of Professions, by Emma Belle Donath (American Federation of Astrologers, 1984): Some unusual and advanced astrological techniques are discussed in this book about career patterns.

APPENDIX

General Career Books

Occupational Outlook Handbook, 1990–1991, by the U.S. Department of Labor, Bureau of Labor Statistics (Career Publishing, Orange, CA): This is a standard directory of hundreds of careers in the United States, current trends, and other important facts about employment, including job descriptions and salary ranges.

The American Salaries and Wages Survey, by Arsen J. Darnay (Gale Research, Inc., Detroit, MI, 1991): A comprehensive collection of occupations and salaries, along with geographical area.

America's Top 300 Jobs, (JIST Works, Inc., Indianapolis, IN, 1990): Describes work conditions, training required, outlook, earning information, related occupations, and further sources.

Guide for Occupational Exploration, by the U.S. Department of Labor, Employment and Training Administration: Thousands of occupations are grouped by interest and ability with skills and training needed and lists of jobs. You can easily use this book once you've selected a few possible areas of specialization in *Star Success*. The *Guide for Occupational Exploration* is designed to be used in conjunction with the *Dictionary of Occupational Titles,* also by the U.S. Department of Labor. This directory lists job definitions.

Your local library has much information available on careers and may have circulating and reference books for your use. Many libraries have separate career sections, but you should also consult the nonfiction section found under 331.702. Specific books can be ordered directly from most bookstores at no additional charge.

POWER ASTROLOGY

MAKE THE MOST OF *YOUR* SUN SIGN

ROBIN MACNAUGHTON

With a depth and insight never before seen in any astrology book, renowned astrologer Robin MacNaughton will help you discover:

* Your sun sign's vital strengths and weaknesses
* Extraordinary self-awareness
* Clearer perceptions of the people in your life
* Access to the full power that lies within you

POCKET BOOKS

Available from Pocket Books

**Unleash Your Creative Potential!
Discover Gifts You Never
Knew You Had!**

DEVELOP YOUR PSYCHIC ABILITIES

AND GET THEM TO WORK FOR YOU IN YOUR DAILY LIFE

LITANY BURNS

Professional medium and teacher Litany Burns helps you tap into your psychic self with the same *effective step-by-step* techniques and exercises that have produced amazing results with her students and clients.

POCKET BOOKS

Available from Pocket Books